IMPERIAL DESIGNS

ALSO BY DEEPAK TRIPATHI

Overcoming the Bush Legacy in Iraq and Afghanistan

Breeding Ground: Afghanistan and the Origins of Islamist Terrorism

RELATED TITLES FROM POTOMAC BOOKS

War, Welfare & Democracy: Rethinking America's Quest for the End of History
—Peter J. Munson

The Other War: Winning and Losing in Afghanistan
—Amb. Ronald E. Neumann (Ret.)

After the Taliban: Nation-Building in Afghanistan
—Amb. James F. Dobbins

The Valley's Edge: A Year with the Pashtuns in the Heartland of the Taliban
—Daniel R. Green

IMPERIAL DESIGNS

War, Humiliation & the Making of History

Deepak Tripathi

FOREWORD BY JOHAN GALTUNG

Potomac Books
Washington, D.C.

Library of Congress Cataloging-in-Publication Data

Tripathi, Deepak.
  Imperial designs : war, humiliation & the making of history / Deepak Tripathi ; foreword by Johan Galtung. — First Edition.
     pages cm
  Includes bibliographical references and index.
  ISBN 978-1-61234-624-3 (hardcover : alk. paper)
  ISBN 978-1-61234-625-0 (electronic)
1. Middle East—History—20th century. 2. Middle East—History—21st century. 3. Middle East—History, Military—20th century. 4. Middle East—History, Military—21st century. 5. Middle East—Foreign relations—Western Countries. 6. Western Countries—Foreign relations—Middle East. 7. Middle East—Colonization. I. Title.
  DS62.8.T75 2013
  956.04—dc23   2012049625

Printed in the United States of America on acid-free paper that meets the American National Standards Institute Z39-48 Standard.

Potomac Books
22841 Quicksilver Drive
Dulles, Virginia 20166

First Edition

10 9 8 7 6 5 4 3 2 1

For Archana

CONTENTS

FOREWORD

This important book by Deepak Tripathi is about the role of humiliation in international politics, specifically in relation to West Asia. Humiliation is a complex and powerful emotion. My experience from many discussions of trauma, violence, and the harm and hurt of the past to body, soul, and spirit reveals two recurrent syndromes—one in the victim, the other in the perpetrator.

Humiliation causes trauma in the victim, an individual, community, or nation-state. Overwhelming thoughts dominate the victim consciously or subconsciously: innocence (it happened for no reason located in me); shame (I have been humiliated and stigmatized); fear (the perpetrator may do it again); hatred (I hate the offender for making me suffer so much); retaliation (make him or her suffer at least to the extent that I have suffered); entitlement (I am offended and entitled to be treated with care); and moral credit (I can draw upon my trauma as assertion of being right).

The humiliator experiences the mirror image of the victim's reactions: legitimacy (violence is bad, but I had good reasons); guilt (I have done something unmentionable and basically wrong); fear (one day the victim will come back and do the same to me); hatred (I hate the victim for what he or she might do in retaliation); and deterrence (I must prevent any retaliation by the victim).

Reconciliation requires coming to grips with such emotions. The victim's humiliation is one such emotion, but we are dealing with a wider phenomenon of an escalating and vicious cycle of violence. This book does not suggest how to end a cycle of violence or turn it into a virtuous phenomenon that leads to a positive future, as happened following World War II. Here the theme is how violence causes behavior that affects societies and their relationships beyond those actually hurt. Trauma becomes part of culture, embedded in monuments and transmitted from one generation to the next.

Deepak Tripathi's book focuses on the Middle East, where antagonists are locked in a deadly embrace. Readers will have no difficulty identifying the dynamic between humiliator and humiliated in Middle East history. The traumas have names—the Shoah (Holocaust) for Jews and the Nakba (Disaster) for Palestinians.

We will get nowhere comparing the levels of horror in these traumas. Traumas are not comparable, for they are intensely subjective, individually and collectively. There is, of course, a major difference between the trauma suffered by the Jews and that suffered by the Palestinians. The Jews were humiliated by Europeans and Germans, not only Nazis, because acts of omission also count. The Palestinians were, and continue to be, humiliated by Jews turned Israelis.

Let us revisit for a moment the then-secret Sykes–Picot Agreement (1916), the Balfour Declaration (1917), and the U.S. recognition of Israel by President Harry S. Truman in 1948—all included among the appendixes in this book. The Sykes-Picot Agreement says little about "an independent Arab state or a confederation of Arab states" (the concept is mentioned in a single sentence); its vocabulary is ambiguous ("recognize and protect" and "suzerainty"). It says much, however, about the lack of independence and British-French privileges that were later known as the four colonies, two for each. Russia and Japan were informed about the agreement, meaning they were in it.

The Balfour Declaration addressed to Lord Rothschild introduces an entity not defined by international law—"a national home for the Jewish people" in Palestine—but with two important conditions: "that nothing shall be done which may prejudice the civil and religious rights of existing non-Jewish communities in Palestine" or "the rights and political status enjoyed by Jews in any other country." There is something prescient and laudable in these conditions, but the document as a whole leaves the United Kingdom open to considerable blame for countless omissions and failures to enforce the conditions. Humiliation rises not only from what is done but also from what is not done.

Before President Truman signed the proclamation recognizing the state of Israel, it had to be edited away from the Balfour Declaration. "The new Jewish state," which sounded like a national home for the Jewish people, became "the new state of Israel," not explicitly linked to Jews. This only added to Anglo-American responsibility.

As Deepak Tripathi points out, "Honor, humiliation, and promises drive behavior." What is humiliation? It occurs when one is not taken seriously as a party to be respected but regarded instead as a nonentity. When the 1978 Camp David Accords between Israel's prime minister Menachem Begin and Egypt's president

Anwar Sadat were signed, Palestinians were reduced to refugees; they were not even seated at the table. Yet, through their past and current labors, they had carried that table on their backs. Maybe the ultimate humiliation is not being defeated or exploited but being ignored as an unworthy victim.

History makes unexpected turns. After some kind of catharsis, with the Soviet Union vanquished and Communism declared dead by its promoters, Russia has risen again from the ashes of a humiliated and fallen empire. And after so many false departures, Palestine, hitherto a humiliated entity, is recognized by the United Nations Educational, Scientific, and Cultural Organization (UNESCO) and assumes a degree of dignity. Then came the General Assembly's overwhelming vote in November 2012 to recognize Palestine as a non-member state.

It is worth considering Arab humiliation under three empires—the Ottomans (actually the Byzantines before that), the West in the form of the Italy-England-France triumvirate, and again the West in the sense of the U.S.-Israel duo. The 1915–1916 uprisings triggered by the fake promises of the Sykes-Picot deal and the Nasser-Gaddafi revolts against England and Italy decades later were two mighty, but in the end unsuccessful, efforts to gain dignity. These efforts were followed by dictatorships engineered by the United States and Israel with the aim of making the world safe for the Jewish nation. It was humiliating for the Arab peoples to be reduced to nonentities, subject to the whims of dictators and those holding the marionette strings.

Then, out of the blue, in December 2010 came the Arab Spring, which promised dignity again, although the jury is still out on that phenomenon. That the Arabs have been humiliated much too much is undeniable, but the humiliators pretend that they are not aware of it. Let us look at Iran. The joint CIA-MI6 effort to overthrow legally elected prime minister Mohammad Mosaddeq and install the shah was an act of humiliation committed upon the Iranian people by treating their hard-won democracy as something that did not merit respect. And look at the state of affairs today. Iran, in turn, has become a source of fear for Israel and the West.

Deepak Tripathi is very well read and has much to say about Alexander the Great that is relevant to this discussion. Tripathi reminds us how Alexander met his end, having come close to what is now Afghanistan—the country where empires went to die some millennia later. A consistent lesson through history is that those who humiliate have to face their own moment of humiliation one day. The simple way to avoid that moment is to abstain from aggressive warfare. Defensive war is a possibility, but not offensive warfare. It is a tragedy that this lesson escaped Alexander, the Roman Caesar, and Emperor Julian the Apostate then; it also escapes the mighty today.

Tripathi further discusses Niccolò Machiavelli and his poor advice to princes—advice elevated to wisdom by Western statecraft. To consolidate a conquest, devastate the conquered, or set up an oligarchy extracting tribute, Machiavelli wrote, employ direct and structural violence. Countless princes-to-be have followed Machiavellian methods, only to harvest what they have sown. For the humiliated, revenge is often the best way out. If the ruler who devastated or exploited is unavailable for revenge, then humiliation can be exacted on somebody else. The lesson is worth remembering, always.

From George W. Bush to Barack Obama, we have seen the controversial Guantánamo Bay detention center, prisoner abuse at Abu Ghraib, special forces operations, bombings by drones, and extrajudicial executions. These acts of master humiliators are amply documented in Deepak Tripathi's book. It should be read widely. The author's knowledge from close observation should be shared and alternatives considered.

Johan Galtung, Professor dr. hc. mult.
Founding director, Peace Research Institute Oslo, Norway
Founder, TRANSCEND, A Peace, Development and Environment Network

PREFACE

This book is the final part of a trilogy. I began working on the manuscript after the publication of *Breeding Ground: Afghanistan and the Origins of Islamist Terrorism* (2011) and *Overcoming the Bush Legacy in Iraq and Afghanistan* (2010). These two books captured much of my work since the 1970s, my understanding of the turbulence from 1970 to 2010, and the conclusions I had drawn to that point. I then went through a period of reflection.

Breeding Ground was a study of Afghanistan from the 1978 Communist coup to 2010. It covered Afghanistan in the last phase of the Cold War (1979–91); the collapse of Soviet and Afghan Communism and the rise of the Taliban (1991–2001); and a brief analysis of the September 11, 2001, attacks on the United States, the American invasion, and the consequences thereof. The historical sequel, *Overcoming the Bush Legacy in Iraq and Afghanistan*, was an assessment of George W. Bush's presidency (2001–9) in terms of the "war on terror"—to use his own language.

The two books were about the political upheaval and tragedy imposed on a vast number of people by relatively few state and nonstate actors. There were, of course, many pawns and even more victims in the Great Game during the U.S.-Soviet Cold War and after. The contest between the two Cold War giants could produce only one victor, and the prize went to the United States. But a decade after the Soviet Union was vanquished came the September 11, 2001, attacks and President George W. Bush's declaration of the war on terror.

I have suggested in the previous books that among the factors contributing to the events of September 11 was a sense of humiliation felt in the Muslim world, particularly in the Middle East. The facets of the U.S. offense—some easier to discern than others—were complex and varied. They included America's lack of interest in Afghanistan, a country devastated in the U.S. proxy war against the Soviet Union, after the end of the Cold War; the humiliation of Palestinians living under Israeli occupation; the conflicts in Kashmir and Yugoslavia; the defeat of Saddam Hussein's army by U.S.-dominated forces deployed to liberate Kuwait from Iraqi occupation in 1990–91; and the West's support of authoritarian and corrupt rulers.

Free market economic policies borrowed from the United States, their harshest versions implemented by totalitarian rulers in the Middle East, created great disparities between the rich and the poor and a small number of elites, who enriched themselves. Extreme wealth in the midst of poverty fostered significant discontent. Unemployment, declining incomes, and a lack of opportunities eroded people's self-respect. When they complained, they encountered state coercion. Increasingly, they held foreign influences responsible for their own plight and that of those around them.

I began to think about the role of humiliation in international politics. A complete international history of conquests and humiliations would fill many volumes. It was particularly important for me to keep my ambition within well-understood limits and to maintain awareness of my focus in such a work. That such a history had some relevance for the contemporary world was also important.

It seemed to me that the focus had to be Middle Eastern oil and geopolitics. The history of Arabs and Persians is rich and interesting. They have certainly fought many wars over the centuries. The meddling of external actors—the Ottomans, the British, and the Americans—in the region is intriguing. The consequences of this meddling have been profound. What other scholars and observers have said about such momentous events is worth learning.

Among the historic events that have shaped the Middle East are the collapse of the Ottoman Empire in the early twentieth century and its repercussions; the discovery of oil in the region and the division of land between Britain and France; the creation of the state of Israel after World War II and its outcome for Palestinians and Arabs, including subsequent wars; the democracy movement in Iran; and the 1953 overthrow of Iran's elected government by British and American intelligence services. Such events are relevant in any study of the role of humiliation in shaping the Middle East and explaining its volatility.

The region has witnessed continuing upheaval for a century, since Ottoman rule was replaced by British and French imperial rule. But the thinking, behavior, and lifestyles of the local peoples had been determined by conflict between tribes and wars with external invaders for centuries before that. Vast sandy deserts, a free spirit, and a warrior instinct are essential characteristics of the cultures of West

Asia, and the Greater Middle East. The history of wars in the region has put these characteristics on display. It has also reinforced them. Where desert communities are sparsely located, interaction is less frequent between them. Interaction between members of each community or tribe is key to survival. For the people of most tribes, personal possessions are few and the traditional lifestyle is frugal. Wealth tends to accumulate with chiefs. Honor, humiliation, and promises betrayed drive behavior. Defending the honor of an individual, clan, tribe, or nation—or regaining it after humiliation—is of utmost importance.

Past injustices and unsettled disputes persist, and more are added to the list as time goes by. Wars, interventions, and broken promises have much to do with present-day hostilities and the insecurities they create. Covering a broad sweep of history, the book includes my reflections on humiliation, a powerful emotion; a discussion of its manifestations; and thoughts on what may lie ahead.

ACKNOWLEDGMENTS

Imperial Designs completes a trilogy of books about West Asia, the wider Middle East, and U.S. policy in the region. I am grateful to Potomac Books, in particular to commissioning editor Hilary Claggett and her colleagues, for making the publication possible. Their support has meant that all three volumes have the Potomac imprint. These books are my attempt to make sense of the region and explain how local and regional conflicts and foreign interventions have shaped the Middle East—a vast area in which Persian, Arabian, and Jewish civilizations live and compete.

I am deeply indebted to Johan Galtung for reading an early draft of the manuscript, making suggestions, and writing the foreword to *Imperial Designs*. His comments were invaluable and I learned a great deal from them, but any imperfections remain my own responsibility. I am also grateful to outstanding scholars such as Mark Juergensmeyer, Hamid Dabashi, Ilan Pappe, and Evelin Lindner for their generous comments on the book. Their sage words have greatly enhanced its value.

I am more grateful to Richard Falk than I can convey. Richard carefully read the drafts of *Breeding Ground* and *Overcoming the Bush Legacy in Iraq and Afghanistan*. He then wrote the foreword to the first book and a review of the second. Richard's encouragement, guidance, and wisdom over a number of years have meant much to me. For their generous reviews of *Breeding Ground*, I owe much to Walter LaFeber, Howard Zinn, Shah Mahmoud Hanifi, and M. Rasgotra. Similarly, for *Overcoming the Bush Legacy in Iraq and Afghanistan*, my thanks go to Marjorie Cohn, Clive Stafford Smith, Ramzy Baroud, and John Tirman, who wrote the foreword.

Finally, I must express my deep appreciation for my wife, who has shown endless patience and given her unstinting support over the last four years. None of this would have been possible without her.

PROLOGUE

A population weakened and exhausted by battling against so many obstacles—whose needs are never satisfied and desires never fulfilled—is vulnerable to manipulation and regimentation. The struggle for survival is, above all, an exercise that is hugely time-consuming, absorbing and debilitating. If you create these "anti-conditions," your rule is guaranteed for a hundred years.

—Ryszard Kapuscinski

The basis of shame is not some personal mistake of ours, but the ignominy, the humiliation we feel that we must be what we are without any choice in the matter, and that this humiliation is seen by everyone.

—Milan Kundera

[Conflict] is the eternal struggle between two principles—right and wrong. They are the two principles that have stood face to face from the beginning of time and will ever continue to struggle. It is the same spirit that says, "You work and toil and earn bread, and I'll eat it."

—Abraham Lincoln

Never underestimate the cost of humiliation. In war, victory is never clean because it empowers the vanquished, or their successors, to struggle in the future. Recent wars in Iraq, Afghanistan, and elsewhere in the Muslim world and beyond confirm this enduring, though often unheeded, lesson of history. Since the era of Alexander the Great, the king of the Macedonian Empire, nearly two and a half millennia ago, imperial powers far afield have sent their rampaging armies to conquer and to humiliate the populations of vast fertile lands, cradles of civilization, close to the four great rivers—the Nile, the Euphrates, the Indus, and the Hwang He. What transpired forms a pattern.

The disputed territories include modern Iran, Iraq, Afghanistan, and the South Asian subcontinent, Pakistan and India in particular. Despite the extreme volatility in this region, a certain consistency has existed for the last 2,500 years. Alexander's campaign of conquest finally ran out of steam on the banks of the Hydaspes, the modern-day Jhelum River. His troops became exhausted. They mutinied, refusing to march any farther. The rebellion continued later at Opis, a Babylonian city on the east bank of the Tigris, where Alexander gave a stirring speech, admonishing his troops. His attempt to rally them failed. Agnes Savill, author of the biography, *Alexander the Great and His Time*, wrote, "A mind of his [Alexander's] calibre never realises how ignorant men dwell on imagined grievances, repeating from mouth to mouth small incidents which assume gigantic proportions. Why, they complained, had their marriages been celebrated with Persian rites? Why did the King and Peucestas wear Persian garments? Why should the army include commanders from Bactria, Sogdiana, Hyrcania, Parthia and other conquered races? They would not obey such officers."[1]

Elsewhere, clans in the Kunar and Swat Valleys had put up extraordinary resistance, forewarning history's greatest military geniuses. However, the message from those uprisings was not enough for Alexander to overcome his own hubris. After the Battle of Hydaspes, he retreated to Persia, leaving governors he had appointed in charge. But they misbehaved. Alexander was exhausted and injured; his aura was not the same as it had been before the battle. He became even more brutal. He died in Persia three years after his retreat. Alexander supposedly remarked, "I am dying from the treatment of too many physicians."

The hills and valleys of Swat and Kunar, together with lands of the vast region of South and West Asia, have been subjected to repeated invasions through the centuries. The soil is soaked in blood spilled in violence between invaders and defenders, communities and tribes, whose fortunes and failings have attracted eagle-eyed predators far and near. And the ground is as fertile for resistance as it is for agriculture. Foreign armies have found this to their detriment time after time.

Subjugation by external forces renders victims helpless but consolidates their long-term resolve. It breeds local resistance to occupiers and their culture. It results in the colonization of lands by foreign troops, mercenaries, and those wearing civilian hats as administrators and advisers. These occupiers engage in activities to extract and sell local assets and goods through market mechanisms created and managed by themselves, not by those who owned the salable items in the first place. Or they use the location of occupied lands to extend their control further.

In chapter 5 of *The Prince*, Niccolò Machiavelli discusses three ways to hold newly acquired states that once had their own sovereign laws: devastate them, live there in person, or maintain the original laws but extract tribute and set up an oligarchy to keep the state friendly. Machiavelli's work is associated with corrupt, manipulative, and totalitarian government. He wrote,

> Examples are provided by Spartans and Romans. The Spartans ruled Athens and Thebes through the oligarchies they established there, although in the end they lost them. The Romans, in order to hold Capua, Carthage, and Numantia, destroyed them and so never lost them. They wanted to rule Greece almost as the Spartans did, freely, under its own laws; but they did not succeed; so in order to maintain their power they were constrained to destroy many cities in that province.[2]

Five centuries after Machiavelli wrote these words, his teachings, a mishmash of cunning and duplicity, live on—despised, if words of condemnation are to be believed, but witnessed extensively in practice.

Since the end of the Cold War and Soviet Communism, the terms of the U.S.-led Western military campaign for unrestrained access to petroleum and other strategic resources have changed. War today is fought for "freedom" against "terrorism," although both remain highly contested terms. Definitions, when attempted, are arbitrary, incoherent, even irrational. The right of the powerful to use unreserved force under the pretext of "self-defense" has superseded the underdog's right to self-defense and resistance.

The logic of brute military power is couched in legal jargon. As an example, the rights of the Israeli state prevail over the basic rights of the Palestinians. Israel is allowed to have its clandestine nuclear weapons program, but no other country in the region is afforded the same privilege. Elections in Iran are "fraudulent" in the absence of clear evidence. But polls are "acceptable" in Afghanistan with plenty of evidence of fraud. High-altitude bombing in Afghanistan, Iraq, and Libya and drone attacks that kill civilians who are posthumously described as "militants" or "terrorists" are justified in the "war on terror." Talk of "night raids"—a euphemism for breaking into Afghans' homes at night—is rare. Those at the receiving end of these raids see them as a humiliating symbol of foreign occupation.

Loss of possessions is one thing; loss of dignity is quite another. And there exists an inverse relationship between humiliation and pride. Take away a people's dignity and they will be ever more determined to seek revenge in the form that their culture and values dictate when the opportunity comes. Time after time, history has shown that great power intervention and national humiliation of a victim leave a legacy that ultimately haunts the intervenor and tempts him or her to resort to more force. In the victor-vanquished relationship, the fewer means the humiliated have, the more precious their honor becomes and the stronger and more determined their retaliatory instinct is in the long run. Imperial powers, such as Britain and Russia—and more recently the United States—have intervened at will in the oil-rich Middle East and its surroundings for resources and access to waterways. And they cannot subdue resistance. The legacy of imperial subjugation continues in the form of conflict and social upheaval.

The region has repeatedly lured external powers and tested their will. At the advent of the twenty-first century, a decade after the Soviet Union's collapse, the United States tried to reshape the region in President George W. Bush's vision but found the spirit of resistance of the peoples radicalized by past interventions to be as strong as before. When Bush left the White House in January 2009, America was involved in costly wars in Iraq and Afghanistan, exhausted, and in deep economic crisis. After eight years in power, the Republican Party had been defeated in the November 2008 general election; the first black president in U.S. history would take office in January.

Unchecked military power and hubris, seeking pleasure in the abuse and humiliation of others, are corrosive. They take the perpetrators on a path to infamy and lead to their own humiliation. David Owen, Britain's foreign secretary in the 1970s and a medical doctor before entering politics, wrote in 2006,

> The hubristic posture has been described by philosopher David E Cooper as "excessive self-confidence, an 'up yours!' attitude to authority, pre-emptive dismissal of warnings and advice, taking oneself as a model." . . . The centralising natures of George W Bush and [British prime minister] Tony Blair were such that they were both in search of more power and were, therefore, particularly susceptible to being swept up with the intoxication of power, following the tragic events of September 2001. . . . Bush and Blair began "trying to create a new legal regime" for avoiding the constraints of international and national law on interrogation and detention after their military intervention in Afghanistan and, later, Iraq. They planned to build a new paradigm to replace the Geneva conventions that were not allowed to apply to al-Qaeda or Taliban prisoners, and they tried to do all this by themselves, with little or no consultation with friends or allies.[3]

The inauguration of Barack Hussein Obama as the forty-fourth president of the United States on January 20, 2009, was the second time in less than a decade that America stood on the threshold of redefining its role in the new century.[4]

After eight years of the George W. Bush administration, millions upon millions of people around the world were ready for an end to America's reliance on overwhelming military force to execute its foreign policy. There was a longing for a return to constitutional government and respect for international law.

Two days after Obama's victory, the *Economist* described American foreign policy as having "an oddly 19th century flavor" under George W. Bush.[5] "Embroiled in foreign wars thousands of miles from home," according to the article, "the Americans, like the British before, are fighting Muslim zealots from Mesopotamia to Afghanistan and Pakistan's Hindu Kush." In an age of unfettered economic deregulation and massively expensive wars abroad, the U.S. economy was entering a crisis unseen since the Great Depression sixty years before. And it was dragging the rest of the world with it. The *Economist* described the recession as a legacy bequeathed by Osama bin Laden and George W. Bush.

Was Obama's election victory a decisive break from a period of extraordinary turbulence? Or was it a false dawn that would lead to another phase of upheaval? Such crossroads in history do not arrive often. The defeat of Nazi Germany at the end of World War II in 1945 was one. Another was a particularly fierce chapter of the Cold War in the 1980s, which ended in the fall of the Soviet Union and the U.S. reign as the only superpower.

The upheaval of the Bush years, Obama's victory in November 2008, and America's role in the twenty-first century are all matters of interest. Together, they tell us a tragic but fascinating story of two important phenomena. One phenomenon concerns the evolution of the alliance among America's neoconservatives, the religious Right, and the Israel lobby since 1980, the year of Ronald Reagan's election as president. The other phenomenon concerns black progress and the ascent of nonwhite groups in American society. The neoconservative alliance was closely associated with the end of the Cold War and the spread of free-market ideas to the Eastern bloc. Under President George W. Bush, American expansion often looked unstoppable. Was Obama's 2008 victory a possible turning point? Or was he no more than a temporary phenomenon? The first black president in American history, a young first-term senator, and a highly educated public speaker with soaring rhetoric, he was also untested for the challenges ahead; the task of changing the course of history was perhaps too much for him. Was he an ideological leader committed to changing the world for the better after a particularly dark period? Or was he a careerist adorned by certain intellect and rhetoric?

The ideological vehicle that took Obama's predecessor, George W. Bush, to the White House in January 2001 was the Project for the New American Century (PNAC). Its avowed mission was to establish "American global leadership."[6] According to its founding statement of June 1997, "cuts in foreign and defense spending, inattention to the tools and statecraft and inconsistent leadership" had made it "increasingly difficult to sustain American influence around the world." The PNAC had professed "to challenge regimes hostile to America's interests and values" and to extend "an international order friendly to the nation's security, prosperity and principles." Granting the United States the right to preemptive attack wherever and whenever it chose, the organization's founders declared, "It is important to shape circumstances before crises emerge, and to meet threats before they become dire."

The PNAC's ideology was a strong assertion of "military strength and moral clarity." The ideologues sold their rhetoric to a nation with an instinct to act in the name of moral values. Their ambition became a reality, steadily and devastatingly, as time went by during the first Bush term. When he departed for the quieter pastures of Texas in January 2009, Bush had left the wreckage to someone else: America at war in Afghanistan and Iraq; a more volatile Middle East after Israel's attack on Gaza in December 2008 and January 2009; the global war on terror; the Guantánamo Bay detention center; Abu Ghraib in Iraq and similar prison camps around the world; and abductions for bounty, torture, and trial by military commissions. Muslims, in particular, viewed these elements of Bush policy as collective punishment for the 9/11 attacks on the World Trade Center and the Pentagon. Eight years after the attacks, Palestinian American columnist Ramzy Baroud wrote,

> Targeting Muslims is a common denominator that now unifies a great proportion of European political elites and media. The reasons are numerous and obvious. Some European countries are at war (which they have chosen) in various Muslim countries; desperate and failed politicians are in need for constant distractions from their own failures and mishaps; associating Islam with terrorism is more than an acceptable intellectual diatribe, a topic of discussion that has occupied more radio and television airtime than any other; also, pushing Muslims around seems to have few political repercussions—unlike the subjugation or targeting of other groups with political or economic clout.[7]

Obama emphasized the theme of change and reconciliation throughout his election campaign.[8] His inaugural address was the first occasion his pronouncements could begin to acquire the status of official U.S. policy. But an inaugural address has its limits; it cannot address policy details. Thus, Obama's speech was short in specifics but lofty in ideals. What the new administration would actually do was still to be seen.

Reconciliation—with the Muslim world above all—was indeed essential. That long-bleeding wound, the Palestinian issue, was the primary cause of instability in the Middle East. An American president in possession of greater understanding, a little healing touch, ingenuity, and diplomatic skills was a necessity as never before. The new president needed to press Israel's right-wing government of Prime Minister Benjamin Netanyahu to be flexible in negotiations with Palestinians over their demands for an end to occupation and an independent state. But, as a candidate, Obama had escaped close scrutiny and vital questions, such as would his dependency on funds from lobbying groups like Jewish Americans for Obama prevent him from confronting Israel on the Palestinian issue? Obama and his Jewish backers stood together in opposing the "Palestinian plan to unilaterally declare statehood," condemning "Palestinian incitement against Israel" and insisting that a "future border accommodate Israel's security and demographic concerns."[9] How could Obama, the president, be different from his predecessor, George W. Bush?

From Abraham Lincoln to John Kennedy to Barack Obama, many presidents have stood up to take the oath of office and made the promises their fellow Americans longed for. However, subsequent events have often confirmed the limits of those promises. On the verge of civil war in March 1861, Abraham Lincoln took the oath of office and declared, "We are not enemies, but friends. We must not be enemies. Though passion may have strained, it must not break our bonds of affection."[10] Regardless, the United States remained painfully split between the North and the South. A hundred years later, President Kennedy, in his inaugural address, spoke of a world that had the power to abolish all forms of human poverty, but also the power to end all forms of life. Therefore, he said, "Ask not what your country can do for you; ask what you can do for your country. . . . Ask not what America will do for you, but what together we can do for the freedom of man."[11] At the time of his death by an assassin's bullet in November 1963, terrible poverty and the threat of nuclear annihilation still haunted the world.

In his inaugural address President Obama referred to the "rising tides of prosperity and still waters of peace" of the past, but also to "gathering clouds and raging storms"—an allusion to the present.[12] In times of turbulence, America had carried on, "not simply because of the skill or vision" of its leaders, but because it remained "faithful to the ideals of our forebears and true to our founding documents." So it has been. So it must be for the current generation of Americans. Implicit in Obama's words was his desire to break from the Bush era. The speech was stirring. But what would the new president do to confront the problems of the day?

The "founding documents" that Obama referred to were the Declaration of Independence and the Bill of Rights. The former announced the thirteen American colonies' intention to secede from the British Empire. According to the document, the colonies' decision to secede was based on two self-evident principles: first, all men are created equal, and second, they are endowed by their creator with certain "unalienable rights," including life, liberty, and the pursuit of happiness. When a government becomes "destructive of these ends, it is the right of the people to alter or abolish it."[13]

The other founding document, the Bill of Rights, contains the first ten amendments to the U.S. Constitution.[14] Among the rights it guarantees are freedom of speech, of the press, and of assembly; protection from search and seizure; due process and trial by jury; a speedy and public trial and legal representation; and the prohibition of cruel, unusual punishment and excessive bail. The Bill of Rights was passed in 1791, and it has been severely tested through history and into the twenty-first century.

The global war on terror was a campaign in which the Bush administration assumed the right to abduct, transport, detain, and interrogate under torture people from anywhere in the world. The sovereignty of other nation-states did not matter. When Obama took over the presidency, he was averse to using the term "war on terror." Nonetheless, he continued his predecessor's use of drone attacks, special forces operations, and assassination operations in other countries. Perhaps nothing illustrated the limits of the Obama presidency more than his failure to close the Guantánamo Bay prison in his first year in office, as he had promised.[15]

Coming to power after his predecessor's eight years of failed foreign policy, which resulted in wars and economic collapse, President Obama faced the challenge of undoing widespread alienation from America in, and making peace with, the Muslim world. His first foreign tour outside the Americas was to Europe and West Asia in April 2009. Turkey was the first Muslim nation he visited, and it was as if he was still on the campaign trail. Obama's message to the Turkish parliament was exactly what the world wanted to hear:

> Let me say this as clearly as I can: The United States is not, and will never be, at war with Islam. In fact, our partnership with the Muslim world is critical not just in rolling back the violent ideologies that people of all faiths reject, but also to strengthen opportunity for all its people.
>
> I also want to be clear that America's relationship with the Muslim community, the Muslim world, cannot, and will not, just be based upon opposition to terrorism. We seek broader engagement based on mutual interest and mutual respect. We will listen carefully, we will bridge misunderstandings, and we will seek common ground. We will be respectful,

even when we do not agree. We will convey our deep appreciation for the Islamic faith, which has done so much over the centuries to shape the world—including in my own country. The United States has been enriched by Muslim Americans. Many other Americans have Muslims in their families or have lived in a Muslim-majority country—I know, because I am one of them.[16]

President Obama's support for Turkey's campaign for admission in the European Union (EU) was music to the ears of the leadership in Ankara, but it did not sit well with the governments in Paris and Berlin. President Nicolas Sarkozy of France repeated his resistance to the idea. The German chancellor, Angela Merkel, reacted by saying that close ties with Turkey did not necessarily mean full membership in the EU.[17] Opinion on making a predominantly Muslim country, a traditional ally of the West, part of the European club had turned steadily negative after the events of 9/11 and through the presidency of George W. Bush.

In Turkey, a Muslim country at the doorstep of the Arab world, Obama pledged that America "is not, and never will be, at war with Islam." Later that April, in Iraq, Obama told his audience that it was time for the Iraqis to "take responsibility for their country." He reasserted his plan to withdraw all U.S. troops from the country by the end of 2011.[18] Then, two months later, in June 2009, he gave his famous speech in Cairo, extending a hand of friendship toward Islam (see appendix B). The sentiment was immediately welcomed but largely forgotten with time, until Obama contradicted himself.

He gave his most celebrated speech of the April 2009 tour of the Middle East and Europe in the Czech capital of Prague. This speech landed him the Nobel Peace Prize merely six months later, in October 2009.[19] In it, President Obama outlined his "vision of a world free of nuclear weapons."[20] He called for a "global summit on nuclear security" and the "forging of new partnerships" to prevent the spread of nuclear weapons. Condemning North Korea's rocket launch only a few hours before, he proclaimed that America had a "moral responsibility to act in ridding the world of nuclear weapons." And Obama pledged to "work to bring the Comprehensive Test Ban Treaty [CTBT] into force" in order to achieve a "global ban on nuclear testing."

First, the United States will take concrete steps towards a world without nuclear weapons. To put an end to Cold War thinking, we will reduce the role of nuclear weapons in our national security strategy, and urge others to do the same. Make no mistake: As long as these weapons exist, the United States will maintain a safe, secure and effective arsenal to deter any adversary, and guarantee that defense to our allies—including the Czech Republic. But we will begin the work of reducing our arsenal.[21]

Among the large group of journalists traveling in the presidential party was the BBC's North America editor Justin Webb. Commenting on Obama's speech, Webb said, "Obama is a seducer, in the nicest possible way of course. He smiles and refers to himself as Hussein and does all the other things that make Europeans swoon."[22]

During the bitter 2012 presidential contest between Obama and his Republican rival, Mitt Romney, talk of the Comprehensive Test Ban Treaty faded away. The United States remained among the countries that had not ratified it. Meanwhile, Obama had vastly expanded the war in Afghanistan and sent pilotless drones on missions inside Pakistani territory.[23] The Associated Press reported a sensational account issued by U.S. intelligence that appeared to justify the extension of American military operations in the Afghanistan-Pakistan (Af-Pak) theater:

> An increase in terrorist attacks in Pakistan and Afghanistan triggered a sharp rise in the number of civilians killed or wounded there last year, pushing South Asia past the Middle East as the top terror region in the world, according to figures compiled by a U.S. intelligence agency. Thousands of civilians—overwhelmingly Muslim—continue to be slaughtered in extremist attacks, contributing to the instability of the often shaky, poverty-stricken governments in the region, the statistics compiled by the National Counterterrorism Center show.[24]

Obama's new Af-Pak strategy was based on three main considerations: the breakdown in order, the inability of both countries to manage the insurgency themselves, and America's declining capacity to sustain the war in Iraq at a time of severe economic crisis. The Obama administration's new strategy would be to cut America's losses in Iraq and raise the level of involvement on the Af-Pak front for a finite period; to disrupt, dismantle, and defeat al Qaeda; and to stabilize the situation in the region enough to begin pulling out American troops. Behind this strategy was the admission that 2008, the seventh year of fighting, had been "the deadliest year of the war for American forces."[25]

To stabilize and to rebuild would require maintaining the military and civilian presence in Afghanistan. It would necessitate using military power to control the cycle of violence. The increased American and allied presence would provide the enemy with many more targets. The result would be higher casualties. Making the occupation finite would involve negotiating with the adversary and determining a specific deadline for expanding the domain of constitutional order and peace. The forces present in large numbers to restore order would also provoke resistance.

Spanish philosopher George Santayana warned of repetitive consequences in his book, *The Life of Reason*. So came his aphorism, "Those who cannot remember the past are condemned to repeat it."[26] From the beginning, President Obama had multiple crises at hand: the economic meltdown, wars in Iraq and Afghanistan; escalating insurgency in a nuclear-armed Pakistan; the Middle East; the loss of America's credibility around the globe; and the nuclear programs of North Korea and Iran. There were other issues too, such as relations with Russia.

A little more than a year after Obama became president, the United States was becoming mired more deeply in the Middle East, Afghanistan, and Pakistan. The United Nations (UN) special investigator for extrajudicial killings, Philip Alston, reprimanded the Obama administration for extending CIA-led drone attacks that killed "hundreds of civilians." Alston's report concluded, "Intelligence agencies, which by definition are determined to remain unaccountable except to their own paymasters, have no place in running programmes that kill people in other countries."[27] The UN investigator described the practice as a "challenge to the international rule of law."

The issues of Palestine and Iran caused the Muslim world to grow more alienated from the United States. And there was an international outcry when, in May 2010, Israeli commandos attacked, in international waters, a humanitarian aid flotilla carrying peace activists, diplomats, and parliamentarians from many countries to the besieged Palestinian territory of Gaza. The attack killed and wounded scores of passengers. UN special rapporteur Richard Falk, a Jewish American, reacted: "As Special Rapporteur for the Occupied Palestinian Territories, familiar with the suffering of the people of Gaza, I find this latest instance of Israeli military lawlessness to create a situation of regional and global emergency. Unless prompt and decisive action is taken to challenge the Israeli approach to Gaza all of us will be complicit in criminal policies that are challenging the survival of an entire beleaguered community."[28]

But the U.S. vice president, Joe Biden, defended "Israel's right to stop" the flotilla: "You can argue whether Israel should have dropped people onto that ship or not—but the truth of the matter is, Israel has a right to know—they're at war with Hamas—has a right to know whether or not arms are being smuggled in."[29]

When a crisis is grave and a person's instinct of revenge powerful, the consequences are catastrophic. As distinguished black American activist and writer Maya Angelou observed, "I've learned that people will forget what you said, people will forget what you did, but people will never forget how you made them feel."

1

DYNAMIC OF IMPERIALISM

Make the best use of what is in your power and take the rest as it happens.

—*Epictetus*

The epigraph for this chapter is from the Greek philosopher Epictetus, who was born a slave and then freed by his master, Epaphroditus. His words have a strange relevance in the twenty-first century. Epictetus belonged to the Stoic school of philosophy, which was based on the belief that all humans had a predetermined fate and that wise men were "free from passion, unmoved by joy or grief, and submissive to natural law."[1] The twenty-first century brought with it a sense that events were uncontrollable, and as a result, large sections of humanity began to feel powerless. The mayhem of September 11, 2001, and conflicts thereafter was the consequence of deliberate human action. War, death, and destruction showed above all that power and wisdom tend not to be companions. As fifteenth-century Italian philosopher Marsilio Ficino had observed, "Wisdom without power helps few, and power without wisdom harms many. Indeed power without wisdom is the more pernicious the greater it is; wisdom which remains distant from power is lame."[2]

History is full of contradictions between what powerful leaders promise and what they are able to deliver. In his inaugural address in 1789, shortly after the U.S. Constitution was ratified, President George Washington spoke of the "eternal rules of order and right" and the "preservation of the sacred fire of liberty."[3] In fact, American Indians and black slaves endured white oppression for a further two hundred years. History records that the Thirteenth Amendment to the U.S. Constitution, adopted in December 1865, abolished slavery—a cause for which

1

President Abraham Lincoln had fought before his assassination in April that year. In truth, re-enslavement occurred quickly under different laws and was to persist for another century. In the early twenty-first century, in the midst of economic crisis, many humans still lived in extreme poverty and squalor in the United States. Workers paid meager wages and often toiling in unsafe conditions produced goods for Western societies in much more impoverished Asia, Africa, and South America. In contravention of the Universal Declaration of Human Rights, these men, women, and children were modern-day slaves. They, too, endured humiliation in their daily lives.

The gap between rich and poor illustrates the dynamic of power between communities in any society. The gap between nation-states with and without access to resources and military capacity reveals the dynamic of imperialist tendencies. These dynamics of power inevitably symbolize strong rivalries, competition for resources, and war. But power has its limits—always.

In a humorous, yet serious, look at America's conduct, Massachusetts Institute of Technology (MIT) political scientist John Tirman said, "When Harry Truman and Joseph Stalin kicked off the Cold War, they probably did not realize what a long game it would be."[4]

In his 1961 inaugural address, President John F. Kennedy pledged to "pay any price, bear any burden, meet any hardship, support any friend, oppose any foe, in order to assure the survival and the success of liberty."[5] Yet the CIA was in close liaison with the South Vietnamese generals who staged a coup in November 1963 and executed the nationalist president, Ngo Dinh Diem, three weeks before President Kennedy was himself assassinated.[6] Over the next twelve years, the military rulers of South Vietnam ran a brutal, corrupt, and incompetent regime. America bombed areas bordering the South and then throughout Cambodia between 1969 and 1973. King Sihanouk of Cambodia was deposed in a pro-U.S. coup by Gen. Lon Nol, whose regime fell to Communists in 1975. America, a nuclear superpower, with a capacity to obliterate its adversaries in Indochina withdrew its forces from the region, wounded. Vietnam also fell under Communist rule. According to a BBC report on the final American evacuation and the surrender by the U.S.-supported Saigon government on April 30, 1975, "The capitulation of the South Vietnamese government came just four hours after the last frenzied evacuation of Americans from the city. President Ford, who has requested humanitarian aid for the Vietnamese, let it be known that he was proud to have saved what Vietnamese he could in the last, frantic helicopter evacuation."[7]

Jimmy Carter ordered the CIA to channel secret American aid to the mu-jahideen in Afghanistan to fight the pro-Soviet Marxist regime. This covert in-tervention in the Afghan War began well before the Soviet military invasion of Afghanistan in December 1979.[8] Evidence of the CIA's aid came to light several years after the Soviet Union retreated from Afghanistan, ending a decade of brutal occupation and ensuring the Soviet state's demise. The mujahideen, America's proxy force, left a trail of brutality of its own. It was wrapped in a CIA-inspired official misinformation campaign as long as the Soviet army occupied Afghani-stan. The group's cover was blown no sooner than the defeated Soviet army had gone home and the Afghan battlefield was engulfed in a new round of civil war. The American proxy war against the Soviet Union in Afghanistan ultimately gave rise to an extreme form of political Islam, represented by the Taliban and al Qaeda, groups that planned and executed the September 11, 2001, attacks on the United States. More than once in history, Afghanistan has shown how conquest can turn into catastrophe.

The day after the last Soviet troops retreated from Afghan soil, the *Guardian* newspaper reported, "As the last Soviet soldier marched out of Afghanistan yester-day, apparently wiping away tears, Pravda said in Moscow that future decisions to send troops abroad should not be taken by a small conclave but by the Soviet Par-liament. Nine years and seven weeks of Kremlin military involvement ended five minutes before noon, when the Soviet forces commander, Lieutenant-General Boris Grosmov, walked across 'Friendship Bridge' linking the Afghan border town of Hayratan with Termez, in the Soviet Union."[9]

Twelve years later, the United States witnessed the horror of September 11, 2001:

All of a sudden the building shook, then it started to sway. We didn't know what was going on. I ran towards the reception area. It was completely col-lapsed, but the receptionist was able to crawl out from under it. People started to panic. We got all our people on the floor into the stairwell, and then people began to calm down. At that time we all thought it was a fire. . . . We got down as far as the 74th floor, and someone there pulled us into their office. They had a TV on, and we saw that a plane had crashed into the building. Then there was another explosion, so we left again by the stairwell. It took about 40 min-utes to get to the bottom. We were trying to get out through the building's lower level when all of a sudden the power shut off and the lights went out. The police yelled, "Run!" Then something behind me collapsed. The build-ing was starting to come down. All you saw was black, it was so dark.[10]

The Taliban were removed from power in Afghanistan barely five weeks after the U.S.-led coalition went to war in October 2001. Achieving the immediate aim—overthrowing the Taliban from the Afghan capital—so quickly led many to claim it had been a perfect war. Writing in *Foreign Affairs*, Michael O'Hanlon described Operation Enduring Freedom as "a masterpiece of military creativity and finesse."[11] It was assumed that al Qaeda had been deprived of its sanctuary, meeting sites, and weapons production and storage facilities. But the Taliban and al Qaeda leaders had escaped. The miscalculations of this Pentagon-nurtured view of the situation in Afghanistan, and later Iraq, came back to haunt the United States and its allies in subsequent years.

After more than four decades and many ruinous conflicts, the Cold War ended in the demise of the Soviet empire. But American triumphalism did not last long. By the end of the George W. Bush presidency, the most pugnacious members of the neoconservative generation had admitted the limits of American power, and assertions of America's "exceptionalism" had become muted. A sense of vulnerability dwarfed claims of America's status as the global hyperpower. Andrew Bacevich, a retired U.S. Army officer, Boston University professor, and critic of the Iraq War, wrote,

> President Bush's depiction of the past is sanitized, selective, and self-serving where not simply false. The great liberating tradition to which he refers is, to a considerable extent, poppycock. The president celebrates freedom without defining it, and he dodges any serious engagement with the social, cultural, and moral incongruities arising from the pursuit of actually existing freedom. A believer for whom God remains dauntingly inscrutable might view the president's confident explication of the Creator's purpose to be at the very least presumptuous, if not altogether blasphemous.
>
> Still, one must acknowledge that in his second inaugural address, as in other presentations he has made, President Bush succeeds quite masterfully in capturing something essential about the way Americans see themselves and their country. Here is a case where myths and delusions combine to yield perverse yet important truths.[12]

Ferdinand August Bebel, one of the founders of Germany's Social Democratic Party in the nineteenth century, said, "In time of war, the loudest patriots are the greatest profiteers." A century after Bebel's death in 1913, the aphorism retained a ring of truth in the context of the war on terror overseen by the Bush-Cheney presidency. The invasions of Afghanistan and Iraq, which led to extended conflicts in the global war, required large armies of soldiers, interrogators, and foreign agents. Free market ideology reached new heights in the George W. Bush administration, which outsourced many operations to private firms such as Blackwater and Halliburton. Dick Cheney was the chief executive of Halliburton from 1995 to 2000, until his election as vice president. Both firms were awarded huge contracts—without open competition—to provide security and logistical services and, after the invasion of Iraq in March 2003, to rebuild Iraq's oil infrastructure.[13] At the end of 2006 Halliburton's contract was downgraded in response to widespread outrage in the United States.

According to the *Washington Post* and Halliburton Watch, a public interest project that monitors the company's activities, Pentagon auditors found about $1 billion in questionable costs.[14] Whistleblowers revealed that the company charged forty-five dollars for a case of soda, billed twice for meals, and allowed troops to bathe in contaminated water. Halliburton predictably denied these allegations. The military defended the company's performance but admitted that reliance on a single company had left the U.S. government vulnerable to risks. By the time the report was released, Halliburton had made almost $15 billion from the war effort.

Writing in Britain's *Independent* newspaper, distinguished war correspondent Patrick Cockburn revealed details of a large-scale plunder of Iraqi wealth after the invasion.[15] A report by America's special inspector general for Iraq reconstruction suggested that more than $50 billion of the $125 billion budget for the U.S.-directed reconstruction effort in Iraq might be missing, making it one of the biggest acts of theft in American history. In 2004–5, for example, the entire military procurement budget of $1.3 billion had been "siphoned off" from the Iraqi Defense Ministry in return for nearly thirty-year-old Soviet helicopters that were too obsolete to fly and armored vehicles that could easily be penetrated by rifle bullets. Iraqi officials were blamed for the missing funds, but actually, American officials had been in control of the Defense Ministry at that time. In his article, Cockburn quoted a U.S. businessman active in Iraq since 2003 as saying, "The real looting of Iraq after the invasion was by U.S. officials and contractors, not by people from the slums of Baghdad." Investigations by American authorities will take years, and the real story might never come out. However, the Defense Ministry incident was indicative of the wholesale plunder of Iraq, part of the tyranny of occupation.

On a monthlong visit to the U.S. East Coast in the summer of 2009, I heard certain assertions from war veterans that astonished me. One said with dead certainty, "War is good for the U.S. economy." Another claimed, "It helps control the population, especially of other countries." These were among the cruelest and most bizarre justifications for war. The veterans' logic was offensive and contradicted reality, for America was in the midst of an economic meltdown. Nearly half a million or more Americans were losing their jobs every month. Homes were being repossessed because homeowners were unable to make mortgage payments. Family splits were on the rise, and I saw children going to bed half fed and without birthday parties. Was war really good for the economy?

War is certainly good for private security firms, eager to make vast profits and unconcerned about sending their employees to distant lands. In the short run, war may also be good for young people from poor backgrounds who have dreams of a college education and good job prospects. High flyers such as Senator John McCain, whose father and grandfather were both four-star admirals in the U.S. Navy, and Colin Powell, son of Jamaican immigrants who achieved career success, are few and far between. In contrast to these stories are examples of many other veterans of American wars—killed, wounded, and traumatized in action; addicted to drugs, mentally ill, and prone to violent behavior and suicide; on the wrong side of the law; forgotten.

An official report commissioned by Congress concluded in 2008 that almost 25 percent of the 700,000 veterans of the 1990–91 Gulf War suffered from war-related illnesses.[16] Around the same time, America's Public Broadcasting System reported that 12 percent of those deployed once in Afghanistan or Iraq between 2001 and 2008 suffered from some kind of mental illness.[17] Among those who had done at least three tours of duty, the figure jumped to 27 percent. The suicide rate among war veterans doubled during this period; attempted suicides and acts of self-harm quadrupled. In 2009 I met a veteran who was preparing for his tenth tour to Iraq or Afghanistan—he did not yet know which country he was destined for this time. He was worried about the risk to his life and what another tour would mean for his family. He was, however, happy that he was making "a lot of money." Across the United States, businesses were collapsing and Americans were becoming jobless. For the first time, the budget deficit surpassed the trillion-dollar mark.

BEING AN EMPIRE

Humans are expansionist by nature; they always want more. Plato's *Republic*, written around 380 BC, includes a dialogue between Socrates and Glaucon about civilized society.[18] They discuss how a society develops from primitive to higher levels of civilization. Trades and occupations multiply, and population grows. The next stage of development, according to Socrates, is an increase in wealth that results in war because an enlarged society wants even more for consumption. Plato's explanation is fundamental to understanding the causes of war. Empires rise from war, as military and economic power are essential to further their aims. A relevant section in the *Republic* reads,

> We shall have to enlarge our state again. Our healthy state is no longer big enough; its size must be enlarged to make room for a multitude of occupations none of which is concerned with necessaries. There will be hunters and fishermen, and there will be artists, sculptors, painters, and musicians. There will be poets with their following of reciters, actors, chorus-trainers, and producers; there will be manufacturers of domestic equipment of all sorts, especially those concerned with women's dress and make-up.[19]

Were Plato to write the *Republic* in the late twentieth or early twenty-first century, the list might have included gas-guzzling automobiles and cheap and plentiful fuel, computer games and PlayStation, and cosmetic surgeons.

Nearly two and a half millennia after Plato, Michael Hardt and Antonio Negri offered a Marxist vision of the twenty-first century in their book, *Empire*.[20] Their core argument in the book, published in 2001, was that globalization did not mean erosion of sovereignty, but a set of new power relationships in the form of national and supranational institutions like the United Nations, the European Union, and the World Trade Organization. According to Hardt and Negri, unlike European imperialism, which was based on the notions of national sovereignty and territorial cohesion, today's concept of empire is based on the globalization of production, trade, and communication. It has no definitive political center and no territorial limits. The concept is all pervading, so the enemy must now be someone who poses a threat to the entire system—a terrorist entity to be dealt with by force. Written in 2000, *Empire* got it right, as events thereafter would testify.

According to Hardt and Negri, the United States occupied "a privileged position in Empire." Its privileges did not necessarily arise from its "similarities to the old European imperialist powers."[21] They derived from the assertion of "American exceptionalism." From the early days of its formal Constitution, the founders of the United States believed that they were creating "a new Empire with open, expanding frontiers," in which power would be distributed in networks. More than two centuries later, the idea had become global. The presidency of George W. Bush was a powerful militaristic expression of America's will:

> We'll be deliberate, yet time is not on our side. I will not wait on events, while dangers gather. I will not stand by, as peril draws closer and closer.

The United States of America will not permit the world's most dangerous regimes to threaten us with the world's most destructive weapons.
[Applause.] Our war on terror is well begun, but it is only begun. This
campaign may not be finished on our watch—yet it must be and it will be
waged on our watch. We can't stop short.[22]

Like "terrorism," the term "empire" is often used disparagingly by those on
the left and the right. The emergence of the United States and the Soviet Union
as the two greatest powers after World War II provided contrasting models of social organization—one based on centrally planned socialist ideology, the other
free market capitalism. Advocates of each accused the other of being an empire,
meaning a large population comprising many nationalities in distant territories
living under subjugation or exploitation. In fact, different concepts of empire have
existed through history. For centuries, the term referred to states that considered
themselves successors to the Roman Empire, but later it came to be applied to
non-European monarchies, such as the Empire of China or the Mughal Empire.
Most empires in history came into being when a militarily strong state took control of weaker ones. The result in each case was an enlarged, more powerful political union followed by its gradual decline.

The dissolution of the Soviet bloc in the late 1980s and early 1990s delivered
a blow to the idea of ruling an empire by brute force. Suddenly, the floodgates
opened for rapid globalization and expansion of the markets to places that had
previously been in the Soviet domain. Capitalism could reach places it had not
been before, from newly independent countries in eastern Europe to Soviet-
style economies in Asia and Africa. Two decades later, the West was to hit the
most serious crisis of its own since the Great Depression. The crisis was brought
about by a combination of impudence after its Cold War triumph, a false sense
of the West's moral superiority, and belief in its power to destroy and re-create
nations at will.

Norwegian scholar Johan Galtung, regarded as the father of conflict and peace
studies, provided a fitting definition for the term "empire" in 2004. He described
it as "a system of unequal exchanges between the center and the periphery." An
empire "legitimizes relationships between exploiters and exploited economically,
killers and victims militarily, dominators and dominated politically and alienators
and alienated culturally." Galtung observed that the U.S. empire "provides a complete configuration, articulated in a statement by a Pentagon planner."[23] The Pentagon planner in question was Lt. Col. Ralph Peters, who wrote, "The de facto
role of the United States Armed Forces will be to keep the world safe for our

economy and open to our cultural assault. To those ends, we will do a fair amount of killing."[24]

The American defense planner's confession, which Galtung referred to, was as revealing as it was terrifying. Economic interest and cultural domination are interwoven in imperial thinking, which is driven by simplistic logic. Imperial powers are expansionist by nature, always inclined to enlarge territories they control. What lies behind their ambition is access to more and more resources—energy, minerals, raw materials, and markets to trade. Imperial behavior drives a great power to expand its domain of direct control or influence by military and other means to territories that have resources and a certain cultural symmetry with the center. The greater the symmetry, the better. Humiliation and subjugation of lesser military powers, endowed with resources, are inevitable consequences of imperial adventure and hubris. Radicalization of the masses who are humiliated, and a will to resist in the long term, follows.

CULTURE AND CONSUMPTION

To appreciate the relationship between economic interest and cultural symmetry, culture has to be understood as a broad concept. Nineteenth-century English anthropologist Edward Burnett Tylor defined culture as "that complex whole which includes knowledge, belief, art, morals, law, customs and many other capabilities and habits acquired by . . . [members] of society."[25] Culture is the way of life that people follow in society without consciously thinking about how it came into being. Robert Murphy described culture as "a set of mechanisms for survival, but it also provides us with a definition of reality."[26] It determines how people live, the tools they use for work, their sources of entertainment, and their luxuries of life. Culture is a function of the homes people live in; the appliances, tools, and technologies they use; and their ambitions.

It is possible to conclude that culture and economic consumption are closely interrelated. Culture defines patterns of production and trade, demand and supply, and social design. Some examples are worth considering. In Moscow, the old Ladas and Wolgas of yesteryear began to be replaced by Audi, Mercedes, and BMW cars in the late twentieth century. The number of McDonald's restaurants in Russia rose after the launch of the first franchise in the capital in 1990. In Russia, China, and India, luxury goods from cars to small electronic goods and jeans became objects of desire for the growing middle classes, while grinding poverty affected vast numbers of their fellow-citizens. Consumption of luxury goods in China and India rose as their economies grew. Following the U.S.-led invasions of Afghanistan and Iraq, sales of American brands in Kabul and Baghdad increased. Such trends form an essential part of the theme that defines societal transformation and, at the same time, represent a powerful cause for opposition.

The hegemon flaunts its power but also reveals its limitations. It invades and occupies distant lands but cannot end opposition from determined resistors. The economic interests of the hegemon and the way of life it advocates are fundamentally interlinked. The hegemon claims the superiority of its own culture and civilization at the expense of its adversary's. Its economic success depends on the exploitation of the natural and human assets of others. The hegemon allows political and economic freedoms and protections to be enshrined for the privileged at home. Indeed, the hegemon will frequently buy influence by enlisting rulers in foreign lands. Rewards for compliance are high, but human labor and life are cheap in the autocracies of distant lands.

The costs of all this accumulate, and their sum total eventually surpasses the advantages. Military adventures are hugely expensive. As well as hemorrhaging the economy, they drain the hegemon's collective morale as the human cost in terms of war deaths and injuries rises. Foreign expeditions by empires tend to attain a certain momentum. But a regal power is unlikely to pause to reflect on an important lesson of history—that adventure leads to exhaustion. Only when the burden of liabilities—economic, political, moral—causes the hegemon's own citizenry to revolt has the moment for change arrived.

There is a simple truth about the dynamic of imperialism. Internal discontent turning into outright rebellion grows as the hegemon's involvement in foreign conflicts deepens and its difficulties mount. However, radicalization of and resistance to the adversary seem to be in direct proportion to the depth of humiliation felt by the victim. Effects of this phenomenon are durable and unpredictable, such is the desire to avenge national humiliation. Whereas every human possession comes with a price tag, honor is priceless.

2

A QUESTION OF SANITY

Insanity in individuals is something rare—but in groups, parties, nations and epochs, it is the rule.

—*Friedrich Nietzsche*

A great power involved in costly military expeditions faces acute dilemmas. The tide of public opinion may turn against leaders who take the nation to war. Eventually, they may be swept out of power and replaced by a new ruling order. The price paid in human lives and economic drain imposes great demands on the population and causes citizens to introspect. There follows alienation against the rulers held responsible, and momentum for change gathers pace. The Vietnam War caused upheaval and change in the United States in the 1970s; the war in Afghanistan in the 1980s not only led to the Soviet Union's defeat in that country but also contributed to the Soviet state's demise. The beginning of the twenty-first century brought with it a conflict between America and an "enemy" that could include any individual, group, or nation not liked in the White House. Whether the acts committed in the name of the war on terror signify chilling rationality involving criminality or mere folly is a matter of intense argument. Voltaire's description of history as a long succession of cruelties seems particularly fitting in this context.[1]

By the end of 2008 American voters had reached a point at which the mandatory departure of George W. Bush after two terms was not enough. John Mc-Cain, the maverick war hero, tried hard to dissociate himself from the outgoing Republican president. As the financial crisis worsened and the prospect of defeat loomed, McCain escalated his criticism of the handling of the economy. He accused the Bush administration of allowing a "mountain of debt to build for

future generations, failing to pay for expanding Medicare and abusing executive powers."[2] McCain was particularly scathing in his remarks about America's
$500 billion debt to China and failure to "enforce and modernize the [finan-
cial] regulatory agencies that were designed for the 1930s and certainly not the
twenty-first century."

The defeat of the Republican Party, and more importantly, the neoconservative ideology that drove America to fight expensive wars, satiated America's public
opinion in part. Alienated citizens are often quick to feel satisfaction at the change
of guard at the top and expect that problems accumulated over a long time will
promptly be solved. A politician on his or her way to power has a vested interest in
promising a "paradise tomorrow." There exists for every power seeker a world of
fantasy and a population yearning for change, anxious to move on from unpleasant
reality to something agreeable.

Contrary to initial expectations in the White House and the Pentagon under
Defense Secretary Donald Rumsfeld and his deputy Paul Wolfowitz, the war in
Iraq had become nasty, brutish, and long by 2008. The number of Americans
killed in Iraq was nearly four thousand and rising. And the conflict had become
multidimensional—between insurgents and occupation forces, between Sunni
and Shiʻa, and within sects. The 2007 U.S. National Intelligence Estimate for
Iraq admitted that the term "civil war" accurately described key elements of the
Iraqi conflict, including the hardening of ethno-sectarian identities, a sea change
in the character of the violence—and population displacements.[3] Earlier, in October 2006, the UN Refugee Agency (UNHCR) had given a stark account of
the expanding crisis:

> Increasing internal displacement is also having reverberations outside Iraq,
> with more Iraqi arrivals monitored in neighbouring countries and beyond.
> "We estimate that up to 1.6 million Iraqis are now outside their country,
> most of them in Jordan and Syria. Others are in Iran," [UNHCR spokes-
> man Ron] Redmond said.
>
> There are an estimated 500,000 Iraqis in Jordan and some 450,000 in
> Syria. Some have been outside Iraq for a decade or more, but many have
> fled since 2003 and UNHCR is noting an increasing arrival rate. Staff
> monitoring the Syrian border, for example, report at least 40,000 Iraqis a
> month arriving there.
>
> Tens of thousands more are moving on to Turkey, Lebanon, Egypt,
> the Gulf States and Europe. Of some 40 nationalities seeking asylum in
> European countries in the first half of this year, Iraqis ranked first. Statistics

received from 36 industrialised countries for the first six months of the year showed a 50 percent increase in Iraqi asylum claims over the same period a year ago.[4]

From that unpleasant reality came the military surge in the final phase of the Bush administration. More than twenty thousand additional U.S. troops were deployed, mostly around Baghdad, the scene of the worst conflict.[5] While American reinforcements defended the Iraqi capital, Washington's proxies in the Sunni Awakening movement were used to suppress al Qaeda violence in Anbar Province covering much of Iraq's western territory. It was the last chance for George W. Bush to claim success in reducing the escalating violence, though, with a Shi'a-dominated regime in Baghdad and a Sunni Awakening unhappy at the prospect of U.S. withdrawal, Iraq remained a highly unstable society.

POLITICS OF ILLUSION

Politicians crave success. When an unpleasant reality threatens success, a politician seeks to create an illusion, or at least a new reality that would make it possible to claim success. To do this, success must be redefined and the politician's own conduct shown to accomplish the goal. Enoch Powell, one of the most controversial British politicians of the twentieth century, said, "All political lives, unless they are cut off in midstream at a happy juncture, end in failure, because that is the nature of politics and human affairs."[6] A political career that ends in failure is the worst nightmare for any politician and utmost effort is employed to avoid failure.

In the wake of the American invasion of Iraq, James Carafano of the Heritage Foundation wrote a commentary, "The Long War against Terrorism." A retired lieutenant colonel in the U.S. Army and a leading neoconservative ideologue, Carafano began with these words: "Two years down the war on terror. How many more to go? We don't know."[7] Boastfully, he argued that America's "long war" against terror was similar in scope and duration to the Cold War. The military establishment, delighted with the enlargement of the Pentagon budget following the return of Donald Rumsfeld as defense secretary in the Bush administration, jumped at the term. It gained currency in the war lexicon within a few months. In 2006 Rumsfeld invented a phrase of his own, describing the war on terror as "a generational conflict akin to the Cold War" and likely to go on for decades.[8]

These assertions were based on flawed thinking, and comparisons with the Cold War were not relevant. America's victory over the Soviet Union was achieved not by bombing the Soviet state out of existence. The victory was achieved by draining the Soviet economy and resolve through an arms race and regional proxy wars. America's enemy of choice in the twenty-first century was a ghost army of guerrillas with little to lose except their lives—something they were only too willing to sacrifice. The world's preeminent military power with overwhelming military technology had decided to confront a loose army of guerrillas with little more than light weapons, explosives, and simple timing devices, able to move at will across frontiers.

In *The Art of War*, regarded as one of the most influential works about war strategy and tactics, Chinese general and military theorist Sun Tzu wrote,

> Warfare is the way of deception.
> Therefore, if able, appear unable.
> If active, appear not active.
> If near, appear far.
> If far, appear near.
> If they have advantage, entice them.
> If they are confused, take them.
> If they are substantial, prepare for them.
> If they are strong, avoid them.[9]

"Shock and Awe"—the doctrine written at the U.S. National Defense University in 1996—was designed to paralyze the enemy and achieve rapid dominance by overwhelming force. The truth is different. If the enemy can remove himself and recover from the shock and awe of high-altitude bombing and missile attacks from unmanned aircraft, in time he will improvise tactics to fight an effective guerrilla war that a conventional army will find difficult to sustain. A major power wants rapid victory. The underdog prefers a long war. This, and not merely the use of overwhelming power and lightning speed, is the essence of Sun's doctrine of warfare.

Gabriel Kolko, a historian of the Left, observes that while most European nations and Japan have gained insights from the calamities that have so seared modern history, the United States has not. "Folly is scarcely an American monopoly," wrote Kolko, "but resistance to learning when grave errors have been committed is almost proportionate to the resources available to repeat them."[10] The United States is by no means the only major power that refuses to learn from past mistakes. When countries with overwhelming destructive power have failed to prevail in war, they have tended to employ even more firepower. But this tactic has not been successful against guerrilla forces. More and more fire-power tends to create a violent culture that threatens security well beyond im-mediate borders.

New Illusion, New Reality

Financial collapse and war brought down the Republican Party at the end of the Bush presidency. Despite growing dissatisfaction among Americans, none of the main presidential aspirants was an antiwar politician. Senator John Mc-Cain, on the Republican side, was an enthusiastic supporter of the military invasions of both Afghanistan and Iraq.[11] If anything, McCain's complaint was that the war in Iraq was not being prosecuted with sufficient vigor. Senator Hillary Clinton on the Democratic side also voted for both military cam-paigns.[12] Obama was a state senator in Illinois in the early period of the Bush presidency. Although he had supported the invasion of Afghanistan following the 9/11 attacks on America, he declared himself firmly against the Iraq War before it started.

In October 2002 Obama, aspiring to become a member of the U.S. Senate in Washington, gave a speech at the Federal Plaza in Chicago. It was a defining public speech that would set him apart all the way to the presidency in 2008 and after. In a move to demonstrate that he was not just some antiwar politician, he repeated a critical sentence again and again: "I don't oppose all wars." Recalling the Civil War and resorting to masterful rhetoric, Obama declared, "It was only through the crucible, the sacrifice of multitudes, that we could begin to perfect this union and drive the scourge of slavery from our soil."

He reminded Americans that his grandfather had signed up for service after the Japanese attack on Pearl Harbor in 1941 and fought in Gen. George S. Patton Jr.'s army, "in the name of a larger freedom, part of that arsenal of democracy that triumphed over evil." And, in the same vein, he reminded his audience that, after the 9/11 attacks on America and upon witnessing the dust and tears, he had sup-ported the Bush administration's "pledge to hunt down and root out those who would slaughter innocents in the name of intolerance." Indeed he pledged that he himself would "take up arms to prevent such tragedy happening again." To fellow Americans, Obama said, "I stand before you as someone who is not opposed to war in all circumstances."[13] Thus began his mission to establish himself as a future commander in chief. It was also the beginning of a political journey that would take him to the White House seven years later.

While Obama did not oppose all wars, he was against a "dumb war"—that is, one America entered without thought and preparation. At a time when Democratic lawmakers in Washington had decided to go along with the Bush administration's war on terror and a large number of them supported Bush in his determination to open another front against Iraq, Barack Obama was constructing a different platform. He described the gathering campaign to invade Iraq as a cynical attempt by "armchair weekend warriors" to impose their own ideological agenda, "irrespective of the costs in lives lost and in hardships borne."[14]

Politicians, especially in critical times, resort to high rhetoric, for it is a powerful weapon for prevailing over their audiences. High rhetoric is a consciously developed form of language that is elaborate and pretentious. Those skilled in the art of rhetoric are especially adept at reminding the masses of the magnificence of history and promising something glorious in future. Rhetoric is a controlling force, hugely inspirational or destructive. The twentieth century gave us both: on the one hand, Winston Churchill, John F. Kennedy, Mohandas Gandhi, Nelson Mandela, and Martin Luther King Jr.; on the other, Adolf Hitler, Benito Mussolini, and Joseph Stalin, to name but a few.

President Obama's June 4, 2009, Cairo speech, titled "Remarks on a New Beginning," was supposed to make peace with the Muslim world.[15] He acknowledged the tumultuous history shared by Iran and the United States: America's role in the 1953 coup that overthrew a democratic government in Iran; acts of hostage-taking violence against Americans since the revolution three decades before; and the Iranian nuclear program more recently. But the American president offered dialogue and peace. Turning to the Palestinian's plight, he said,

> For more than 60 years they [Palestinians] have endured the pain of dislocation. Many wait in refugee camps in the West Bank, Gaza, and neighboring lands for a life of peace and security that they have never been able to lead. They endure the daily humiliations—large and small—that come with occupation. So let there be no doubt: the situation for the Palestinian people is intolerable. America will not turn our backs on the legitimate Palestinian aspiration for dignity, opportunity, and a state of their own.

A year after this speech President Obama was besieged with problems at home: an ailing economy, ever more mutinous Republicans in Congress determined to block legislation, Democratic members reluctant to support their president, the BP oil spill and its political fallout. As Obama found his domestic agenda compromised, his foreign policy became more and more aggressive.

Unable to tame Israel's willful refusal to stop the construction of illegal Jewish settlements in the occupied West Bank and to ease the blockade of Gaza against worldwide criticism, essential for any improvement in relations with the Muslim world, the Obama administration lurched into a routine of condemning Iran. The president's rhetoric degenerated: "The international community is more united, and the Islamic Republic of Iran is more isolated. And as Iran's leaders continue to ignore their obligations, there should be no doubt: They, too, will face growing consequences. That is a promise."[16]

His secretary of state, Hillary Clinton, said at the U.S.–Islamic World Forum in February 2010,

> Iran leaves the international community little choice but to impose greater costs for its provocative steps. Together, we are encouraging Iran to reconsider its dangerous policy decisions. We are now working actively with our regional and international partners, in the context of our dual track approach, to prepare and implement new measures to convince Iran to change its course.
>
> And of course, our concerns about the Iranian government's intentions are intensified by its behavior toward its own people. The world has watched the events of the past several months in Iran with alarm. We know of the large-scale detentions and mass trials, political executions, the intimidation of family members of the opposition, and the refusal to extend Iranian citizens the right to peaceful assembly and expression, as we have seen again in just the last few days.[17]

AFTER BUSH'S IRAQ WAR, OBAMA'S AFGHAN-PAKISTAN WAR

Those who expected a radical shift in American policy after the Bush-Cheney administration were to be disappointed. Obama had established before his election that he was no antiwar politician, but rather one with a more cautious disposition and with intellect. The original justification for the Iraq War—that Saddam Hussein was developing weapons of mass destruction—had long been discredited. Five years after President Bush announced that America and its allies had prevailed in Iraq, the occupation forces had still not suppressed the insurgency. The vicious civil war had not only caused much loss of life and property but also polarized the country, with millions of Iraqis fleeing as refugees to Jordan, Syria, and other destinations.[18] The International Crisis Group concluded its report on the refugee situation with the following comments:

The refugee crisis has presented a test that virtually all involved are failing. The three neighbouring host countries have performed best. There is much in their attitude toward Iraqis that is open to question and, as time elapsed, they unfortunately have hardened their policies. Still, Syria and Jordan in particular opened their borders and provided sanctuary at significant cost to their already fragile socio-economic fabric. Nothing of the sort can be said of the Iraqi government or of those in the international community primarily responsible for the refugees' plight. The Iraqi government, neighbouring host countries, the U.S. and EU have a joint obligation to do more for the refugees' welfare.[19]

The worst of the Bush administration's legacy included a long trail of abuse by the CIA and the private contractors and the political fallout they left behind. Afghanistan had become a sideshow, an underresourced mission with inevitably poor consequences. Obama, the successor, promised to redefine American policy by repudiating the decision to go to war in Iraq and the worst excesses committed in the war on terror. He called Bush's Iraq invasion "a war of choice"; it was part of the reason Afghanistan had been neglected and America could not go after Osama bin Laden as aggressively as it should have. As a consequence, America had "paid an extraordinary price in blood and treasure" and fanned the anti-American sentiment that "actually makes it more difficult for us to act in Pakistan." Despite this, "we have to, as much as possible, get Pakistan's agreement before we act." However, America should "not hesitate to act when it comes to al Qaeda."[20]

Afghanistan thus became Obama's war, just as Iraq had been Bush's. In July 2008, nearly four months before he was elected, candidate Obama pledged to reinforce the U.S. occupation forces by ten thousand troops.[21] In February 2009, after a review of U.S. policy in Afghanistan and Pakistan, Obama sanctioned reinforcements on a bigger scale for Afghanistan.[22] He appointed Gen. Stanley McChrystal, a counterterrorism specialist, commander of the occupation forces in Afghanistan.[23] Pilotless drone attacks across the Afghanistan-Pakistan frontier became more frequent and killed "militants" and civilians in greater numbers. The findings of an opinion poll conducted by the Gallup Organization in Pakistan were published in August 2009.[24] Almost 60 percent of Pakistanis thought the United States was the greatest threat to their country; about 18 percent thought India was the greatest threat and 11 percent thought the Pakistani Taliban were. An even bigger majority of two-thirds opposed U.S. military operations in Pakistani territory. These were depressing statistics for a country that had spent billions of dollars in Pakistan and Afghanistan.

August 2009 was a bad month for the Obama administration in Afghanistan. Elections were held amid allegations of widespread fraud and intimidation. Despite a partial news blackout, it emerged that voting was low outside Kabul because of Taliban threats and general indifference. And according to the *Daily Telegraph*, as few as 10 percent of Afghans went to polling stations in many areas.[25] The occupation forces, in particular American and British troops, took a high number of casualties during the summer of 2009 as the Taliban consolidated their hold in the south and penetrated new areas north of the capital.

Russia's ambassador in Afghanistan, Zamir Kabulov, who was the senior KGB officer in Kabul in the 1980s, made some insightful remarks as the Obama presidency approached. In Kabulov's view, the American enterprise in Afghanistan faced grim prospects if Washington failed to learn from mistakes made by the Soviets when they occupied the country. The Americans "had already repeated all our mistakes" since overthrowing the Taliban regime in 2001. They underestimated the resistance, showed an overreliance on airpower, and failed to understand the Afghan "irritative allergy" to foreign occupation. Even worse was the belief that sweeping into Kabul was all that was necessary. In his remarks to the *New York Times*, Kabulov further warned, "We abused human rights, including the use of aggressive bombardment. . . . Now, it's the same, absolutely the same. Some Soviet generals gave instructions to wipe out the villages where the mujahedeen were entrenched with the civilian population. Is that what your generals are going to do?"[26]

Another flaw in the American strategy was assuming that sending more troops would turn the tide of the war. Fighting an insurgency requires a difficult balance. Too few soldiers in the battlefield impede an army's ability to secure territory in a country of vast mountainous terrain such as Afghanistan. However, determined insurgents find many more targets when reinforcements are sent to subdue them. Regimes installed by external powers and obedient to their masters come to be seen as corrupt and weak. Communist rulers installed in Kabul by the Soviet Union suffered this fate in the 1980s. In the early twenty-first century, the U.S.-installed government of President Hamid Karzai similarly could not avoid that image.

When an occupation force carries out military operations that cause significant numbers of civilian casualties and the leadership of the country can do nothing except occasionally complain, the state of occupation is primed for political failure. As Afghanistan became Obama's war, 2009 turned out to be the bloodiest year in terms of military fatalities among U.S.-led coalition troops.[27] The credibility of the presidential election giving victory to Karzai lay in tatters. And the effort to create a centralized state in Afghanistan appeared doomed.

The summer of 2010 brought more violence and upheaval. General McChrystal was dismissed by President Obama after *Rolling Stone* magazine quoted him and his staff making intemperate comments about the Obama administration. American reinforcements brought the total strength of foreign troops to 140,000, almost the same number as in the Soviet occupation forces at their peak in 1987. And the Russian ambassador's comments from a year before acquired added poignancy: "The more foreign troops you have roaming the country, the more the irritative allergy toward them is going to be provoked."[28]

3

THE AXIS OF EVIL AND THE

GREAT SATAN

America is the Great Satan, the wounded snake.

—*Ayatollah Khomeini*

States like [Iran, Iraq, North Korea] constitute an axis of evil, arming to threaten the peace of the world.

—*President George W. Bush*

Spoken two decades apart, the epigraphs to this chapter sum up the troubled history between Iran and the United States. Nietzsche once said, "There are no facts, only interpretations." His observation holds true about the manner in which Tehran and Washington remained preoccupied with each other in the second half of the twentieth century and the early twenty-first. Almost thirty years after the overthrow of Iran's autocratic ruler and America's policeman in the oil-rich Persian Gulf, Mohammad Reza Shah Pahlavi, the legacy continues to haunt the two countries.

No significant event in Iran could go without repercussions for relations with the West. The presidential election of June 2009 was no exception. Mahmoud Ahmadinejad, the conservative incumbent, was seeking reelection after four turbulent years. A range of internal and external peculiarities affected the 2009 campaign, which was both exciting and unique. In a country of more than 70 million people, nearly two-thirds were under thirty years of age, and the rate of literacy exceeded 75 percent.[1] Iran's economy, facing ever-tightening sanctions since the 1979 revolution, had suffered a steady decline. Oil revenues had failed to benefit the population. The downturn in the world economy had affected Iranian oil exports particularly badly, and its balance of payment difficulties were acute. Iran's financial reserves were low.[2]

Inflation had risen to more than 30 percent in 2008, when the Central Bank intervened to limit lending to prevent the expansion of money supply. In 2009 inflation had come down, but still hovered around 24 percent. Unemployment was 17 percent, about a third higher than it was in 2005, when Ahmadinejad became president. The chorus of criticism of Ahmadinejad for economic mismanagement grew louder as the election approached, not only from his political opponents but sometimes from onetime supporters. The Islamic Revolution Devotees Society, a grouping of revolutionary veterans cofounded by the Iranian president, accused him of launching huge state-funded projects while Iran's poor suffered, and his stated goal of social justice was undermined.[3] A number of senior Iranian clerics were outspoken in their criticism of Ahmadinejad, including a leading traditionalist conservative, Ayatollah Mohammad Reza Mahdavikani, a former prime minister: "We shift problems and fault onto others and in order to say we are innocent we blame others. . . . In my meeting with Mr Ahmadinejad I told him not to use us [clerics] as instruments. We were combatants before the [1979] Revolution. We fought against corruption and what was against religion."[4]

Ahmadinejad routinely dismissed such complaints. He said they were a product of intervention by hostile media. He blamed "secret networks" for rising house prices. Ahmadinejad had a doctorate in engineering, but he often made light of complaints about the economy by telling jokes. He told members of the Iranian parliament to visit his grocer to find out the truth about the rising price of tomatoes. He then suggested that he often took advice about the economy from his local butcher, who knew all the economic problems of the people. And he said that he prayed to God that he never learned about economics.

The electoral system of Iran was by no means perfect. In other countries in the region—for example, Saudi Arabia, small gulf emirates, and Egypt—elections were either nonexistent or held under extreme restrictions. Rigging was widespread. But these states were ruled by America's allies. In the 2009 presidential election, Ahmadinejad faced three challengers. Mir-Hossein Mousavi was seen as the leading opposition candidate. He had been Iran's last prime minister (1981–89) before a presidential form of government was introduced.[5] Three others had been rejected by the Council of Guardians, which vetted all candidates. Former president Mohammad Khatami, a relative liberal, announced his candidacy but later withdrew and declared his support for Mousavi. Another ex-president, Ali Akbar Hashemi Rafsanjani, often described as a centrist-pragmatic conservative, was known to be unhappy with the state of affairs.[6]

A high percentage of young voters, economic decline, and restlessness among influential Iranians encouraged many inside and outside the country to believe that Iran was ripe for change. President Obama's Cairo speech, seeking "a new beginning between the United States and Muslims," came a few days before polling day in Iran. The American president's words of reconciliation were a source of new hope for moderates and liberals in the country. They enlivened the prospect of improvement in U.S.-Iranian relations, perhaps for the first time since the 1979 revolution.

In the end Ahmadinejad was declared reelected by a two-thirds majority. Traditionalist voters in the countryside and the merchant class did not abandon him, and liberals in urban areas were no match to them. After an exciting campaign, sharp exchanges during television debates, and overly optimistic reports in the foreign press, it was a bitter disappointment for Iran's opposition. Its supporters came out in large numbers in cities and towns, but their protests did not grow into a movement powerful enough to replace the existing regime. Coercive instruments of the Iranian state—the military, the intelligence services, and the police—held together. And a clampdown on opponents of the Islamic order followed. There were protests in the United States; the most vocal were from the Republican right, the Israel lobby, and human rights groups. They only helped the conservatives around the regime who denounced external criticism as outside interference. President Ahmadinejad criticized President Obama for interfering in Iran's affairs.[7] And the Iranian authorities took specific retaliatory action against Western news organizations. Iran's foreign minister accused Britain of seeking to sabotage the presidential election and ordered the BBC's Tehran correspondent to leave within twenty-four hours: "Great Britain has plotted against the presidential election for more than two years," Manouchehr Mottaki told foreign diplomats in Tehran in comments translated into English by state-run Press TV.[8]

Relations between Washington and Tehran had sunk to a new low following the September 11, 2001, attacks on America and Bush's description of Iran as part of the "axis of evil."[9] Two factors in particular had come to the fore: Iran's nuclear program, assisted by the United States when Reza Shah Pahlavi was Washington's proxy in the region; and accusations of the Islamic Republic's support for international terrorism. In a leaked letter obtained by the Associated Press in September 2006, the International Atomic Energy Agency (IAEA) described as "outrageous and dishonest" claims made in a report of the U.S. House of Representatives Intelligence Committee that Iran's nuclear program was geared toward making weapons.[10]

The IAEA specifically said that "the report is false in saying that Iran is making weapons-grade uranium at an experimental enrichment site." In fact, the agency said, the material produced was only in small quantities far below what can be used in nuclear weapons. The clash between Washington and IAEA experts was reminiscent of the earlier disputes between them over claims that President Saddam Hussein of Iraq was involved in developing weapons of mass destruction. Those claims in Washington and London were given as the principal reason for the invasion of Iraq in 2003 but were discredited when no such weapons, or traces of such weapons, were found. However, the Iraq experience did not prevent the United States from using similar tactics against Iran; both America and Israel repeatedly warned Iran that its nuclear research facilities could be bombed. Vice President Dick Cheney said in an interview in January 2005, "One of the concerns people have is that Israel might do it without being asked. . . . Given the fact that Iran has a stated policy that their objective is the destruction of Israel, the Israelis might well decide to act first, and let the rest of the world worry about cleaning up the diplomatic mess afterwards."[11]

The failure of the U.S.-led invasion forces to produce evidence of Iraqi weapons of mass destruction was one reason that deterred an attack on Iran at the time. Another was the outbreak of full-scale war following the dissolution of the Iraqi state structure by Paul Bremer, head of the American-led occupation administration after the invasion. The conflict in Iraq defied the Bush administration's calculations and prevented the Americans from moving with force against other adversaries. However, diplomatic pressure and threats continued to the end of the Bush presidency and into the Obama administration. During a visit to Israel, Secretary of State Clinton said, "Patience does have finally its limits and it is time for Iran to fulfill its obligations and responsibilities to the international community and accepting this . . . would be a good beginning."[12]

Only a month before, in September 2009, the IAEA director general, Mohamed ElBaradei, had delivered his last report to the Board of Governors before he retired. ElBaradei said that although Iran had "cooperated with the agency on some issues," several critical areas remained "unaddressed."[13] Tehran had not suspended its enrichment-related activities or its heavy water–related project, as required by the UN Security Council. Choosing his words carefully, ElBaradei said that these issues needed to be clarified "in order to exclude the possibility of there being military dimensions" to Iran's nuclear program. President Ahmadinejad had by then ruled out further concessions from Iran. He told journalists in Tehran, "From our point of view, Iran's nuclear issue is over. We will never negotiate over the obvious rights of the Iranian nation."[14] Tehran also accused Washington of faking documents and other intelligence reports suggesting that Iran "had studied ways to make atomic bombs."[15] Ali Asghar Soltanieh, Iran's envoy to the IAEA, wrote to ElBaradei, "The government of the United States has not given original documents to the agency because it does not actually have any credible documents."[16]

The outgoing IAEA director general ElBaradei was also highly critical of the United States and its allies, France and Israel in particular. Both had earlier accused ElBaradei of "suppressing damning evidence" of Iranian attempts to build nuclear weapons. The IAEA chief said, "I am dismayed by the allegations . . . which have been fed to the media that information has been withheld from the Board. These allegations are politically motivated and totally baseless."[17] ElBaradei complained that such attempts to influence the work of the IAEA Secretariat undermined its independence and objectivity, were in violation of the IAEA statute, and should cease forthwith. As he prepared to retire, there were accusations and counteraccusations between all concerned parties. A stalemate over the nuclear issue persisted. And the United States and Iran remained engaged in brinkmanship.

After months of negotiations and "major concessions" by American officials, the UN Security Council agreed on a statement imposing a fourth round of sanctions against Iran's nuclear program.[18] It was a much watered-down statement, which President Obama still hailed as "the toughest sanctions ever faced" by Iran. Twelve of the fifteen member-states of the Security Council voted for the sanctions; Turkey, a North Atlantic Treaty Organization (NATO) member, and Brazil voted against them; and Lebanon abstained. The sanctions agreed to were against "military purchases, trade and financial transactions carried out by the Islamic Revolutionary Guards"—the corps that controlled Iran's nuclear program and played a "central role" in the economy. America and the European Union immediately embarked on further sanctions, banning investment in Iran's energy sector.[19] The move gave new business opportunities to China and Russia, as the Bloomberg news service reported, "Iranian Oil Minister Masoud Mir-Kazemi and Chinese officials pledged for their countries to cooperate more closely in the energy sector during talks in Beijing on Aug. 6, Iran's government-run Press TV reported. Russia's state-controlled OAO Rosneft and OAO Gazprom Neft may step up fuel shipments to the Islamic republic this month, the Iran Commission of the Moscow Chamber of Commerce and Industry said in July."[20]

As President Obama's reelection in November 2012 approached, he faced increasing pressure to act against Iran. Israel's right-wing prime minister Benjamin Netanyahu intensified the pressure on the Obama administration to possibly take military action against Iran. If it didn't act, Netanyahu repeatedly warned, Israel would do so unilaterally. Although Obama's rhetoric against Iran continued, with further sanctions, he appeared less keen on attacking Iran than the Israeli hawks did. America's war in Afghanistan had gone from bad to worse.

NATO's war in Libya had brought down Col. Muammar Gaddafi's government, and he had been assassinated by NATO-backed rebel forces.[21] The situation in Syria, in contrast, was much more difficult. The "humanitarian" intervention in Libya approved by the UN Security Council had become NATO's mission to overthrow the Gaddafi regime.[22] And Russia and China blocked moves in the Security Council to authorize external intervention in Syria.[23] President Bashar al-Assad proved far more durable than Gaddafi in Libya—a country devastated and fragmented into fiefdoms under control of competing militias after the war.

THE ROOTS OF IRAN'S ALIENATION

Iran had been an object of desire in the strategic rivalry called the Great Game between the British and Russian imperial powers in Central Asia from the early nineteenth century. The twentieth century had been a traumatic journey for the Iranian people, who endured foreign intervention, manipulation, and revolutions. These transformational events were, to a large degree, imposed on the country. Mules and camels were the normal means of transport at the beginning of the twentieth century. A hundred years on, Iran was officially a theocracy; Tehran city had extremely heavy and dangerous motor traffic; Iranian scientists were engaged in stem cell research with a vast potential in the treatment of serious illnesses—the kind of research that America's right-wing lobbies opposed; and Iran had a nuclear research program, a major cause of brinkmanship between Tehran and Washington.[24]

In a hundred years Iran transitioned from a country without an effective bureaucracy, communication network, or standing army to a major power in Central and West Asia—a country of vast energy resources. At the beginning of the twentieth century, local tribal leaders, notables, clergy, and powerful merchants ran the country in the name of the shah of the reigning Qajar family in Tehran. Internal conflict in a weak state brought insolvency and foreign intervention by the Russian and British imperial powers and the United States. Each intervention was followed by further upheaval that shaped Iran into an Islamic republic vehemently opposed to the West by the end of the century.

Like many ruling dynasties of the time, the Qajar family suffered decline in the early part of the twentieth century. Qajar rulers had been on the throne for more than a hundred years, not so much because of bureaucratic institutions and coercion, but thanks to systematic manipulation of social divisions.[25] The jurisdiction of the Qajar state was really limited to Tehran and surrounding areas. But wearing grand titles, including that of Supreme Arbiter, the shah was content with clan and tribal chiefs and powerful notables exercising real authority in the outer reaches of his kingdom. Some of them married into the royal family to cement their relationship with the ruling family.

Facing an economic crisis brought by bankruptcy and high inflation in 1904–5, the Qajar ruler, Muzaffar al-Din Shah Qajar, threatened a steep rise in land taxes and turned to Britain and Russia for loans on top of the £4 million Iran had already borrowed. The imperial powers forced him to hand over control of Iranian customs to Belgian administrators, who promised that repaying the outstanding loans to Britain and Russia would be a priority. The crisis triggered what became Iran's Constitutional Revolution. Speakers at sermons in the capital mourned the loss of their nation's sovereignty. One protested that the country had been "reduced to such a condition that our neighbors of the north and south already believe us to be their property and divide our country between themselves."[26] Widespread protests shook the monarchy, and attempts to suppress them were unsuccessful. On August 5, 1906, Muzaffar al-Din Shah finally signed a royal proclamation to hold national elections for a constituent assembly.

In October an elected assembly convened and drew up a constitution that provided for strict limitations on royal power; an elected parliament, or Majlis, with wide powers to represent the people; and a government with a cabinet subject to confirmation by the Majlis. The shah signed the constitution on December 30, 1906. He died five days later. The Supplementary Fundamental Laws approved in 1907 provided limited freedom of press, speech, and association and security of life and property.[27]

The attempt to replace Muzaffar al-Din Shah's despotic rule with a written code of laws debated and approved by an elected assembly was short-lived. The 1907 Anglo-Russian pact signed by the two imperial powers, who were fearful of Germany, divided up much of Iran. Isfahan in the north went to Russia, and areas in the southwest, including Baluchistan, Kerman, and Sistan, went to Britain. Furthermore, the empires in the north and the south agreed to keep the Belgian customs officials to collect taxes and use the revenues to recover the loans. The rest of Iran was declared a "neutral zone," leaving the constitutionalists to deal with the shah. As a keen observer was to write later, the pact "taught Iranians a hard lesson in realpolitik—that however predatory the two neighbors were, they were even more dangerous when they put aside their rivalries."[28] Conflict broke out between the shah and the constitutionalists, spreading far afield, and instability continued until the middle of the century.

Fifteen years of internal conflict and intervention by Britain and Russia, soon to become the Soviet Union after the fall of the czarist regime in 1917, left Iran in a fragmented state in 1920. The Qajar shah had been forced to grant Britain access to Iranian oil fields, including in the north, which was under Russian influence. In return, Britain would offer weapons, ammunition, and military advisers to the Iranian ruler. The Anglo-Iranian agreement, issued by the British foreign secretary Earl Curzon, turned Iran into a virtual British protectorate and was widely condemned, most notably by France and the United States.[29] Soon the Red Army threatened to march on Tehran. Amid all the turmoil, Gen. Reza Khan, commander of a Russian-trained Cossack brigade in Qazvin to the west, marched into Tehran. Reza Khan declared martial law, took control of the capital, and told the Qajar ruler, Ahmad Shah Qajar, that he had come to save him from the Bolsheviks.[30] In reality, though, the Qajar dynasty was coming to an end. Reza Khan was the new shah of Iran by 1925, and he declared his own Pahlavi dynasty a year later. In the end, "the Qajar dynasty fell with a whimper. In many ways there had been no real contest. Reza Khan's opponent [Ahmad Shah Qajar] had been a timid and selfish young man who did not care about his country.... Long before Reza Khan had come upon the scene the Qajars had been discredited and Ahmad Shah had acquired a reputation for greed, profiteering, self-indulgence and indifference to the fate of his country."[31]

The Iranian state's systematic humiliation and consequent weakness had made it progressively susceptible to external forces. A lack of infrastructure and instruments of enforcement at the state's disposal were responsible for two distinct phenomena in the country. The Qajar dynasty collapsed because it had little to give its subjects and few means of control in Iranian territory. A state without means is a state without authority. Its fate is in the hands of those who move in to fill the void created by the state's inability. The Qajar dynasty lasted more than a century (1794–1925), but in the end it was a puppet of whichever external power was ascendant.

Social upheaval of such order frequently leads to radicalization. The 1906 Constitutional Revolution had raised hopes that the Iranian parliament would assert itself and be a counter to manipulations of the Qajar regime and imperial powers. In the end, the Qajar dynasty and the constitutionalists both failed, and a new order emerged under the leadership of Reza Shah, who in February 1921 staged a coup that made him Iran's effective ruler. Four years later he proclaimed the Pahlavi dynasty. The last king, Ahmad Shah Qajar, went into exile in Europe.

His successor, an autocrat, was clear about what was wrong with the country. He abrogated the Anglo-Iranian agreement and signed a pact with the Soviet Union.[32] The British retreated. The Soviets were persuaded to withdraw to Gilan Province in northwestern Iran and cancel most of the czarist debt and claims. However, the new Communist rulers in the Kremlin gave Iran a guarantee that they would intervene if a third power ever invaded the country and posed a threat to the Soviet Union.

Reza Shah consolidated his rule through state building in two areas: the bureaucracy and the armed forces. By bolstering the bureaucracy he meant to create a hierarchy of authority from the center down to the local level. Government officials would implement laws, gather information, and perform the vital function of tax collection. Reza Shah's attention to the armed forces reinforced the nation's primitive defenses. It was the beginning of a trend that would turn Iran into a major power in the Persian Gulf in the next half century.

At this stage, Reza Shah appointed an American, Arthur Millspaugh, to the post of treasurer-general.[33] Educated at the University of Illinois and Johns Hopkins, where he also lectured, Millspaugh had worked at the drafting office at the State Department and then as a trade adviser. Reza Shah's decision to hand over the responsibility of reorganizing the economy to an American technocrat looked like a master stroke. It reduced British and Soviet interference in Iran's affairs. Moreover, Millspaugh and Reza Shah worked well together for some time, and the economy improved dramatically.

Using the shah's personal authority and the coercive power of Iran's expanding military, Millspaugh started collecting taxes from those who had been avoiding paying. He made the Majlis raise the tax rates every time more revenues were needed for expansion of the military or bureaucracy. He appointed full-time civil servants to run departments. All this strengthened the authority of the central government under Reza Shah—a remarkable turnaround in a country squeezed between two major imperial powers of the day. Millspaugh stayed in Iran for five years, until 1927. Many Iranians saw him as the man who could liberate them from British and Russian domination and the United States as a friend of their country.

The advent of the United States as the third significant power in the region did not prevent Britain and the Soviet Union intervening again in Iran, most notably in the early 1940s and a decade thereafter. In 1941 Reza Shah Pahlavi was seen as sympathetic to Germany's Nazi regime in World War II.[34] The British and the Soviets forced him to abdicate and his son, Mohammad Reza Shah Pahlavi, became shah. The Allied forces promptly occupied Iran and transported armaments to the USSR to repel the Nazi advances. And the American CIA and the

British MI6 staged the 1953 coup in which the democratically elected prime minister, Mohammad Mosaddeq, was overthrown. Gen. Fazlollah Zahedi, who had collaborated with the Western intelligence services, became prime minster. The 1953 overthrow of Iran's democratically elected nationalist government in a U.S.-inspired coup plot sank deep in the Iranian psyche and determined the nation's state of mind and actions leading to the 1979 Islamic Revolution and beyond. Writing about the radicalized generation of Iran, Farhad Khosrakhavar observed,

> The youth of the 1970s was raised on stories about the hostile British and U.S. attitude toward Prime Minister Mohammad Mossadeq, the nationalist hero who had been opposed and ultimately overthrown in a 1953 coup d'état fomented by the U.S. Central Intelligence Agency and the British secret service, MI6. These two factors—one perceptible in daily life (in 1978 there were some forty thousand Americans in Iran, including a contingent of military personnel who had diplomatic immunity) and the other experienced by the older generations and partially transmitted by the youth—helped to nourish strong misgivings about the meaning and value of democracy. In addition, the Marxist left, under an Iranian communist party, the Tudeh, had a strong tendency to identify democracy with bourgeois or imperialist domination. All of these factors hindered the formation of a strong democratic turn of mind in Iran during the 1970s.[35]

4

IRAN'S DIALECTIC

OF ANTI-AMERICANISM

Iran has informed the [International Atomic Energy] Agency that it is constructing a second plant for uranium enrichment.

—*Press TV, September 25, 2009*

On the day Iran announced that it was constructing a new plant for uranium enrichment, President Obama said that the United States, Britain, and France had been tracking the construction of the plant, in remote mountains northeast of the holy city of Qom, for some time.[1] The Iranians had realized that Western intelligence agencies had been keeping an eye on work on the facility since 2006.[2] The three Western powers were about to confront Iran with the evidence they had gathered while international attention was focused on Iran's known facility at Natanz. Their claim was that the secret plant was only months away from acquiring the ability to produce weapons-grade uranium.

In his announcement, President Obama asserted that Iran's action of building a nuclear facility without informing the IAEA amounted to "a direct challenge" to the basic rules of the nonproliferation regime. Iran was refusing to live up to its "international responsibilities, including specifically revealing all nuclear-related activities." But, in an article in the *Guardian*, Scott Ritter, a former UN weapons inspector, cautioned against believing Obama's politically motivated hype.[3] According to Ritter, the rules Iran was accused of breaking were clear.

Under Article 42 of Iran's Safeguards Agreement and code 3.1 of the general part of the Subsidiary Arrangements (the "additional protocol"),[4] Iran was obliged to inform the IAEA of any decision to build a facility with operational centrifuges—devices used to enrich uranium. Ritter pointed out that Iran had signed this agreement in December 2004. However, as the Iranian parliament had not ratified the additional protocol, the obligation was not legally binding. In Iran's view, when it agreed to allow international inspectors to visit the previously secret facility, its cooperation was voluntary, a "confidence building" gesture rather than an obligation. Furthermore, Ritter concluded, "While this action is understandably vexing for the IAEA and those member-states who are desirous of full transparency on the part of Iran, one cannot speak in absolute terms about Iran violating its obligations under the nuclear non-proliferation treaty." So, according to Ritter, when Obama announced that "Iran is breaking rules that all nations must follow, he is technically and legally wrong."

The 2009 U.S.-Iranian confrontation over Tehran's nuclear program was only the latest in the history of conflicts between Iran and external powers going back hundreds of years. The country had been at the center of an imperial rivalry, the Great Game, between Russia and Britain in the nineteenth and twentieth centuries. Reza Shah had modernized his army and strengthened central rule in Iran by the time World War II broke out in 1939. He wanted to remain neutral and refused to support the Allies in the 1940s.[5] According to Abbas Milani,

> When the war began, a large number of German technicians and advisors were already living in Iran. Their presence became a source of apparent alarm for the Allies. Soviet and British propaganda began to repeat the claim that "thousands of Germans" lived and worked in Iran, a potentially dangerous "fifth column." The BBC's alarming programs on the subject notwithstanding, the actual number of Germans was less than a thousand, and British authorities definitely knew the real number. Two facts that no doubt came closer to the Allies' real concerns were that Iranian oil was needed for the war effort and that the Iranian railroad was an asset of enormous strategic significance.[6]

In 1941 the Allies invaded and occupied Iran and forced Reza Shah to abdicate in favor of his twenty-two-year-old son, Crown Prince Mohammad Reza Shah Pahlavi. It was a brutal operation. The British told Reza Shah, "Would His Highness kindly abdicate in favour of his son, the heir to the throne? We have a high opinion of him and will ensure his position. But His Highness should not think there is any other solution."[7] The deposed ruler was sent into exile in South Africa, where he died three years later. The United States sent military units to maintain and operate sections of the trans-Iranian railway. The entire episode was a national humiliation for Iran.

Strong currents of anti-imperialism, nationalism, and opposition to autocratic rule have played a transformational role in the development of Iranian society. Persia had been home to ancient civilizations from early history, around 3200 BC, and became a battleground for ambitious rulers and invading armies in subsequent millennia. Then the Industrial Revolution began in the United Kingdom in the late eighteenth century and machine-based production started to replace manual labor in Europe. Imperial Russia, Britain, and France established their influence in what is now Iran.

Iran was forced to cede territory to Russia under the Treaty of Gulistan (1813) after the first Russo-Persian War and the Treaty of Turkmenchay after the second war (1828). Then, with the discovery of oil in Khuzestan in 1908, the British Empire's interference in Persia intensified.[8] So did competition between Britain and Russia—and cooperation, when it suited them. These and other interventions served to strengthen anti-imperial and nationalist sentiments among the Iranians. Reza Shah's determined but ultimately fruitless effort to maintain his country's neutrality in World War II was a sign of the Iranians' mind-set—and ultimately led to his overthrow and the occupation of Iran by the Allies in 1941. Later, an observer of Iran's history remarked, "For the Iranians, the Allied occupation was a deep psychological shock and political affront, evoking memories of the earlier occupation by the great powers that revived strong feelings of resentment against both occupying powers. Dislike was particularly focused on the British from whom a less insensitive response had seemed likely: little better was expected from the Russian government."[9]

In the twenty years that Reza Shah was in power, Iran went through an unprecedented degree of centralization. It was his answer to the Iranian state's weakness and fragmentation under the Qajar dynasty. Reza Shah intended to turn Iran into a modern, secular country.[10] To achieve this goal, he suppressed tribes that challenged his authority.[11] He dominated all state and many non-state institutions; the Majlis, bureaucracy, and political parties—all functioned at His Majesty's pleasure. But as a leading authority on Iran commented, "Personal dominance and control should not be confused with legitimacy and staying power. The personalization of the system undermined its consolidation in relation to society and the regime continued to be relatively fragile."[12]

Reza Shah's autocratic rule and his modernization program led to a confrontation with the traditionalists and the clergy. He introduced a dress code, replacing the Pahlavi cap with the "international" fedora. The same decree encouraged women to reject the veil. He obliged his senior officials to bring their wives to public functions without veils and decreed that female teachers could no longer come to school with head scarves. He also opened the Majlis himself without an officiating cleric—an affront to religion and convention. The drive to modernization continued beyond Reza Shah, during his son's rule; so did reaction against it. Tehran University, which had opened in 1934, began to produce educated men and women. University campuses, mosques, and the bazaar came to provide the main base for opposition networks.

The dynamic of forces thus created shaped Iran's complex psyche. Iran emerged as a regional power destined to play a major role in the oil-rich Middle East, Central Asia, and the Arabian Sea; it was a vibrant nation, a rich civilization, where young, educated people came to dominate. Their history made them proud. External manipulations and interventions made them distrustful of foreign powers. Attempts to impose Western values offended Iran's traditionalist, devout followers of Shi'a Islam. A failing state with a corrupt, weak center of power led to demands for a constitutional system in the early twentieth century. Attempts of heavy central intervention and modernization too quickly alienated important sections of Iran's conservative society. The center remained unable to gain wide support and legitimacy.

Ten years after the British-led occupation of Iran and the overthrow of Reza Shah in favor of his young son, the opposition tide was on the rise again. In 1941 Britain had invaded Iran to make certain that a supply route was open to its ally, the Soviet Union, and that Germany did not obtain access to Iranian oil. A decade later the humiliation of that episode formed the roots of a confrontation between the opposition forces and Mohammad Reza Shah. The Anglo-Iranian Oil Company, founded in 1908 and controlled by the British government since 1914, had managed to retain control of Iran's oil fields several years after World War II had ended and the British and Soviet invasion forces had withdrawn from the country.[13]

The company renewed its agreement with Reza Shah in 1933. But local employees grew increasingly restless over its failure to fulfill its promises to improve their living conditions, training, and promotion opportunities.[14] Many Iranian nationalists saw the British government's hand behind these broken promises. In their view, Mohammad Reza Shah was a mere puppet of the British. In reality, though, some of the previous brutality against opponents eased after the British and Soviets had withdrawn at the end of World War II, giving nationalist activists a better opportunity to gather forces. The treatment of oil workers catalyzed the new political environment and turned their protests into "a radical and widespread revolt."

In 1947 a major strike was called by workers at the Abadan Refinery, for they had "no vacation day, no sick leave, no disability compensation."[15] They lived in a shantytown with no running water and no electricity. The protests were crushed when British-instigated mobs clashed with the striking workers, and the oil company used the disturbances as a pretext for suppression by force. The workers' strike and its suppression propelled Mohammad Mosaddeq to the leadership of the National Front and ultimately to the office of prime minister.

The Iranian parliament voted to nationalize its oil resources in April 1951.[16] Mosaddeq was chairman of the Oil Committee, and the parliamentary vote was called at his insistence. At the Oil Committee's recommendation, the Iranian Majlis had unanimously approved the resolution nationalizing Iran's oil on March 8. The Senate passed it on March 20. The following month's vote was to be the confirmation of the parliament's will; the scene was set for a confrontation with the Anglo-Iranian Oil Company, Britain, and the United States. In London, Clement Atlee's Labour government was caught off guard: "It labeled the Iranian nationalists 'ungrateful,' 'paranoiacs,' 'thieves' and 'unreliable,' to cite just a few of epithets wielded by British ministers and diplomats at the time. Labour's obdurate and reactionary attitude was quite paradoxical for a government that made 'nationalization' a pillar of its political program and was undertaking several operations of that kind in Great Britain."[17]

In August 1951 Britain imposed severe sanctions on Iran, resorting to the extraordinary accusation that Iran's decision to nationalize its oil was "theft." As a result, those who assisted Tehran in producing and exporting oil, and those who bought Iranian oil products, were considered accessories to a crime punishable under international law. Western companies, in collaboration with BP, participated in "the oil blockade." Iran's economic crisis appeared to be deepening.

This put the certainty of cheap oil for the West under threat during the Cold War with the Soviet Union. The competition for the world's resources was intensifying. In the final months of Harry Truman's presidency, the United States grew increasingly anxious. Truman received a top-secret National Security Council report in November 1952.[18] His administration's strategic thinking had started from the premise that Mosaddeq and the nationalists were the strongest barrier against a Communist (Tudeh) takeover in Iran. However in the final months of his presidency, Truman had started to change his mind.

The NSC report he approved said, "In the event of either an attempted or an actual seizure of power, in one or more of the provinces of Iran or in Tehran, the United States should support a non-communist Iranian government, including participation in the military support of such a government if necessary or useful."[19]

Preparations to this end included (1) plans for specific military, economic, diplomatic, and psychological measures; (2) politico-military discussions with the British government; (3) preparatory measures for the implementation of special political operations in Iran and adjacent Middle Eastern areas; and (4) perfection of plans concerning the UN handling of the matter if and when that became necessary.

The Truman administration, in its twilight months, was not prepared to take concrete action in Iran. That, however, did not prevent British intelligence from hatching its own plot to overthrow Mosaddeq. The architect of the 1953 plot, named Operation TPAJAX, Donald Wilber, wrote in his secret history of the coup that British intelligence officers met their American counterparts in Washington in November–December 1952: "In attendance for British Intelligence were Mr. Christopher Montague Woodhouse, recently Chief of Station for British Intelligence in Tehran; Mr. Samuel Falle of British Intelligence Station in Tehran; and Mr. John Bruce Lockhart, SIS [also known as MI6] Washington representative. . . . Although it was not on the previously agreed agenda of the meeting, British Intelligence representatives brought up the proposition of a joint political action to remove Prime Minister Mossadeq."[20]

The Americans were surprised, and the meeting "concluded without any decision being made." In any case, the matter was too important to be decided at the meeting. The Americans said they would "study" the proposal. President Dwight Eisenhower succeeded Harry Truman in the White House in January 1953. By that time, the plot had taken a definite shape. Donald Wilber wrote that "the Tehran [intelligence] station had informed Washington that General [deleted] had contacted the assistant military attaché" and requested the U.S. ambassador's views as to "whether or not the US Government was interested in covertly supporting an Iranian military effort" to overthrow Prime Minister Mosaddeq. The name of the Iranian general and any information suggesting possible links remained a secret even after the *New York Times* disclosed in 2000 the existence of Wilber's account of the 1953 coup, which indicated Britain's role in the operation was greater than had been thought for nearly a half century.

A progress report after Eisenhower became president in early 1953 dealt with a much narrower focus. The report said that "in the event of either an attempted or an actual communist seizure of power" in parts of Iran or the capital of Tehran, America "should support a non-communist Iranian government, including participation in the military support of such a government if necessary or useful." Preparations for such an eventuality were to include military, economic, diplomatic, and psychological measures.[21] Something had clearly happened between the American and British intelligence officers' meeting in late 1952 and March

1953. The overthrow of Mosaddeq's democratic government led to almost three decades of absolute rule by pro-U.S. Mohammad Reza Shah Pahlavi.

The 1953 CIA-led coup was primarily motivated by oil. In his account, Donald Wilber wrote that the United States put forward two conditions before it would approve the coup plot. First, the Eisenhower administration stipulated that America "could provide adequate grant aid to a successor Iranian Government" to sustain it "until an oil settlement was reached." Second, Britain would have to signify in writing to the State Department's satisfaction "its intention to reach an early settlement with a successor Iranian Government in a spirit of good will and equity."[22] Wilber further wrote,

> In mid-July 1953, the Department of State and the British Foreign office granted authorization for the implementation of the TPAJAX project, and the Director of CIA obtained the approval of the President of the United States. . . . Arrangements were made jointly with the SIS [MI6] whereby operational liaison would be conducted on Cyprus where a CIA officer would be temporarily stationed, and support liaison would be conducted in Washington. Rapid three-way communications were arranged through CIA facilities between Tehran, Cyprus and Washington. The time set for the operation was mid-August.

At this point, the British government was becoming increasingly fearful of losing control of Iran's energy resources. The Cold War was escalating. The Union of Soviet Socialist Republics (USSR) was not an ally but a superpower adversary, driven by communist ideology and also interested in Iran's strategic location. The emerging covenant between Washington and London seemed to be that America would ensure the survival of a proxy regime in Iran, and Britain would deliver a quick oil settlement with the new government. This would minimize the cost to the Eisenhower administration of sustaining the new regime; the political uncertainty in Iran and its relationship with the Soviet Union would be kept to a minimum; and the outlook for oil supplies for the West would improve relatively quickly. The escalation of the Cold War required that Iran remain in the Western domain and that the waterways in the Persian Gulf and the Arabian Sea continue to be open for the United States and allies.

The plot to overthrow the Mosaddeq government encountered early problems. Under the CIA-MI6 plan, Mohammad Reza Shah Pahlavi had to be "forced to play a specific role" and steps had to be taken to rid him once and for all of his pathological fear of the British hidden hand. Distrust of Britain had run deep in the Iranian consciousness since Reza Shah had been deposed in 1941. In the months before the plot was implemented, the shah had to be assured that "the United States and the United Kingdom would firmly support him [the shah] and had both resolved that Mosaddeq must go."[23]

The first attempt went badly wrong on the night of August 15, 1953.[24] According to Donald Wilber's account, the plan was "betrayed by the indiscretion" of one of the Iranian army officers and because "most of the participants proved to be inept or lacking in decision at the critical juncture." Mosaddeq learned of the plot early and took countermeasures. Army units loyal to government came out in Tehran, and the forces assembled around Gen. Fazlollah Zahedi, who would be prime minister after Mosaddeq had been deposed, "lost heart and went into hiding."

Top plotters believed that success was still possible, provided they could persuade the public that Zahedi was the lawful prime minister appointed by the shah.[25] At the CIA's instigation, several Iranian newspapers carried reports of two decrees signed by the shah: one dismissing Prime Minister Mosaddeq and the other appointing General Zahedi in his place. The shah had fled to Baghdad. Some newspapers published a fake interview with Zahedi claiming that his was "the only legal government in existence." The news spread by word of mouth, and crowds began to gather to discuss this. CIA agents appeared to give the gathering crowds the lead. Offices of the Iranian Tudeh Party were ransacked.

Only two days before, Tudeh supporters had begun to attack symbols of the monarchy and demand that the monarchy be abolished.[26] This would have violated the constitution, and Mosaddeq had ordered a crackdown on the demonstrations. Perhaps fatally, Mosaddeq also dissolved the Iranian parliament, the source of his own democratic mandate. On the other hand, pro-shah crowds were encouraged to gather and demonstrate. As the situation spiraled out of control, the prime minister's chief of staff, Gen. Tahi Riahi, informed Mosaddeq that "he no longer controlled the army."[27]

Events went against Mosaddeq from thereon. Soon there were "pro-shah truckloads of military personnel at all the main squares."[28] On the afternoon of August 19 Tehran radio "broadcast the first word of the success of the royalist effort, including a reading of the *firman* [royal decree]."[29] Later that afternoon General Zahedi, the CIA-installed pro-shah prime minister, addressed Iranians in a national broadcast claiming legitimacy for his government. As the Mosaddeq government collapsed, the Soviet Union was caught totally unprepared. Until 11:00 on the evening of August 19, Radio Moscow was still carrying news of the coup's failure. According to Donald Wilber,

Its Persian program that reached Iran early in the afternoon was built around the text of the earlier Pravda article entitled "The Failure of the American Adventure in Iran," and this program was repeated early in the evening. The same Pravda article was broadcast throughout the late afternoon and early evening from Moscow in English, Arabic, Bulgarian, Polish, Czech and Slovak, German, Dutch, Italian, Portuguese and Turkish, although by that time nearly every one of its listeners must have known that this material was no longer applicable.[30]

The overthrow of Prime Minister Mosaddeq reminded the Iranian people of centuries of trials and tribulations that had resulted from external interventions in, and manipulations of, their country. The upheaval and its aftermath not only deepened the people's sense of helplessness at the hands of external powers and a handful of internal players willing and ready to act as proxies; it also fueled the nation's rage. Thereafter, the United States—and to a lesser extent Britain—benefited from Iran's oil wealth. The U.S. government assisted an increasingly autocratic Iranian regime in building a large military and a notorious intelligence agency, SAVAK, created by the CIA. Successive American administrations worked to build a security system anchored in Iran, on one hand, and Israel, on the other. The close liaison between Tehran and Tel Aviv fanned anger throughout the Muslim world. And the more Iran's pro-U.S. regime postponed its demise through suppression of internal opposition, the more that opposition multiplied. The 1979 Islamic Revolution and the overthrow of the Pahlavi dynasty amounted to a revenge unparalleled in scope and consequences in the history of Iran.

In 2006 former foreign secretary of Britain Douglas Hurd remarked in the House of Lords that "Iran is an ancient country with a huge history"—and very conscious of it. He said this was a relevant political fact, not a mere platitude for after-dinner speeches. "We have forgotten so much of our history," Lord Hurd said, "and, in a way, the Iranians remember too much of theirs." They remember past glory, as well as humiliation—"at our hands, Russian hands; and the coup of 1953 against Mosaddeq—things which we never knew or have forgotten." Hurd concluded, "Out of this comes a deep reluctance to be told by other people how they [Iranians] should behave."[31] The burden of forgetting and ignoring weighs heavily in relations with contemporary Iran.

5

AMERICAN EMPIRE IN CHAOS

When the tide of misfortune moves over you, even jelly will break your teeth.

—*Persian Proverb*

A quarter century after the 1953 Anglo-American coup overthrew Iran's democratic government, the pro-U.S. regime collapsed in a popular revolution. In mid-January 1979 Mohammad Reza Shah Pahlavi left his kingdom, never to return. On February 1, seventy-six-year-old cleric Ayatollah Ruhollah Mousavi Khomeini returned after fourteen years in exile in Turkey, Iraq, and briefly in France. On April 1, following a landslide vote on a new constitution, Ayatollah Khomeini declared Iran an Islamic republic. He had already announced the constitutional future of Iran on March 13, 1979, during the referendum campaign: "Don't listen to those who speak of democracy. They all are against Islam. They want to take the nation away from its mission. We will break all the poison pens of those who speak of nationalism, democracy, and such things."[1]

America's grand strategy, which had been evolving since World War II, was in trouble. That grand strategy began with the 1953 coup, which reimposed the Pahlavi family's absolute rule. The objective was to create an American security system in the Middle East to guarantee oil supplies for the industrialized world and to challenge Soviet power in West Asia, North Africa, and beyond. The American security system was to be anchored in Israel, a state created when the British relinquished their mandate in 1948,[2] and Iran, a U.S. proxy after the 1953 coup. American aid sustained the Iranian regime after the 1953 turmoil. The total amount of assistance from Washington in that decade was $1.135 billion—more than $600 million in economic assistance and $500 million in military aid. Only a quarter of this total was in loans. All the military and more than half of the economic assistance was in the form of grants.[3]

Several years after Iran's revolution, a U.S. military strategist, Thomas L. Mc-Naugher, wrote that "Iran remained the critical buffer between the Soviet Union and the Gulf" and U.S. policy must be based on this fact.[4] America had to think all the time about "its interests in the Gulf with ideas grander than the mere defense of oil wells" if the Soviets were to be denied any opportunity to acquire influence, or the appearance of influence, over the flow and price of oil. McNaugher was a graduate of the U.S. Military Academy at West Point and known for his close links with the military-industrial complex. He would rise to become a vice president of the RAND Corporation, a military-strategic think tank founded in 1948 and largely financed by the U.S. government. Given McNaugher's association with the global policy and defense establishments, his views on America's aims need to be taken seriously:

> The United States must make clear to Moscow that Iran as a whole is critically important to the interests of the United States and that Moscow should not regard as irreversible any Iranian move toward the Soviet camp. The United States must also devise a diplomatic strategy that provides Iran with alternatives to greater reliance on the Soviet Union. If it is too soon for the United States and Iran to deal with one another, then U.S. allies should be encouraged to forge links with Tehran.[5]

The Islamic Revolution in Iran was a huge shock to American strategy. The Soviet Union was active in the region and apparently on the ascendancy following the 1978 Communist coup in nearby Afghanistan. Israel had taken a hit in the 1973 Arab-Israeli War, the toughest for the country since its creation. The Arab oil embargo, from October 1973 to March 1974, had delivered a strategic blow to the United States and its allies; the State Department described it as a "major threat."[6] It was a direct retaliation against "the U.S. decision to re-supply the Israeli military during the war."

The embargo was also extended to other industrialized countries supporting Israel. In addition to the economic cost, the Arab action had political consequences. European countries and Japan began "to dissociate themselves from the Middle East policy," a development that "created a strong rift in the Atlantic alliance." The State Department later admitted that America had been forced to negotiate an end to the embargo "from a weaker international position"—on condition that America would make efforts to "create peace" in the region.

Although the effects of turmoil in the Middle East were still being felt several years after, the United States lost Iran in the 1979 revolution. The political upheaval threatened to have both immediate and long-term consequences for the industrialized world's economic dominance and security. America itself imported about 5 percent of its oil from Iran in 1978–79, but other allies, including Western Europe and Israel, were much more reliant on oil from the region. The United States pledged to fill Israel's shortfalls.[7] Saudi Arabia increased its own production; so did Iraq and Kuwait. But the overall output was still down by more than 2 million barrels per day—"more than enough to supply all the daily needs of Britain or Canada." All this because Iran's production had suffered a dramatic collapse from 6 to 1.5 million barrels a day owing to strikes in the oil industry.[8]

Beyond the immediate consequences of the revolution—a decline in energy supplies and escalating prices—there were serious implications for the security system America had been working on. One of its two allies in West Asia, where that security system was anchored, had collapsed, and modern weapons supplied to Iran had fallen into the hands of a fervidly anti-Western regime. Not only was the new Iran a threat to Saudi Arabia and Israel but it was also no longer an assured oil supplier and certainly not a regional policeman for the West. With Iraq's Baʿathist regime already in the Soviet camp, the revolution was the beginning of a nightmare for President Jimmy Carter. On February 11, 1979, the Iranian military stepped aside, and the government headed by the shah's last prime minister, Shapour Bakhtiar, fell, completing Iran's transformation. *Time* magazine, in a story titled "The Khomeini Era Begins," acknowledged the sense of powerlessness in Washington: "Anything that carries Washington's approval is now anathema in Iran. Some Administration advisers admit that open endorsement of Bakhtiar was a serious mistake, and that U.S. policy in Iran should have remained noncommittal once the Shah's ruling days were clearly over. Particularly unfortunate was a statement by President Carter in January rebuking Khomeini and urging him to support the Bakhtiar government."[9]

U.S.-Iran relations plunged after the establishment of the Islamic republic at the end of March. On November 4, 1979, revolutionary students stormed the American embassy in Tehran and took dozens of employees hostage, accusing them of being spies. The crisis was to last 444 days. In April, only months before the November 1980 presidential election, Carter ordered a secret military mission to rescue the fifty-two hostages. The operation ended in failure when two aircraft collided at a remote rendezvous point where the rescue mission had landed, killing eight American soldiers.[10] The fiasco was largely responsible for President Carter's election defeat to Ronald Reagan in November. Iran's revolutionary government freed the American hostages only after Carter had handed the presidency over to Reagan in January 1981. The hostage crisis had far-reaching consequences for the United States and its strategy in West Asia. In Iran, the provisional prime minster, Mehdi Bazargan, a moderate, resigned when he failed to get the hostages released to end the crisis. Years later British academic John Dumbrell offered this assessment of the crisis in the Islamic republic's initial months: "With the fall of the Shah, the State Department attempted to encourage 'moderate' factions in Tehran. Whatever the virtues of this policy, Washington still did not fully comprehend the strength of the Islamic fundamentalist opposition. Any hopes for a 'moderate' succession were destroyed by the taking of the American hostages."[11]

Imperial powers seek to capture, control, or take advantage of what rightfully belongs to others. Empires have done this by coercion, manipulation, and deception throughout history. By April 1979 Iran was out of America's sphere, ruled by Islamic clerics. For more than a quarter century, the United States had made a huge investment in Iran, but this investment was lost. The likelihood that Khomeini's Iran would join the Soviet camp was remote. The Ba'athist regime of Iraq was Moscow's traditional ally in the region, and memories of 1941, when the Soviets, along with the British, had invaded the country, had not faded. Even so, by mid-1979 it was of utmost importance for the United States to deprive the Soviet Union of any opportunity to move into Iran. But by late 1979 America's hopes of exercising any influence on Iran were all but destroyed. A report in the *Guardian*, quoting Reuters news agency, gave an account of the last-minute dismantling of a U.S. listening post close to the Soviet border:

> The "Voice of the Revolution" radio station in Tehran said last night that a US listening post taken over by revolutionary forces at Kabkan near the Soviet border was the most important of its kind in the country.
>
> Quoting unidentified "American authorities," the radio said that 20 American technicians evacuated from the Kabkan base, 40 miles from the Soviet border in north-east Iran, had destroyed equipment worth $500 million after Mojahadeen guerrillas took the base over. The radio said the loss of the base was regarded as a major defeat for the United States.[12]

THE CIA'S BEAR TRAP IN AFGHANISTAN

Afghanistan fell to a Soviet client regime in a coup in April 1978. By 1979 the ruling People's Democratic Party of Afghanistan (PDPA) was deeply split along ideological, ethnic, and tribal lines. Personal rivalries played no minor part in the Communist regime's internal conflict.[13] Its support base was narrow; in addition to the infighting, it was struggling with popular resistance. To survive, the regime was employing brute force on the domestic front and desperately looking to the Soviet Union for help.

Three months after Iran became an Islamic republic, on July 3, 1979, President Carter signed a directive that tempted the Soviets to invade Afghanistan in December of the same year. But the move also helped America achieve its aim of ensuring that the Soviet leadership did not consider moving into Iran and the Persian Gulf. In an interview with the French newspaper *Le Nouvel Observateur* nearly twenty years later, Carter's national security adviser, Zbigniew Brzezinski, revealed the story of the CIA trap for the Soviets in Afghanistan's inhospitable mountains.[14]

Brzezinski dismissed the official version of history, widely promoted in the West, that "CIA aid to the Mujahideen began during 1980," after the Soviet invasion of Afghanistan. Contrary to the official version, Brzezinski revealed that Carter ordered the provision of secret CIA aid to opponents of the Soviet client regime in Kabul in mid-1979 in order to bait the Kremlin to take action in the region. Robert Gates, a career CIA officer, was the first American official to disclose this information in his memoir in 1996.[15] Brzezinski's revelations confirmed Gates's account, but Carter maintained his silence.

In his interview with *Le Nouvel Observateur* Brzezinski also revealed that, on the day Carter authorized covert aid to the mujahideen, he wrote a note to the president saying that in his opinion "the aid was going to induce a Soviet military intervention."[16] Brzezinski admitted that "we knowingly increased the probability" that the Soviets would intervene in Afghanistan. Throughout Soviet occupation of the country in the 1980s, Kremlin leaders asserted that their intention was to fight America's "secret involvement in Afghanistan." Many in the West did not believe them. The interviewer noted that there was indeed truth in the Soviet assertion and asked Brzezinski if he had any regrets. Carter's former adviser responded, "Regret what? The secret operation was an excellent idea." On the day the Soviets officially crossed the border into Afghanistan, he wrote to President Carter, "We now have the opportunity of giving the USSR its Vietnam war." For almost ten years Moscow had to "carry on a war unsupportable by the government, a conflict that brought about the demoralization and finally the breakup of the Soviet empire."

The CIA intervention in Afghanistan thus tempted the Soviets to increase their involvement in a country that had long been a graveyard for intervening empires. The Americans ambushed the USSR in Afghanistan, and fighting the Soviet occupation forces became a major U.S.-led enterprise involving Pakistan, Saudi Arabia, Egypt, China, and others. The eventual victory over Soviet and Afghan Communism was not clean, however. Its consequences were to haunt the conqueror in the years to come.

ROMANCING PAKISTAN'S MILITARY RULERS

Carter's decision to provide secret aid to the mujahideen in Afghanistan in July 1979 opened a new front to draw the Soviet Union away from Iran and the oil-rich Persian Gulf. Pakistan's collaboration in the effort was critical, but Washington's relationship with Islamabad was strained. Pakistan's military chief, Gen. Mohammad Zia-ul-Haq, had overthrown the democratically elected prime minister, Zulfiqar Ali Bhutto, in July 1977. Zia believed that the country's survival "required it to be an ideological state, carefully run under the guidance of the military and the intelligence services."[17] He hated "Hindu India, sought national unity in the name of Islam, and hoped that the United States could be persuaded to foot the bill for Pakistan's security and economic development." His dream was for Pakistan to become a client state of America and to give Islamic clerics and religious parties a significant role in the state's affairs:

> While Zia ul-Haq's secular critics perceived him as cynically manipulating Islam for the survival of his own regime, some Islamic ideologues felt he was not going far enough in recreating a puritanical state. Exigencies of statecraft required compromises instead of ideology, and Zia ul-Haq compromised. If Zia's predecessors had been totally cynical in using Islam as a unifying ideology for an otherwise disparate populace, Zia was only partly cynical. Part of him actually believed in the notion of Islamic revival through political means.[18]

The chain of events—Iran's Islamic Revolution and then America's decisions to open a front to engage the Soviets in Afghanistan's mountains and to channel secret aid to the anticommunist mujahideen factions—offered General Zia a perfect opportunity. Advantages for him were many. The isolation of his regime would end; billions of dollars in American aid, military and civilian, would flow into Pakistan, alleviating the nation's crisis; and Zia, in talks with Western leaders, would look like an international statesman. It would bring legitimacy to his military dictatorship while he continued to oppress Pakistanis at home. All Zia had to do was lend Pakistan's territory, its military intelligence, and its infrastructure, including roads, railways, and air services, to the Americans in their war against the Soviets.

Pakistan had had a nuclear weapons program since 1972. In 1971 its eastern territory had seceded to become an independent country, Bangladesh, following a bitter war of liberation. Its foe India had intervened on behalf of the Bengali population, leaving what remained of Pakistan in the west of the South Asian subcontinent a much reduced entity. Soon after the war, Zulfiqar Ali Bhutto, Pakistan's firebrand leader, committed his country to developing the atomic bomb. India, a Soviet ally, already had a nuclear program.[19] The 1971 war between India and Pakistan and the search by both nations for the bomb had resulted in Western sanctions against them. But the American sanctions had hit Pakistan harder. India was the first South Asian country to test a nuclear device in the Thar Desert of Rajasthan in May 1974—an event that reinforced Pakistan's determination to continue its program:

> Pakistani interest in nuclear weapons to counter the Indian nuclear development got a major boost following the Indian nuclear test in 1974. Dr A. Qadeer Khan, a Pakistani nuclear scientist working in the Netherlands, convinced Bhutto of the efficacy of uranium enrichment technology and Pakistan started developing a plant of its own design. In a significant policy departure, Pakistan refused to put its facility under IAEA safeguards. Relentless US pressure to abandon the nuclear programme transformed it from a diplomatic issue to a question of national pride and sovereignty for the general public in Pakistan.[20]

However, by 1979 all had been forgiven in the interests of America's new strategy following Iran's Islamic Revolution and of executing the CIA's plot to trap the Soviets in Afghanistan. The first Carter directive authorizing covert aid for the mujahideen in July 1979 consisted of only about a half million dollars.[21] The American support soon acquired momentum, and by late August General Zia was pushing the White House to supply weapons to the Afghan opposition. At the same time, Pakistan's most secretive military intelligence organization, Inter-Services Intelligence (ISI), was also pressing for the Afghan insurgency to be expanded.

As a result, CIA director Stansfield Turner gave his approval for a number of "enhancements." They included provision of communications equipment for the guerrillas via Pakistan and Saudi Arabia and funds for Pakistan's military regime to buy weapons for the insurgents. The United States also provided Pakistan with a similar amount of arms and equipment to be distributed among the mujahideen groups. There is evidence that ISI officers put the CIA in touch with their preferred anticommunist Afghan leader, Gulbuddin Hikmatyar, in May 1979, even prior to Carter's approval of secret aid to the mujahideen.[22]

The guiding principle of the new relationship between America and Pakistan had begun to evolve even before the invasion of Afghanistan. It was sealed at a meeting between Brzezinski and General Zia in Islamabad in January 1980.[23] Zia demanded that all weapons and ammunition, money, and training for the insurgents "be provided through Pakistan and not directly by the CIA." Brzezinski readily agreed, saying the decision had approval from "the top echelons of the Carter administration." An ISI officer, Brig. Mohammad Yousaf, head of the Afghan Bureau in the Pakistani military intelligence service from 1983 to 1987, later confirmed, "As soon as the arms arrived in Pakistan, the CIA's responsibility ended. From then on, it was our pipeline, our organisation that moved, allocated and distributed every bullet that the CIA procured."[24] As long as Pakistan's military rulers allowed their country to be used as a base to fight America's war against the Soviet Union, they were left to pursue the atomic bomb.[25] A year before Ronald Reagan assumed the U.S. presidency and escalated America's proxy war against the Soviet occupation forces in Afghanistan, the Carter administration advised its missions abroad to make these points to host governments:

> The Soviet invasion of Afghanistan has created a serious threat to the states of the South Asia region, particularly Pakistan. President Carter has announced that the United states would provide military equipment, food and other assistance to help Pakistan defend its independence and territorial integrity.
>
> The administration plans to seek urgent Congressional approval for a substantial amount of economic and security assistance to Pakistan over 18 months. We view this assistance as part of a larger multilateral effort to help Pakistan at this critical time.[26]

After a decade of occupation, the Soviets retreated from Afghanistan in February 1989. The Soviet state was extinct by the end of 1991. Afghan Communism collapsed soon after. The enemy was vanquished, and the United States moved on to what imperial powers do—rebuild to fight the next war. As Soviet Communism was collapsing, America fought a brief war to end Saddam Hussein's occupation of Kuwait in early 1991. However, other U.S. concerns in the aftermath of the Cold War took priority over making further big military commitments.[27] President George H. W. Bush was defeated in his 1992 reelection bid; the main focus of his successor, Bill Clinton, became reconstruction of the American economy and market enlargement in other parts of the world. To achieve this, Russia and the newly independent ex-Soviet republics had to be stabilized. Afghanistan and Pakistan, of critical importance in the decisive phase of the Cold War, were no longer on Washington's priority list.

Almost a decade later came the September 11, 2001, attacks on America. Pakistan was once again under military rule; Gen. Pervez Musharraf had seized power in a 1998 coup. Three years on, Musharraf's military regime faced growing opposition at home and disapproval abroad, just as the previous military dictator, General Zia, had a quarter century before. The events of 9/11 restored Pakistan's now-familiar status as a frontline state in the war against al Qaeda and its hosts, the Taliban, in Afghanistan. General Musharraf was one of the first foreign leaders to phone President George W. Bush to express his shock and outrage and to offer his full support. Musharraf's promise established Pakistan as a client state of America in the global war on terror:

> We regard terrorism as an evil that threatens the world community. Concerted international effort is needed to fight terrorism in all its forms and manifestations. The carnage in New York and Washington has raised this struggle to a new level. Pakistan has been extending cooperation to international efforts to combat terrorism in the past and will continue to do so. All countries must join hands in this common cause.
>
> I wish to assure President Bush and the U.S. Government of our unstinted cooperation in the fight against terrorism.[28]

Thus Musharraf officially cut ties with the Taliban and joined in America's war on terror. He did so for three main reasons: (1) deep fear of what refusing President George W. Bush would mean, especially its consequences for Pakistan's traditional rivalry with India and the Kashmir dispute; (2) the need to revive Pakistan's economy; and (3) protection of Pakistan's nuclear weapons program. Musharraf had little choice, and he made this clear to the Pakistani people a few days later:

> We do not have any details from the U.S. of the exact nature of the support from us. But we do know that they have the support of the UN Security Council. The UN resolution specifies punishment for those committing terrorism. This has been supported by all the Islamic countries.

We in Pakistan are facing a very critical situation. Perhaps as critical as the events in 1971 [the year East Pakistan seceded to become Bangladesh]. If we make the wrong decisions our vital interests will be harmed.[29]

Musharraf's military regime "stood aside as the U.S.-led coalition assisted its detested antagonist, the Northern Alliance, to rout its own clients and their al Qaeda accomplices and seize power in Kabul."[30] Pakistan's military launched "counterterrorism operations" in its territory on behalf of the United States for a price. Such operations included kidnap, torture, and transportation of "suspects" to other destinations, including Guantánamo Bay detention center.[31]

In return, the Bush administration "provided almost $10 billion in overt security and economic assistance" between 2001 and 2008. It compensated the Pakistani military for counterterrorism operations with roughly $1 billion annually. At Camp David on June 24, 2003, as General Musharraf looked on, George W. Bush declared that key al Qaeda terrorists had been neutralized thanks "to the effective border security measures and law enforcement cooperation throughout [Pakistan], and . . . to the leadership of President Pervez Musharraf."[32] But as Ashley Tellis reminded readers four years later, "The Bush administration has been compelled to revise the president's earlier, more optimistic, assessment." The July 2007 National Intelligence Estimate, "The Terrorist Threat to the U.S. Homeland," acknowledged that al Qaeda had protected or regenerated its capability to launch attacks and that its leadership and operatives had found a safe haven in Pakistan's Federally Administered Tribal Areas. The war continued well beyond George W. Bush's presidency under his successor, Barack Obama.

AMERICA'S CLUB OF "HONORARY DEMOCRACIES"

In his book, *War and the Liberal Conscience*, eminent British military historian and ex-soldier Michael Howard made a telling observation about the U.S. relationships with client regimes during the Cold War that continued in the post-Soviet international order:

Every state and every regime whose interests coincided with the United States automatically became part of the "Free World," honorary democracies whatever the nature of their political system. The criterion of "freedom" rapidly ceased to be that defined by [President] Truman: "Free institutions, representative governments, free elections, guarantees of individual liberty, freedom of speech and religion and freedom from political oppression." It became, rather, accessibility to American influence and willingness to fall in line with the wishes of the United States.[33]

America's actions in Pakistan and, before 1979, its western neighbor Iran were driven by motives that deserve comparison. As the leader of the capitalist world, the United States was primarily interested in Iran's oil fields and those in the Gulf. At the same time, it sought to deny the Soviet Union primacy in the region. Iran turned into America's frontline proxy in the world's most volatile region. Rapid industrialization was necessary to achieve two goals: development of the oil industry for the West's sake and buildup of Iran's military and centralized regime.[34] Resistance from the clergy, traditionalists, and nationalists was met with force. The United States stuck with the shah to the bitter end in early 1979.

Pakistan was different. The country neither had oil, nor was it of strategic importance to the degree Iran was. Episodes during and after the Cold War made Pakistan's territory useful, most notably in the decade of Soviet occupation of Afghanistan in the 1980s and then following the 9/11 attacks on America in 2001. Unlike Iran, where Shi'a Islam was suppressed, Pakistan encouraged Sunni fundamentalism. General Zia, with American help, was the pioneer of the Islamization of Pakistani society. It suited the United States to fight the Soviet Union and served Zia's own interests to consolidate his regime, but Iran and Pakistan each had to ultimately pay a high price.

6

ARABIA AND THE WEST

Aside from his anti-Zionism, the Arab is an oil supplier.

—*Edward Said*

In his 1978 literary masterpiece *Orientalism*, Palestinian-American intellectual Edward Said presented a critical analysis of Western attitudes toward the East. Said examined the set of beliefs behind the Western ideology known as Orientalism, that is, the tendency for colonial administrators, philosophers, and writers to treat the East as alien, exotic, and inferior. For several centuries, this ideology emphasized "the difference between the European and Asiatic parts of the world," as if each were a distinct and single entity.[1] Said described Orientalism as "fundamentally a political doctrine willed over the Orient." Orientalism determines the relationship between the exploiter and the exploited, based on power. It is aggressive, judgmental, and unsupported by a wholesome body of knowledge. Often orientalists applaud Christian or Western colonial intervention in large parts of Asia, saying it has modernized these regions. They minimize, or ignore, the devastating effects imperialism can have on rich cultures and focus instead on the benefits of foreign ideas, political systems, and lifestyles. They are inclined to generalize rather than explain the causes and consequences of each unique situation. In his essay "The Roots of Muslim Rage," published in *The Atlantic*, orientalist historian Bernard Lewis wrote in 1990,

For a long time now there has been a rising tide of rebellion against this Western paramountcy, and a desire to reassert Muslim values and restore Muslim greatness. The Muslim has suffered successive stages of defeat. The first was his loss of domination in the world, to the advancing power of

Russia and the West. The second was the undermining of his authority in his own country, through an invasion of foreign ideas and laws and ways of life and sometimes even foreign rulers or settlers, and the enfranchisement of native non-Muslim elements. The third—the last straw—was the challenge to his mastery in his own house, from emancipated women and rebellious children. It was too much to endure, and the outbreak of rage against these alien, infidel, and incomprehensible forces that had subverted his dominance, disrupted his society, and finally violated the sanctuary of his home was inevitable. It was also natural that this rage should be directed primarily against the millennial enemy and should draw its strength from ancient beliefs and loyalties.[2]

The British East India Company arrived in the subcontinent to trade and then ruled large parts of India for a century until the 1857 rebellion.[3] In the following year the British Crown assumed direct control of India. The Great Game for supremacy in Central Asia had been ongoing between the British and Russian Empires since the early nineteenth century. With the advent of the twentieth century came the discovery of oil in modern-day Iran, Iraq, Saudi Arabia, and smaller Gulf states. A certain body of scholarship and thought evolved in the West. Philosophers, writers, and colonial administrators associated with these ideas came to be known as Orientalists.

Orientalism caused the biggest wave of commercialization of knowledge and gave birth to the idea that knowledge is power. Knowledge for knowledge's sake—the basis for ambitious, open-ended inquiry since ancient times—had had its day. The distinction Edward Said drew between pure and political knowledge is important here. Inquiry in an area of pure knowledge, he said, has no predetermined goal for overtly political and economic ends, even though its broader significance for such purposes may not be in dispute. However, political knowledge, directed and financed by powerful entities, for economic gain at the cost of someone else is different. Its aims are narrow, are often unjust, and lead to conflict.[4]

Colonialism and colonial behavior are often defended in Western arts, literature, films, and popular culture by assertions of the East's "ignorance and darkness."[5] Intellectual and popular discourse clearly emphasizes the development of Eastern societies by colonial powers. The building of schools, hospitals, roads, and railways under colonial rule is celebrated. One-way flow of ideas and philosophy from the West to the East is emphasized. And, in the aftermath of September 11, 2001, many Eastern societies, or significant sections of them, have been portrayed as living in an uncivilized age. Political and social studies of the East have come to be dominated by terrorism in a narrow sense. Peoples of Eastern appearance, Muslims in particular, are viewed as terrorists or suspects in general, resulting in social schism and targeting of individuals. In a 2006 *USA Today*/Gallup survey, 40 percent of Americans admitted to feeling prejudice against Muslims:

> Substantial minorities of Americans admit to having negative feelings or prejudices against people of the Muslim faith, and favor using heightened security measures with Muslims as a way to help prevent terrorism. Personally knowing someone who is Muslim—which 41% of Americans say they do—corresponds with more favorable attitudes on these questions. These are the key findings of a July 28–30, 2006 *USA Today*/Gallup Poll focusing on U.S. attitudes toward Muslims living in the United States.
>
> Americans' personal discomfort with Muslims is reflected in survey questions dealing with their reaction to being near Muslims in different situations. Nearly one quarter of Americans, 22%, say they would not like to have a Muslim as a neighbor. Slightly fewer, 18%, say they would feel nervous if they noticed a Muslim woman flying on the same airplane as themselves, while significantly more—31%—say they would feel nervous if they noticed a Muslim man on their flight.[6]

A government-funded survey in the United Kingdom in early 2010 showed an alarming rise in the anti-Muslim sentiment there. Ironically, another survey conducted among Muslims across Europe a month before found that British Muslims were much more likely to identify themselves with their adopted country: "Among the findings are that 55 per cent of the population would be strongly opposed to a large mosque being built in their area, while only 15 per cent would be against a new church."[7]

Western imperialists do not want "them" (that is, the Eastern members of their colonies) but instead want "their" wealth. Imperialism is about expanding control beyond state frontiers to areas rich in raw materials and markets. It is not "free trade"—a term increasingly used in the postcolonial age. Colonial powers that grant countries independence but continue to dominate them by controlling their raw materials or using them as markets for manufactured goods are exhibiting a form of imperialism. Use of aggressive means in the form of military or economic pressure to achieve these ends is an essential characteristic of new imperialism. Many of the poorest newly independent nations in Asia, Africa, and Latin America have found themselves in this situation. They have fallen under heavy debt in relation to their economic capacities. Corrupt rulers installed or favored by ex-colonial powers have contributed to these countries' miseries.

Power and humiliation are the cause and effect of human behavior. In chapters 3 and 4, I discussed interventions by Russia, Britain, and the United States in Iran and the consequent radicalization of the Iranian population. In a seminal study, Evelin Lindner analyzed humiliation and its consequences at the personal, national, and global levels. She observed, "It is a universal human experience to feel terrible if put down and humiliated."[8] In my observation, the greater the scale of mobilization by opposing sides locked in a conflict, the deeper, more long-term reaction the conflict generates. The greater the defeat, the more intense and long-lasting the determination in the vanquished to extract the price for humiliation.

The contemporary phenomenon of terrorism originating from the Middle East and America's response can be seen within this framework. Lindner said that the forefathers of Americans in most cases had themselves felt unwelcome, misunderstood, and humiliated before they made it to the United States.[9] She pointed out that America had been a target of major external attacks twice in its history—in 1941 at Pearl Harbor and on September 11, 2001, in New York and Washington. She called it a remarkable record of national security. But the same history and accumulated mind-set made the country respond with intense aggression when threatened militarily and economically.

SAUDI ARABIA

Much of the Arabian Peninsula fell under the Ottoman Empire's nominal rule in the sixteenth century, although, in effect, tribal leaders remained in control.[10] Two centuries later the influential al Saud family and a puritanical religious movement named after its founder Mohammad ibn Abd al Wahhab forged an alliance. Al Wahhab was a religious scholar who sought protection from al Saud and granted legitimacy to the House of Saud in return. In 1744 the House of Saud founded what came to be known as the First Saudi State, which included most of the territory of modern Saudi Arabia. In the face of invasion by the Ottomans and Egyptians in 1818, the Saudi state collapsed. But soon the Saudis reestablished a second kingdom in Najd, the central region, with its capital in Riyadh, the city from which the Egyptian garrison was expelled.[11] A period of interfamily rivalries and civil conflicts weakened al Saud's hold on power at the end of the nineteenth century, forcing the ruling family to go into exile in Kuwait.

The development of modern Saudi Arabia can be traced back to around 1902 and the campaign of Abd al Aziz ibn Saud, who was battling his way back to power in central Arabia and Riyadh. By 1906 the Ottomans had recognized him as their client. Within a decade, the House of Saud family expelled the Ottomans from an area in central Arabia and then waited as the rival Hashemite ruling family in the western region of Hejaz rebelled against the Turks with the aid and encouragement of the British.[12] Ibn Saud resumed his advance after the war, capturing Mecca and Medina in the mid-1920s. He renamed his kingdom Saudi Arabia in 1932.[13]

Fifteen of the nineteen hijackers who committed the 9/11 atrocities seven decades later came from Saudi Arabia; two came from the United Arab Emirates, and one each came from Egypt and Lebanon. In October 2001 came U.S. retaliation against Afghanistan, initially to remove the Taliban regime, for giving sanctuary to al Qaeda. The Iraq invasion was next in March 2003, resulting in the overthrow of Saddam Hussein. That no action was taken against Saudi Arabia after 9/11 raises questions about America's relationship with the kingdom.

Saudi Arabia had an immensely important role as a U.S. ally against the Soviet Union during the Cold War. In the post-Soviet international order, the kingdom remained vital for the United States in the Middle East and beyond. In her study of U.S.-Saudi relations, Rachel Bronson recalled the joint operation to fight the Soviet Union in Afghanistan in the 1980s. America and the Saudi kingdom each spent $3 billion to arm and finance religious extremists. Both countries thought it was a price worth paying to bring down Soviet Communism.[14] Referring to events that led to the decisive East-West confrontation, Bronson cited three major reasons for the U.S.-Saudi alliance in the 1980s. These were the challenge posed by the Shi'a clergy's rise in the Islamic Revolution in Iran and the American hostage crisis in Tehran in November 1979; seizure of the Grand Mosque of Mecca by Saudi and non-Saudi Sunni extremists in the same month; and the Soviet invasion of Afghanistan a month later. These events caused serious crises for the Saudi rulers at home and abroad. And a particularly zealous and fundamentalist form of Sunni Islam became the chosen instrument to deal with these crises. The joint American and Saudi strategy was to direct extremist Islamic rage toward the external enemy, the Soviets:

> It is unclear whether it was American or Saudi officials who first initiated what was to become a multibillion-dollar partnership to challenge the Soviets in Afghanistan. What is apparent is that both parties had their own vested interests in hurting the Soviets. For his part, Brzezinski was determined to bleed them for their activities in Africa and Southeast Asia. The Saudis, religiously motivated and viscerally anti-Soviet, were natural

partners given the vast resources at their disposal and the ease with which they would fund religious groups.[15]

Other factors played a part in the development of U.S.-Saudi relations through the twentieth century. America's ever-increasing dependence on oil supplies from a friendly, reliable producer and the Saudi kingdom's need for access to the industrialized world's markets meant that the two sides bought and sold each other's products on a huge scale. A senior State Department official and former academic, Anne-Marie Slaughter, suggested that the benefits of relations with Saudi Arabia could be seen through three different lenses—a functional lens, a lens of partnership, and a more global lens.[16]

For the same reasons, the U.S. relationship has had historical significance for Saudi Arabia. In the early 1930s King Abdel Aziz bin Abdel Rahman al-Faisal al-Saud found that his sources of revenue, including British assistance and taxes on the pilgrimage to Mecca (the hajj), were not enough. King Ibn Saud, as he was known in the West, told his British confidant Harry St. John Philby that for a million pounds he would grant all the rights anyone wanted over his land.[17] Ultimately, the king granted Standard Oil of California the concession in return for a total of fifty thousand pounds in two interest-free loans, which the king promised to pay back from future oil income if it materialized. Thus began a relationship with the United States that was to prove highly profitable and enduring. Regarding the depth of the relationship, the U.S.–Saudi Arabian Business Council, an organization of business leaders from both countries, explained,

> Business has always been at the forefront of the U.S.-Saudi relations. For the past four decades, the United States has been Saudi Arabia's largest trading partner, while the Kingdom is the largest market for American products in the Middle East. Bilateral trade between Saudi Arabia and the U.S. has increased from $160 million in 1970 to over $26 billion in 2004. Additionally, American companies are the Kingdom's leading joint venture partners, with about 360 projects valued at more than $20 billion. . . . The U.S. is also a leading foreign direct investor in Saudi Arabia, accounting for more than 25 percent of total inward Foreign Direct Investment.[18]

Since the mid-twentieth century America's Middle East policy has been anchored in Israel and Saudi Arabia, more so following the overthrow of the pro-U.S. Pahlavi dynasty in the 1979 revolution in Iran. Unlike its relationship with Israel, a state founded in 1948, the U.S.-Saudi relationship is older, much more discreet, and it can be argued, more important and rewarding for both countries. With two of the holiest religious sites, Mecca and Medina, in Saudi Arabia, the country has high status in Islam. That status and the royal family's wealth and willingness to align with the West have earned Saudi Arabia greater respect from the United States than most countries in the region. But I argue that the relationship is uneven within the imperialist context. Overall, the Saudis gave more to the United States than they received in return.

In 2010 Saudi Arabia was the world's largest producer and exporter of petroleum liquids and the second-largest crude oil producer after Russia. Figures indicated that about 90 percent of Saudi Arabia's export earnings and total state income came through oil sales.[19] The kingdom was a far more reliable supplier to the industrialized world than its adversary, the Soviet Union and its successor state Russia after the end of the Cold War, could ever be. As an Islamic theocracy, the Saudi state was highly susceptible to communist assault in the early days of oil exploration, limiting the Saudi royal family's options. The demand in the United States for its oil treasure was insatiable. The capitalist world could sell whatever the Saudi rulers wanted.

The United States was one of the world's biggest oil producers at the end of 2000s but still imported around two-thirds of its oil needs annually.[20] Only in 2009, the year of the economic meltdown, did U.S. imports drop to 61 percent. One of the two leading members of the Organization of the Petroleum Exporting Countries (OPEC) selling petroleum to America between the early 1970s was Saudi Arabia; the other was Venezuela. An analysis of global oil trends in 2007 noted that four of the five biggest oil-producing countries—Saudi Arabia, Iraq, the United Arab Emirates, and Kuwait—were in the volatile Gulf region in close proximity to each other. But others—Russia, Venezuela, Libya, and Nigeria— were each either "fraught with political uncertainty or run by strongmen hostile to U.S. interests."[21]

Twenty-two percent of the world's known oil reserves were in Saudi Arabia, according to the same analysis. A historically friendly country, the Saudi kingdom was of immense value for the United States, other industrialized countries, and corporate businesses based in the emerging economies producing low-cost goods for the rich world. Of the daily global consumption of approximately 80 million barrels per day, Saudi oil production was just 10 million barrels. Before the economic crises came, as the global economy expanded and the demand for oil rose, the Saudis said they would raise their daily production by 2 million barrels.

Saudi Arabia's spare production capacity was substantial and of vital importance for the United States. One estimate in 2005 indicated that this capacity enabled the Saudis to start pumping and exporting a half million extra barrels per day almost overnight in the hour of crisis. They could boost production by 2 million barrels within three months and by 3 million per day within eighteen months.[22] However, this spare capacity did not always benefit the United States.

The capacity to vary production was used to devastating effect in the wake of the October 1973 Arab-Israeli War. The Arab oil embargo, with Saudi Arabia the leading producer, cut the total output by 5 million barrels a day. The oil price rose from three dollars to twelve dollars per barrel, and the world faced acute energy shortages and dramatic price increases.[23] The Arab oil producers' power was demonstrated when the initial embargo spread throughout OPEC members following pressure from Arabia, led by the Saudi kingdom. Modest increases in production by Iran, Nigeria, and Indonesia quickly dried up.[24] In the immediate wake of the Arab boycott in October 1973, oil prices went up by about 70 percent. In December the OPEC conference in Tehran announced a further price increase of 130 percent and a total embargo on the United States and several other nations.[25] The prices had quadrupled. The boycott was lifted in March 1974, only after Secretary of State Henry Kissinger negotiated disengagement between Israel and Syria.

At other times the Saudi kingdom's spare production capacity was very helpful. For most of the 1980s and 1990s Saudi Arabia's spare capacity was instrumental in increasing oil production to offset demand and supply shocks. One expert described the country as the "cornerstone of world oil market stability" even though the overall cushion of this capacity had been on the decline.[26] These were decades of major conflicts and internal turbulence in the Middle East: the aftermath of Iran's Islamic Revolution, the Iran-Iraq War, the East-West confrontation in Afghanistan in the 1980s, the Gulf War to evict Iraq from Kuwait, and its impact in the following decade. Once the immediate shock of the outbreak of war had dissipated, increased production contributed to periods of glut and lower prices. This occurred in the mid-1980s and again in the mid-1990s.[27] A global analyst, Ashraf Laidi, observed, "The outbreak of the Iran-Iraq war in autumn 1980 had the potential to produce further escalation in prices as the war involved two leading world producers of the fuel. But Saudi Arabia, the biggest producer, flooded the world market with inexpensive oil in 1981 and on into the mid-1980s, raising production to make up for the loss of Iranian and Iraqi production."[28] And Colin Wells, an expert on Saudi Arabia, wrote, "The kingdom currently produces about 8 million barrels a day, and took steps in the 1990s to raise their overall capacity to 10 or even 11 million barrels a day if needed. The Saudis have repeatedly led OPEC in keeping the production high during market shortages, so that prices would stay down to between $25 and $30 per barrel."[29]

By the early twenty-first century the situation had changed dramatically. The 9/11 attacks had a depressing impact on the world economy. The rise of Russia, Venezuela, and Nigeria as major oil producers acted as a counter to Saudi Arabia's leading position. In 2003, the year of the U.S.-led invasion of Iraq, Saudi oil imports to the United States increased to 1.77 million barrels a day, up from 1.55 million barrels in the previous year.[30] Even so, with the world's largest proven reserves around 261.7 billion barrels according to January 2001 estimates, Saudi Arabia's role as an energy supplier in helping to build the U.S. empire was indisputable and substantial. Saudi oil was a vital component in building the industrialized economies and, more importantly, America's military complex after World War II.

Saudi Arabia was a leading member of the U.S.-led coalition against the Soviet Union in the Afghan War in the 1980s. Riyadh contributed millions of dollars to support the Contra forces fighting the left-wing government in Nicaragua once it became clear that Congress would not increase direct U.S. support to the group.[31] Saudi Arabia was in the anticommunist coalition that backed Jonas Savimbi's União Nacional para a Independência Total de Angola (UNITA) forces in the Angolan Civil War. The coalition also included other pro-U.S. Arab states, Israel, and South Africa.[32] Saudi Arabia was the frontline state in the Gulf War to end Iraq's brief occupation of Kuwait in 1990–91. And the kingdom became involved in a border conflict with the Houthi rebels in Yemen in late 2009.

Saudi Arabia's religious and political standing in the Muslim world is of immense help to America in the Middle East, especially as a counter to Iran. Saudi Arabia's role in the Afghan War in the 1980s has been widely discussed and well documented. A program officer with the Third World Network's Africa Secretariat in Accra wrote about the Saudi kingdom's clandestine help for the UNITA rebels in Angola:

> Starting in 1981, Saudi Arabia supplied Morocco with $50–70 million annually to train UNITA personnel. The Clarke amendment fell during Reagan's second term in office, thus clearing the way for direct covert aid to UNITA. The scale of the resulting aid can be gleaned from the following: $15 million in 1986, $15 million in 1987, $30 million in 1988 and $50 million in 1989.
>
> With US material support, and with joint military operations with South Africa, Savimbi expanded operations and escalated the fighting over Angola. Already by 1987 one million people, or 12% of the population, were displaced. In addition, telecommunications facilities were blown up; government health clinics were burned down; 10,000 classrooms were

ravaged; grain storage facilities and hydroelectric grids were destroyed; over 200 bridges were smashed.

Land mines were put in agricultural fields. Between 1980 and 1988, the government lost about $30 billion in revenue; and the amount of physical destruction stood at $22 billion.[33]

THE ROOTS OF A CURIOUS RELATIONSHIP

On the surface, the United States and Saudi Arabia appear to have a symbiotic relationship, each benefiting from the other and causing no harm to its partner. The U.S.-Saudi relationship is based on the exchange of oil and manufactured goods and defense and political cooperation. However, beneath the surface are finer details that determine the overall balance and character of the relationship. These details raise questions about the substance of the benefits and consequences for each country. These questions relate to the challenges and choices confronting each side, considerations that came into play as the relationship developed, the impact of external events, and their objectives above all.

Oil is a commodity of great importance for defense, security, and industrialization. Ownership of petroleum brings significant advantages but also threats from eagle-eyed predators. As a leading producer of oil, the Saudi kingdom's international importance has been unquestioned since the resource was discovered there. In time, however, West Asia, Africa, Europe, and the Americas joined the oil-producing club, and Canada and the United States themselves became significant producers. The enlargement of the producers' club opened up America's options for access to energy sources. However, Saudi Arabia remained competitive because its oil was close to the surface and relatively cheap to retrieve. In addition, the strategic objective of countering the Soviet Union remained important.

When Saudi Arabia granted oil exploration rights to Standard Oil of California in the 1930s, Britain had replaced the Ottoman Empire as the dominant power in the Middle East. What the new Saudi rulers found attractive in the Americans was that they were not "colonialists, like the British, and therefore uninterested in restructuring domestic Saudi politics."[34] To the deeply conservative Saudi ruling clan, American businesspeople represented their companies, not government. Too much familiarity with the British had bred a certain degree of suspicion among the Saudis. Unlike Britain, the United States was far away and tended not to interfere in domestic Saudi politics. This suited Saudi Arabia's conservative social system:

The United States, already active in Saudi Arabia's oil fields provided a natural counter to British hegemony in the region. British influence surrounded the kingdom. The British had treaty obligations with every Persian Gulf state, maintained a colony at Aden with protectorates around it (which eventually became South Yemen), placed its allies on thrones in Iraq and Jordan, and held the Palestinian mandate. A fear of encirclement, which guides Saudi Arabian foreign policy even today, pushed the new king away from the British and toward the Americans.[35]

After World War II and Britain's decline as an imperial power, Soviet influence grew around the kingdom, and this worried the royal family. The Soviet Union shared borders with Iran and Turkey, whose ethnic and linguistic groups also lived on the Soviet side.[36] The end of World War II brought the end of the U.S.-Soviet alliance against the Axis powers and the beginning of the Cold War. The Middle East's oil resources and shipping lanes were of interest to both superpowers. The Cold War resulted in a split among countries in the Middle East as elsewhere.

Egypt was the first major Arab state to fall into the Soviet sphere in the early 1950s. Gamal Abdel Nasser, a young army officer, led the 1952 coup that overthrew King Faroukh and was the undisputed leader of the most powerful Arab state by 1954. Nasser's anti-Western pan-Arab nationalism inspired others in the region. Col. Muammar Gaddafi emerged as Libya's strongman after the 1969 coup that overthrew King Idris. Gen. Hafiz al-Assad and his Ba'ath Party rose to power in Syria, a state rocked by coups between 1946 and 1970.[37] The 1958 Ba'athist revolution ended the monarchy in Iraq. New regimes in Egypt, Syria, and Iraq were all guided by a brand of Arab nationalist socialism that looked to the Soviet Union rather than the West. They worshipped, but never achieved, the goal of Arab unity. The political union between Egypt and Syria, known as the United Arab Republic, lasted a mere three years, from 1958 to 1961. And the Ba'athist parties of Iraq and Syria were afflicted by bitter rivalries. All this upheaval was of grave concern to the Saudi kingdom's royal family.

Saudi Arabia thus made the critical decision to align itself with the United States to protect its vast wealth and theocratic model. The kingdom's early preference for the Americans over the British was vindicated. As the British Empire declined and Soviet Communism became ascendant, America was the only safe option. And the Saudis persevered with this option. Conflicts within the Arab world made it imperative for the Saudi kingdom to maintain its alliance with the United States. The establishment of a Shi'a theocracy in the Islamic Revolution in Iran was a serious challenge to the Sunni theocracy of Saudi Arabia.[38]

In the overall scheme of regional and global politics, it is difficult to envisage the Saudi rulers taking a different route. They had to maintain a consistent, long-term alliance with the United States for the survival of the kingdom's model and their wealth. The alliance served both ends in a narrow sense. In the broader context involving the United States and its adversaries, the U.S.–Saudi Arabian alliance brought unintended consequences, most notably but not exclusively in Afghanistan. Saudi support for Islamist groups in America's war against the Soviet Union created a radical force that was to become a threat to the United States and its allies. An article in the *Middle East Quarterly*, published by the conservative pro-Israel think tank Middle East Forum, acknowledged in 2006 (a bit late),

> The 1979 Soviet invasion of Afghanistan was, in the eyes of those cautioning against a Western cultural attack, affirmation of their assumptions. The struggle for Afghanistan gave young, religious Saudis—graduates of the kingdom's new religious universities—an opportunity to defend Islam. A few hundred traveled to Afghanistan to join Muslim guerrilla fighters, the mujahideen. The United States, Saudi Arabia, and Pakistan assisted them financially and logistically. For the Saudi regime, their activity was a blessing: not only did it portray Saudi Arabia as a leading force in the liberation of Afghanistan without the kingdom having to directly intervene in the conflict, but it also kept the most radical and adventurous young Saudis far from Saudi Arabia. Instead of fighting the U.S. presence on Saudi soil, the kingdom's young radicals fought Soviet penetration of Afghan soil.[39]

The story of Saudi Arabia's involvement in the U.S. war against the Soviet Union in Afghanistan at the end of the twentieth century is part of a bigger picture of the Cold War that deserves a closer, more detailed examination.

7

IRAQ UNDER OCCUPATION
AND DICTATORSHIP

A hostile act thou shalt not perform, that fear of vengeance shall not
consume you.

—Ancient proverb

Modern Iraq was once part of Mesopotamia, which also included northeastern Syria, southeastern Turkey, and southwestern Iran. Situated around
the Tigris-Euphrates river system, Mesopotamia was a cradle of civilization with
origins going back more than six thousand years. Wealth made it a target of invasions. Bruce Preston points out in *A Brief Modern Political History of Iraq*, that
Persian ruler Cyrus was an early conqueror; he was followed by Darius I. In 331
BC Alexander the Great of Macedonia overran Mesopotamia in the Battle of
Gaugamela and rendered the Persian Empire of Darius III impotent.[1] Alexander
encountered a resurgent Persian Empire under the Parthian and Sassanid dynasties
and wars over the land of two rivers continued.

Arabs invaded from the south and made Baghdad, and for a while Samara, their
capital in the year AD 762. In the era of the Abbasid caliphate, the terms "Arab"
and "civilization" became synonymous, and Mesopotamia entered a period of
great glory. Baghdad was "not just the hub of a huge empire but also the location
of a wondrous outburst of learning and culture"—of arts, literature, medicine,
mathematics, and much more.[2]

In 1055 a new wave of invaders, the Seljuq Turks, entered Baghdad from Iran;
these people did not alter the institutions of state or religion in any significant way.

That, however, changed two centuries later. In 1258 the Mongols under Hulagu, grandson of Genghis Khan, attacked the land, killed the last Abbasid caliph, and plundered Baghdad. According to historian Efraim Karsh,

> The terrified [Abbasid] caliph, Mu'tasim, accompanied by his sons, ministers and other members of his coterie, produced himself to Hulagu. He was forced to disclose his treasures and was ridiculed for having failed to put them to good use in the city's defense. Ten days later the hapless suzerain was taken to a neighboring village and executed, apparently by being rolled in a carpet and trampled to death by horses, as the superstitious Mongols would not shed royal blood by the sword. Meanwhile, Baghdad was thoroughly ravaged and plundered, with most of its inhabitants brutally slaughtered.[3]

The three principal territories of modern Iraq, based in Baghdad, Basra, and Mosul, became part of the Ottoman Empire gradually during the sixteenth and seventeenth centuries. As the Ottoman Turk rulers from Istanbul extended their domain to the fertile lands between the Tigris and Euphrates Rivers, it was necessary to check the ambitions of the Safavid shahs of Persia. The region known in Europe as Mesopotamia became a battleground for influence between the two powers. The consequence was that "the imperial and doctrinal rivalries between Sunni Ottomans and Shi'i Safavids touched the histories of the peoples of these frontier lands."[4] The Shi'a-Sunni divide and mutual fear between Iranians and Arabs dated back to the era of Arab invasions. Those divisions were reinforced. Kurds, an Iranian ethnic group spread over the Kurdistan region of Iran, Iraq, Syria, and Turkey, were to become the third force. Already a battleground for influence of regional powers for centuries, the region became a target of growing attention from the Western industrializing powers beginning in the early twentieth century with the discovery of oil. The collapse of the Ottoman Empire and Britain's entry as the new colonial power led to the establishment of the modern Iraqi state after World War I, but not without conflict, which was to continue. As Charles Tripp wrote in his seminal work, *A History of Iraq*,

> The British invasion and occupation of the Ottoman provinces of Basra, Baghdad and Mosul and their subsequent consolidation into the new state of Iraq under a League of Nations Mandate administered by Great Britain radically changed the political worlds of the inhabitants in these territories. . . . Narratives that had made sense of people's lives in one setting were be-

ing overtaken by changed circumstances as the emerging state became the vehicle of distinctive ideas and forms of order, prefigured by, but not necessarily identical to, those of the late Ottoman state. The Iraqi state became a new centre of gravity, setting up or reinforcing the structures that would shape a distinctly Iraqi politics.[5]

The Ottomans had reconquered Basra, Baghdad, and Mosul in the early 1830s and established direct rule under the sultan's governors. Prior to that Ottoman victory, the region had been ruled by Mamluk pashas, who had been taken as boys from Christian families in Georgia and converted to Islam. They ran the local administration, often in accordance with the wishes of the powerful local tribal chiefs. Tripp described the chain of events that led the Ottoman sultan Mahmud II (1808–39) to reassert the central government's authority in outlying provinces. The main reasons were the growing power of other European states and of the provincial governor of Egypt, Muhammad 'Ali Pasha:

> The *Nizam-i Cedid* (the New Order) implied the consolidation of power in the hands of the sultan and his government and left little room for semi-autonomous provincial governors. It was not long, therefore, before Istanbul turned its attention to Baghdad, Basra and Mosul. In 1831, when Da'ud Pasha, the *mamluk* governor of Baghdad, refused to comply with the sultan's edict that he relinquish his office, an army under the governor of Aleppo, 'Ali Rida Pasha, marched on Baghdad, capturing the city and Da'ud Pasha himself. With his capture the rule of *mamluks* in Baghdad ceased abruptly.[6]

The Ottoman army went on to capture Basra, ending Mamluk rule in the city, and in 1834 Mosul too came under the direct central authority of Istanbul.

With the outbreak of World War I in the summer of 1914, the end of the Ottoman Empire was near. British imperial administration was firmly in place in India, and the balance of power was to undergo a dramatic change in a relatively short period. The decline of the Ottomans meant the emergence of Britain, France, and to a lesser extent, Italy. Both France and Italy had their eyes on Libya, but Italy attacked first and seized Libya from the Ottomans in 1911. The British invasion of Mesopotamia began with two infantry brigades of Indian Expeditionary Force D. They occupied Basra, a port city, on the Shatt al-Arab River.[7]

It was no coincidence that during this period oil was first discovered in the region. The objective of the British forces was threefold: to secure a strategic position at the head of the Persian Gulf, to reinforce the Anglo-Persian Oil Company's installations in Abadan in Persia, and to confirm the loyalty of the local Arab personalities and tribal leaders in Basra and its vicinity. However, what was originally designed to be an expedition "on the beach of the Persian Gulf" turned into a major military campaign in March 1917, and Britain went on to capture the Ottoman provinces of Baghdad, Mosul, and Basra.

The retreat of one empire and the arrival of another to fill the vacuum are usually violent and chaotic. The British objective during the occupation of Mesopotamia was to "extract local resources of manpower, food and fodder." This required mobilization and state building. The British had to "penetrate local political, economic and social patterns and intervene in the fabric of colonial society" to divert civilian resources for military purposes. The process was all the more messy because of a "lack of information on the part of the British and Indian administrators."[8]

The forced entry of a new colonial power into society inevitably brought "the new administration in conflict with tribal and nationalist elements and the construction of an administrative framework based on the lines of an Indian province." The colonial administration was "wholly unsuited to local Mesopotamian conditions."[9] Extraction of resources and imposition of administrative control resulted in open revolt between July and September 1920. The legacy of that revolt played a crucial role in defining the nature of the modern Iraqi state, which emerged in 1922 and lasted until the U.S.-led invasion of Iraq in 2003.[10] The 1920 Arab revolt provided for the Sunni minority's control over the larger Shi'a population and the Kurds.

Britain was granted a League of Nations mandate to rule Iraq at the San Remo Conference in Italy in April 1920.[11] What was in effect the incorporation of Mesopotamia into the British Empire provoked local fears of European imperial rule and seemed to belittle the local political leaders' pride. Shi'a and Sunni communities united, and large mass meetings were held to denounce the mandate.[12] An armed revolt broke out in late June 1920. British authorities attempted to crush the rebellion by arresting a number of tribal chiefs in the Euphrates area, but the action fueled the rebels even more. By July the rebellion had spread to many areas of the lower Euphrates and districts in the north, east, and west of Baghdad.

Kurds seized several towns near the border with Persia. By late October the British had regained control of its lost territories, but the revolt had taken the lives of some five hundred British and Indian soldiers and six thousand Iraqis. Iraqi nationalism was born, and the people of Mesopotamia realized the meaning of the identity and interests of a new Iraqi state. Sir Percy Cox arrived in Baghdad to take over as Britain's first high commissioner under the mandate. London had realized that direct rule was too costly, prompting Cox to persuade the elderly Naqib Al-Ashraf of Baghdad, Sayyid Abd al-Rahman, to accept the presidency of the appointed Council of Ministers, which would function under British supervision.

Whitehall was under domestic pressure to devise a formula that would provide the maximum control over Iraq at the least cost to the British taxpayer. The British replaced the military regime with a provisional Arab government, assisted by British advisers and answerable to the supreme authority of the high commissioner for Iraq, Cox. The new administration provided a channel of communication between the British and the restive population, and it gave Iraqi leaders an opportunity to prepare for eventual self-government. The provisional government was aided by the large number of trained Iraqi administrators who returned home when the French ejected Faisal from Syria. Like earlier Iraqi governments, however, the provisional government was composed chiefly of Sunni Arabs; once again the Shi'a were underrepresented.[13]

The reasons for the apparent breakdown of the Sunni-Shi'a alliance of the early stage of the revolt and the failure of the revolt in general were complex. The armed opposition began to run out of steam because the rebels had spread themselves too thinly. The British authorities employed greater coercive military power and intelligence, and many Sunni notables of Baghdad became increasingly apprehensive of the growing power of Sunni tribes and Shi'a influence.[14]

In particular, the tribal sheikhs of the Kut and Amara regions "not only refused to join the revolt, but also worked against it." They were unwilling to jeopardize their extensive landholdings, which the British authorities had recognized. Such "geographical limits to the revolt allowed the British forces to regroup and to counterattack with a formidable modern arsenal" at their disposal. The effort culminated in the surrender of Najaf and Karbala and the end of the revolt. The British prevailed, but they had to give concessions to the Sunni elite. Shi'a "had to watch others benefit from the opportunities that their sacrifices had helped to create."[15] As a result, long-term resentment against the emerging political order remained in what was to become the state of Iraq, with a Shi'a majority and a powerful Sunni ruling class.

With the arrival of Sir Percy Cox, the creation of the new Iraqi state in Mesopotamia had begun. It soon became clear that the British were restoring the Sunni-dominated ruling order of the Ottoman era. The exclusion of Shi'a from important administrative positions under the Ottoman Empire meant that few Shi'a were left with the necessary qualifications and experience or not tainted with accusations of disloyalty.[16] In contrast, there were plenty of unemployed Sunni ex-Ottoman officials looking for jobs. There was a sizable Sunni Arab ruling class in waiting.

Imperial powers are as calculating in strategy as they are hungry for the resources of the lands they conquer. Realism is a common characteristic among empires. The objective of the British Empire was to defeat the Ottomans, but as a victorious power, Britain (along with France) faced the challenge of administering its conquered territories. The lessons of India could not be applied in Iraq. A British-trained army of local soldiers and civil service officials were not available in this newly occupied land.

The initial haste in imposing strict central authority proved disastrous in 1920, and realism soon prevailed. The result was a classic formula to control a restless mixed population: divide the people; support the underdog against the larger, more confident and rebellious section of the population; and rule indirectly from behind the facade of devolution to local administration. The old Ottoman administrative units were restored down to the municipal councils.[17] The Iraqi army too was reconstituted with former Ottoman officers, mostly Sunnis. An ex-Ottoman officer, Ja'far al-'Askari, was installed as defense minister. His brother-in-law, Nuri al-Sa'id, was to become chief of the general staff in February 1921.

State building was proceeding rapidly. The politicians and bureaucrats in London began to think there might be a need to translate the changes on the ground into a more definitive text or constitution. Winston Churchill was secretary for the colonies in the British government of Prime Minister David Lloyd George. He decided to create a Middle East department in the Colonial Office, in a move that would give Churchill a major voice in the formulation of policy in Mesopotamia, Palestine, and other Arab territories that had come into the British sphere.[18]

Deciding the political future of Mesopotamia came first. The high cost of dealing with the Arab uprising and World War I made for a strong economic argument for convening the Cairo conference in March 1921. Britain had to determine how its interests could be "safeguarded as economically as possible." Many British troops were withdrawn, and the air force was strengthened with additional squadrons of aircraft to "maintain order and provide security against extreme threats."[19]

The most important decision made at the Cairo conference was to install the Hashemite Amir Faisal I, an outsider who had been the king of Syria under the French mandate for a year before France threw him out, as king of Iraq. Churchill saw Faisal I as "reliable and inspiring." With the decision to appoint Faisal already made in Cairo, the Council of Ministers promptly declared him king. Next, "a bogus 'referendum' was held in which it was claimed that 96 per cent of the population of Iraq accepted the new king."[20] On August 23, 1921, Faisal was enthroned with pomp and ceremony. As part of the deal, his brother Abdullah became emir of Transjordan (simply called Jordan since 1949). But the wings of Faisal I had to be clipped:

> As a counterforce to the nationalistic inclinations of the monarchy and as a means of ensuring the king's dependence, the British cultivated the tribal shaykhs, whose power had been waning since the end of the nineteenth century. While the new king sought to create a national consciousness, to strengthen the institutions of the emerging state, and especially to create a national military, the tribal shaykhs supported a fragmented community and sought to weaken the coercive power of the state. A major goal of the British policy was to keep the monarchy stronger than any one tribe but weaker than a coalition of tribes so that British power would ultimately be decisive in arbitrating disputes between the two.[21]

The preeminence of Sunnis over Iraq's Shi'a is illustrated by the fact that during a fifteen-year period (1921–36), a mere five out of fifty-seven ministers were Shi'a or Kurds. Further, during the entire period of monarchy until 1958, the prime minister and the ministers of foreign affairs, defense, interior, and finance were almost all Sunni. The domination of Sunni Arabs replicated down to the district level and was out of proportion with the population.[22] The Iraqi state, the monarchy in particular, suffered from a legitimacy crisis. Not only had it deliberately been made weak, but Faisal I was not an Iraqi and the people viewed the monarchy as a British creation. Nevertheless, Churchill took pride in the outcome of the Cairo conference, which he had presided over himself. Britain had nearly forty battalions of troops stationed in 1921, but not a single regular battalion, British or Indian, was left in Iraq by 1929.[23] Expenditure was cut from £20 million to just £1.5 million in this period. Churchill may have had reasons to congratulate himself for running Iraq on the cheap in 1929. It is doubtful "whether he understood, or even followed closely, the tide of events in the Middle East." Opposition to British rule by mandate remained strong in Iraqi society, and the British government had to think of other ways to control the country and its resources.

The Anglo-Iraqi Treaty of Alliance was conceived in 1922 and thereafter became a template to be used in occupied lands again and again. The treaty created the impression of an alliance of two sovereign countries and recognized Iraq's independence. However, its terms authorized Great Britain to appoint advisers to the new government, to supervise its military, to protect foreigners, and to make recommendations on financial and foreign policy matters.[24] With defense, foreign, and military policies firmly in British control, the Council of Ministers of "independent Iraq" looked like a body of puppets.

The Council of Ministers, emboldened by continued opposition to what was seen as British supremacy in Iraq, insisted that the treaty be ratified by the Constituent Assembly to be elected soon. That condition had the effect of linking the treaty with the "constitutional framework of the new state."[25] After much opposition and heated debate, the Anglo-Iraqi Treaty was ratified two years later. It was signed for twenty-five years. Britain retained the right to full military access to Iraqi land for strategic purposes; and the treaty took into account Britain's interests in oil discoveries made in Iraq in 1927. The oil exploration rights had first been granted to the Turkish Petroleum Company before World War I. However, Ottoman and German shares in the company were forfeited to a group of Allied interests, including the Anglo-Persian Oil Company, Royal Dutch Shell, and an American consortium later owned by Standard Oil and Mobil. Because the British government had a substantial stake in the Anglo-Persian Oil Company, Britain came to dominate.[26]

Britain, with a new Labour government in power, announced negotiations on a new treaty with Iraq in 1929, hoping to end the mandate.[27] In November of the same year, the Iraqi Constituent Assembly passed the treaty. Iraq became a member of the League of Nations three years later in October 1932, but British influence remained strong. King Faisal I, installed by Churchill a decade before, was still on the throne; ministries and other state institutions devised by British advisers were in place; and under the treaty, Britain had a right to use all Iraqi military facilities, in addition to leasing two bases:

> The British had therefore succeeded in holding Iraq together by introducing a system of government dependent upon the continued existence of a pliant monarch and his ability to garner support among Sunni Arab elites.... The heterogeneity of Iraq's society had not been lost on the king. Shortly before his death in 1933, he provided an ominous and accurate analysis of the problem confronting Iraq. He lamented that "In Iraq . . . there is still no Iraqi people, but unimaginable masses of human beings, devoid of any patriotic ideal . . . connected by no common tie, giving ear to evil, prone to anarchy, and perpetually ready to rise against any government whatsoever."[28]

From 1932 to 1941 Iraq was officially a fully independent state, a Hashemite monarchy. When King Faisal I died of a heart attack in Switzerland in 1933, his twenty-one-year-old son, Ghazi, succeeded him on the throne. Under Ghazi's rule, Shi'a resentment grew, starting with the resignation of two key Shi'a ministers after the cabinet diverted funds from the Gharraf Dam to the Iraqi army in late 1933. The diversion was an indication that "the government was less concerned about the largely Shi'i communities which would have benefited from the dam."[29] Further moves by the Sunni-dominated regime contributed to tension with the population. The decision to start a conscription program and expand the armed forces pleased the Sunni elite but was seen with suspicion by many Shi'a and Kurds. In August 1934 Ali Jawdat became prime minister. Immediately, Jawdat persuaded the king to dissolve parliament and call new elections, which were massively rigged. Many tribal sheikhs from the mid-Euphrates region were excluded from the new parliament, laying the foundation for tactical alliances against the regime.

The point about British supremacy in Iraq after the Ottoman Empire's defeat has been made. Britain was to remain preeminent in Iraq until 1958, when a military coup ended the monarchy. One historian has observed that the history of the new state in this period and after can be rewritten as "an endless series of coups and countercoups, conspiracies, purges and counter-purges, violent seizures of power, ruthless suppression of dissent and wars," followed by adventures and sanctions that came in the late twentieth century.[30] This upheaval left manipulator and manipulated, victor and vanquished, humiliator and humiliated, gainer and loser, favorite and underdog in its wake. It radicalized the population against foreign powers and classes and communities against each other. In such an artificial state as Iraq, created by an imperial power, tensions are often kept in control through suppression by central authority. This is the story of much of the Middle East.

Britain was to invade Iraq again in 1941, during World War II. The previous decade had been one of considerable upheaval, and in the midst of political chaos, Iraq grew close to Nazi Germany. Nazi sympathies in Iraq led to British troops marching into Baghdad. King Ghazi, young and immature, was on the throne for less than six years from 1933 to 1939. Growing anti-British sentiments and admiration for European fascist dictatorships seemed to have convinced many in the Iraqi military that only a strong militaristic regime could handle the problems of fragmented and backward countries. Gen. Bakr Sidqi, a Sunni nationalist of Kurdish descent in command of the Iraqi army, staged a military coup in October 1936.[31] The civilian government of Yasmin al-Hashemi was overthrown, but King

Ghazi remained on the throne. Hikmat Sulaiman, an anti-reformist figure, became prime minister.

General Sidqi was assassinated in August 1937, and Hikmat Sulaiman too was overthrown by the army. King Ghazi was killed in a car accident in April 1939 and was succeeded by his infant son Faisal II under his uncle, Prince Abd al-Ilah.[32] The deceased king, Ghazi, had shown an unusual degree of independence from Britain, unlike his father, Faisal I. This annoyed London and prompted the British ambassador, Maurice Peterson, to say that King Ghazi "must either be controlled or deposed." And the British undersecretary for foreign affairs (later a conservative foreign secretary and deputy prime minister) R. A. Butler discussed with Peterson the "relative merits" of finding other members of the royal family to replace Ghazi "in case any emergency might arise."

Only a few days after these conversations, King Ghazi died in the car crash. The damage to the car was minimal, and two other passengers in the car "disappeared without trace." The British got the infant king, Faisal II, on the throne with Prince Abd al-Ilah, whom they trusted, acting as regent. But the episode inflamed the anti-British sentiment in Iraq. Riots broke out, and the British consul in Mosul was assassinated.

In all, seven coups took place between the first military coup of Bakr Sidqi in October 1936 and Britain's reoccupation of Iraq in May 1941, but no military plotters made any serious attempt to change the constitution.[33] As one scholar put it, "The most significant constitutional step taken during that period was the decision of Rashid Ali . . . and the colonels to replace the existing regent after he fled the country in April 1941. But although successive army interventions made little attempt profoundly to change or overthrow the constitution and political order, they undermined the parliamentary system and sank political life in Iraq to sinister and murderous levels. Plots and assassinations became a frequent occurrence."[34]

The colonels, also described as the Golden Square, played an important part in Iraqi politics in the 1930s and 1940s. The members of the Golden Square were Col. Salah al-Din al-Sabbagh, Col. Kamal Shahib, Col. Fahmi Said, and Col. Mahmud Salman. These Arab nationalists were seen as having anti-British and pro-Axis views during a period when the German ambassador, Fritz Grobba, was actively networking in Baghdad.[35]

When World War II broke out in Europe in September 1939, Britain, invoking the treaty, made a number of demands on Iraq: that it break off relations with Germany, intern all Germans living in Iraq, and offer whatever help Britain required in its war effort. The Iraqi government of Nuri al-Sa'id responded by meeting the demands quickly and assuring Britain of full support. The Iraqi regime went even further by imposing censorship and curfew, introducing rationing and requisitioning of national resources, and taking all the steps necessary to put Iraq on a war footing. The government assumed the power to rule by decree, which caused great resentment among the Iraqi people. The results were counterproductive and probably contributed to pro-German sentiments in the populace.

As the war progressed and the Germans achieved a series of victories in Europe, Iraq's political climate was transformed. Iraqi nationalists witnessed the Germans overrunning France and other Allies in Europe and the Italian fascist leader Benito Mussolini's decision to formally enter the war as Hitler's ally in June 1940. These developments emboldened the nationalists and split the Iraqi cabinet and the ruling class. One section, including the regent and Nuri al-Sa'id, were seen as strong advocates of a pro-British policy and supporters for the Allies; the Golden Square and Arab nationalists thought the Axis Powers were going to win the war and that Iraq should not provoke them.

The ensuing power struggle led to the coup by Rashid Ali and nationalist officers on April 1, 1941, which forced Nuri al-Sa'id and the regent to escape to Transjordan. Rashid Ali promptly appointed an ultranationalist civilian government that gave "only conditional consent to British requests . . . for troops landings in Iraq."[36] It was too much for the British to take in the midst of the war. Great Britain accused the Iraqis of violating the Anglo-Iraqi Treaty of 1930 and launched the second occupation of Iraq. In the same year Britain and the Soviet Union invaded Iran. Many Iraqis saw the occupation of their country as "an attempt to restore British rule." They rallied in support of the Iraqi army. The Germans, who were already busy preparing for their invasion of the Soviet Union, did not offer enough assistance. As the British occupation army advanced from Basra to Baghdad, Rashid Ali and his nationalist government fled to Egypt. The regent, Abd al-Ilah, returned to power; Rashid Ali and the four generals were tried in absentia and sentenced to death. The generals returned to Iraq and were executed. Rashid Ali stayed in exile.

World War II made Iraq's economic and social problems much more acute. Rising prices and shortages of goods depreciated the salaries of middle-class civil servants, teachers, and army officers. The gap between the rich and poor was widening as wealthy "landowners were enriching themselves through corruption."[37] Peasants had to pay a high price. There was a mismatch between the popular anti-British sentiment and a government in Baghdad dominated by the pro-British Nuri al-Sa'id. It created a leadership crisis that would haunt the constitutional legitimacy of the Iraqi ruling order for more than a decade. In 1955 the Iraqi regime announced that it was joining the Baghdad Pact, later known as the Central

Treaty Organization (CENTO), a British-sponsored military alliance including Iran, Pakistan, and Turkey.

For the monarchy and Nuri al-Sa'id, pro-British policies turned out to be a fatal mistake. The series of coup attempts that began in 1936 finally culminated in the coup of July 14, 1958—officially termed the July 14 Revolution—with virtually no opposition. Crowds poured out into the streets of Baghdad demanding death for the leaders of the ousted regime. Nuri al-Sa'id, Abd al-Ilah, King Faisal II, and several other members of the royal family were executed. Angry crowds attacked the British embassy in the Iraqi capital. The power of the landed sheikhs and the absentee landlords was destroyed. Iraq was now a republic, but internal divisions would soon plague the new military junta, led by Brig. Abd al Karim Qasim and Col. Abd al Salaam Arif. The coup in Iraq in some ways echoed the 1952 revolution in Egypt, in which Col. Gamal Abdel Nasser and fellow young officers of the Free Officers' Movement seized power and overthrew the pro-Western monarchy.[38] The Egyptian revolution ended Britain's influence in the country, which had been under colonial rule from 1882 to 1922 and then functioned as an independent monarchy with close British ties. With anticolonial fervor and harnessing the widespread discontent over economic and social problems and humiliation throughout the Arab world, Egyptians looked up to Nasser. In 1956 the new Egyptian leadership nationalized the Suez Canal and thwarted the 1956 Anglo-French military invasion, supported by Israel, to reoccupy the waterway, built almost a century before, to connect Europe with Asia.

In London an editorial in the *Times* described the 1958 Iraq coup as a "disaster for the west."[39] The editorial went on to say, "The [Iraqi] conspirators may feel that they are simply following an Egyptian lead, and that the slogans of unity, nationalism and neutralism provide them with a policy. But it is far from a true parallel. The Egyptian monarchy was ramshackle and corrupt. Iraq, led by a conscientious royal house, has risen to unimagined prosperity. Now it is the forces of disorder, rather than reform, that are released."

The 1952 Egyptian revolution was a major event that encouraged opposition to pro-Western rulers in the Middle East and North Africa. The coup in Iraq was one of many violent overthrows at the time. In Iran, the nationalist government of Prime Minister Mosaddeq was emboldened as it proceeded to nationalize the country's oil wealth. As discussed in chapter 4, that attempt was crushed in the CIA-MI6 coup, and absolute monarchy closely allied to the West was restored in 1953. However, the 1958 coup in Iraq succeeded, marking a break from Britain. Iraq's neighbor, Syria, underwent a coup that brought the Ba'ath Party to power in 1963. After years of turmoil and several internal coups, Hafiz al-Assad, a general in the Syrian air force, captured power in 1970 in a bloodless coup officially named as the Corrective Revolution.[40] Prior to that decisive change in Syria, in 1969, Muammar Gaddafi, a twenty-seven-year-old army colonel, had led a coup that overthrew King Idris of Libya, and the country became an Islamic Socialist republic.[41]

After the 1958 military coup, Iraq withdrew from the Baghdad Pact. Membership in a military alliance with Iran, Turkey, and Pakistan had been a symbol of British and Western domination of Iraq and was no longer acceptable to Iraq's new military regime. Further, the Iraqi regime established diplomatic relations with the Soviet Union. Baghdad sought military and technical assistance from Moscow and a fifteen-year Soviet-Iraq Friendship Treaty was signed in 1972.

When in 1961 Kuwait was granted independence from Britain, the regime in Baghdad demanded that the small emirate integrate into Iraq. The claim ultimately became the pretext of Iraq's invasion and brief occupation of Kuwait in 1990 under Saddam Hussein.[42] Saddam's rise to power began during a period of considerable turmoil in the Iraqi military, involving a series of coups between 1958 and 1979. Saddam was appointed a member of the ruling Revolutionary Command Council and its vice president in 1969. One by one, he eliminated his adversaries, real or suspected, until he seized absolute power and was sworn in as president in 1979. He ruled Iraq until the U.S.-led invasion that overthrew his regime in 2003.

8

THE BETRAYAL OF PALESTINIANS

We must expel Arabs and take their places.

—*David Ben Gurion*

This is my homeland; no one can kick me out.

—*Yasser Arafat*

We will have to face the reality that Israel is neither innocent, nor redemptive. And that in its creation, and expansion; we as Jews, have caused what we historically have suffered; a refugee population in Diaspora.

—*Martin Buber*

Several epoch-making events happened in the Middle East within a brief period in the twentieth century. After seven years of exploration, the first major oil discovery was made in Iran in 1908, and the Anglo-Persian Oil Company was incorporated a year later.[1] It was the beginning of an oil bonanza, principally for Britain and the United States. During the same period turbine engines powered by oil began to replace coal-fired technology in a race to make imperial navies and road transportation more efficient.[2] The change would have major consequences.

In May 1916, after the fall of the Ottoman Empire in World War I, the British and French governments concluded a secret agreement to carve up their spheres of influence. Sir Mark Sykes of Britain and Georges Picot of France negotiated what came to be known as the Sykes–Picot Agreement. Imperial Russia had a minor role in the exercise, acquiescing with Britain and France.[3] The agreement

stipulated that Britain and France "shall be allowed to establish such direct or indirect administration or control as they desire and as they may think fit" in areas
designated to them. It led to the division of Turkish-held Syria, Iraq, Lebanon, and
Palestine under French and British administration. The Arabs were shocked when
the agreement was exposed by the Bolsheviks in 1917; they realized that two
European powers had planned to divide the fertile crescent into colonies.[4] In the
same year the British foreign secretary, Arthur Balfour, made a policy statement
in a letter to Baron Walter Rothschild, a leader of Britain's Jewish community.
The Balfour Declaration said, "His Majesty's government view with favour the
establishment in Palestine of a national home for the Jewish people, and will use
their best endeavours to facilitate the achievement of this object, it being clearly
understood that nothing shall be done which may prejudice the civil and religious
rights of existing non-Jewish communities in Palestine, or the rights and political
status enjoyed by Jews in any other country."[5]

The British cabinet approved the Balfour Declaration not merely because
politicians such as David Lloyd George, Winston Churchill, and Arthur Balfour
were ideologically of a Zionist bent. They also recognized that the Zionist project
would serve as "a tool with which to cloak and to further imperial ambitions."[6]
In part the aim was to limit Jewish immigration from Eastern Europe to the West,
but in addition, "Western states found that Zionism could bring greater political advantages." The minutes of a meeting between Balfour and U.S. Supreme
Court Justice Louis Brandeis in 1919 were instructive of the thinking in London
and Washington. Brandeis said that "as an American he was confronted with the
disposition of a vast number of Jews, particularly Russian Jews pouring into the
United States year by year." And he came to the conviction that "Zionism was
the answer." In agreement, Balfour responded, "Of course, these are the reasons
that make you and me such ardent Zionists."

The 1917 Balfour Declaration was an act of war, a calculated masterstroke
with a number of objectives. It was designed to get international Jewry onside
and encourage U.S. entry into World War I. At the same time, the Zionist project
would counter support in Western Europe for Russian Bolsheviks, who had destroyed the czarist monarchy in a series of revolutions in the same year. Further,
Great Britain could gain "Palestine as the strategic northern flank of the Suez canal—the gateway to India."[7] All this even though in 1917 Palestine was not under
British control, but still part of the Ottoman Empire. Great Britain had neither
the title of Palestine nor any claim over the territory. A century later the Balfour
Declaration remained central to the main conflict in the Middle East, giving rise
to many disputes.

Scholars have described the Balfour Declaration as ambiguous.[8] Actually, it was far from vague. Saying that the British government viewed with favor the creation of a homeland for the Jewish people and making the promise that Britain would use its best endeavors to achieve this objective was hardly ambiguous. Further, in suggesting that "it be clearly understood that nothing shall be done which may prejudice the civil and religious rights of existing non-Jewish communities in Palestine," Balfour neither gave a guarantee nor set up a mechanism to safeguard the Palestinians' existing rights and lifestyle.

Balfour also contradicted the Sykes-Picot Agreement, which provided for an international administration, the nature of which was to be decided after consultations with Russia, other allies, and the representatives of the shereef of Mecca. With the Balfour Declaration, those promises lay in ruins. In the five years after World War I, Jews continued to immigrate to Palestine, increasing the size of the Jewish community there to 12 percent of the total population by 1923. Alarmed by the developing trend, the First Palestine National Congress met in Jerusalem in early 1919. It rejected the Balfour Declaration and demanded independence for Palestine, but in April 1920 the Supreme Council of the San Remo Peace Conference assigned the Palestine mandate to Britain, a move formally approved by the League of Nations in July 1922.[9] Worse was to come. Several Jews were killed and more injured in violent protests; the British removed the mayor of Jerusalem, Musa Kazim Pasha al-Husseini, from office for opposing their policies; and Palestinians tried to convene the Second National Congress in May 1920 to discuss the matter but were prevented.

Violent incidents continued between Palestinians and the Jewish immigrants as the League of Nations Council prepared to give its approval to the San Remo Peace Conference's decision to assign the Palestine mandate to Great Britain. In February 1922 another Palestinian delegation to London repeated its rejection of the Balfour Declaration to the British colonial secretary, Winston Churchill, and demanded independence again. Despite growing protests, in 1922 Churchill issued a white paper that set out policy with regard to Palestine's future. He seemed to lay the blame on Palestinians, and his subsequent assertions demonstrated why the Palestinians' sense of betrayal is so deep and permanent. Churchill wrote, "The tension which has prevailed from time to time in Palestine is mainly due to apprehensions, which are entertained both by sections of the Arabs and by sections of the Jewish population. These apprehensions, so far as the Arabs are concerned, are partly based upon exaggerated interpretations of the meaning of the [Balfour] Declaration favouring the establishment of a Jewish National Home in Palestine, made on behalf of His Majesty's Government on 2nd November 1917."[10]

Churchill's white paper accused the Palestinians of making unauthorized statements to the effect that the purpose is to "create a wholly Jewish Palestine." He condemned the use of phrases such as "Palestine is to become Jewish as England is English." He asserted that the British government regarded "any such expectation as impracticable" and had "no such aim in view." Nor had London "at any time contemplated, as appears to be feared by the Arab delegation, the disappearance or the subordination of the Arab population, language or culture in Palestine." The white paper was a masterpiece in doublespeak, as the following passages illustrate:

> The Zionist Commission in Palestine, now termed the Palestine Zionist Executive, has not desired to possess any share in the general administration of the country. Nor does the special position assigned to the Zionist organization in Article IV of the Draft Mandate for Palestine imply any such functions. That special position relates to the measures to be taken in Palestine affecting the Jewish population, and contemplates that the organization may assist in the general development of the country, but does not entitle it to share in any degree in its government.

Then Churchill went on to write,

> It is necessary that the Jewish community in Palestine should be able to increase its numbers by immigration. This immigration cannot be so great in volume as to exceed whatever may be the economic capacity of the country at the time to absorb new arrivals. It is essential to ensure that the immigrants should not be a burden upon the people of Palestine as a whole, and that they should not deprive any section of the present population of their employment.[11]

The British mandate for Palestine officially came into force on September 29, 1923. A fourth wave of sixty-seven thousand Jewish immigrants, more than half from Poland, were granted permission to settle in Palestine between 1924 and 1928. The Jewish population increased to 16 percent of the total of Palestine, and meanwhile, in 1925 the Revisionist Party, founded by Polish Zionist Vladimir Jabotinsky, demanded establishment of an independent Jewish state.[12] In the 1930s a further wave of a quarter million Jewish people arrived, increasing the Jewish population to about one-third of Palestine. The trend of Jewish immigration to Palestine had been established. It would continue, leading to tensions and conflict, both within and without, before the creation of Israel in 1948 and beyond.

Amid escalating turmoil the British government convened the St. James Conference in 1939, to which both Arab and Jewish delegations were invited, each side representing disparate groups with their own internal differences.[13] The Jewish side had Zionist and non-Zionist factions; the Arab side had Palestinians and Arabs from Egypt, Iraq, Saudi Arabia, Transjordan, and Yemen. So tense was the environment that the British were forced to negotiate with each delegation separately, and British proposals encountered resistance from both sides. In the absence of any agreement at the St. James Conference in February, the British government announced its own policy in May 1939 in a white paper published by Malcolm MacDonald, colonial secretary in Neville Chamberlain's cabinet.

The 1939 white paper, in the making for several months, was seen as a significant reversal of "the British commitment to a Jewish homeland in Palestine, dating back to 1917." Germany's Nazi regime was looking increasingly menacing in Europe, and the outbreak of World War II was only months away. In the white paper on Palestine, the limitation of Jewish immigration was made permanent: "Seventy-five thousand Jewish immigrants would be allowed to enter Palestine over a five year period and any subsequent increase would require the acquiescence of the Arabs." The situation for the Jews was desperate. It looked as though "the British repudiated the Balfour Declaration and their commitment under the League of Nations just at the time of greatest need for a sanctuary for Jewish refugees."[14]

The 1939 white paper appeared to be in violation of the Balfour Declaration, but the Palestine mandate still remained with Britain. The Jews of Palestine and the rest of the world were outraged at this "British betrayal." For the Arabs, the white paper "did not go far enough" because "it was British policy that Palestine should be converted into an Arab state." These developments contributed to the environment that gave rise to Zionist groups such as Irgun and its breakaway wing, Lehi. According to *A History of Jewish People*,

Anti-British activities were intensified by the Irgun and Lehi. Until that time the founder of Lehi, Abraham Stern, and several of his associates had been the only element in the Yishuv [pre-state Jewish residents] that took a consistently anti-British stand and tried to contact the Axis powers, particularly Italy, so as to achieve the political objectives of Zionism with their help, in a common struggle against Britain. Such an attitude could not be accepted by the Yishuv at a time when the war against the Nazis and their satellites was at its height, and this group [Lehi] therefore became isolated.

Finally, it was almost entirely annihilated when Abraham Stern was captured by the British police in February 1942 and murdered on the spot.[15]

The 1940s were decisive years in several respects. The developments signified Britain, the power with the mandate to administer Palestine, losing control. The Balfour Declaration had signaled the beginning of Palestinian estrangement. MacDonald's 1939 white paper appeared to be doing something comparable in the 1940s. Large-scale Jewish emigration from Europe and the consequential involuntary transfer of property to new arrivals in Palestine heightened social tensions. Some of that anger was now directed at the British, who attempted to suppress it by force. Jewish terrorism became a distinct phenomenon.

Police officers were assassinated. Sir Harold McMichael, the assistant inspector general of Palestine, was assassinated by the Irgun and Stern gang.[16] But the most high-profile assassination was that of the British minister of state, Lord Moyne, in Cairo. As he arrived for a luncheon date on November 6, 1944, Moyne was shot to death by two members of the Stern gang, whose leader had been killed by the British police a little more than two years before. As historian Robert Kumamoto remarked, "This bold and daring act horrified Great Britain and served notice to the world that serious events were indeed unfolding in the Middle East."[17]

World War II ended in Europe in May 1945. In September large-scale Jewish immigration to Palestine, organized by Haganah, the Jewish paramilitary organization that later formed the core of the Israel Defense Forces, resumed.[18] From 1945 until the creation of the Israeli state in 1948, Haganah's main activity was to smuggle tens of thousands of illegal immigrants into Palestine. During World War II, the United States had become the center of world Zionist activity. In May 1942 an American Zionist conference in New York made the first open demand for a Jewish state, "embracing all Palestine," on the basis of a proposal put forward by David Ben Gurion, head of the executive committee of the Jewish Agency for Palestine, a group created by the Sixteenth Zionist Congress, held in Zurich in 1929, to facilitate Jewish settlement in Palestine.[19] Growing American pressure under the Roosevelt and Truman administrations prevailed over Britain and transformed the Palestinian landscape in coming decades. According to Malcolm Kerr, "Britain was undoubtedly opposed to Palestine's partition, but it could not force this solution in the face of strong American pressure and escalating Jewish terrorism. Ernest Bevin [the British foreign secretary] pointed out that from the Zionist point of view, 100,000 immigrants was only a beginning and that the Jewish Agency talked of millions."[20]

Amid deteriorating Anglo-Jewish relations, a plan was devised by the Anglo-American Committee set up that year to agree on a policy regarding the admission of Jews to Palestine. The plan was to turn the mandate into a British trusteeship, under which Palestine was to be divided into a Jewish province, an Arab province, and a purely British-administered area including Jerusalem and Negev.[21] The idea was to no one's satisfaction. Even so, if the United States agreed to share the financial cost, 100,000 Jews would be allowed to migrate to Palestine in the first year, and thereafter the number of immigrants would be "determined by the economic absorptive capacity."

President Truman rejected the proposal, known as the Morrison-Grady Plan. Jewish opposition was also vehement, and more violence worsened the crisis between Britain and the Jewish population. The Jewish Agency, meanwhile, secretly approved a resolution accepting a sovereign Jewish state in a "partitioned Palestine," provided it had full control of immigration and economic policies. The United States and Britain were "quietly informed" of the decision.[22]

In another desperate attempt, the British government invited the Arab governments, the Arab Higher Committee for Palestine (the central political organ of the Arab community of Palestine, created in April 1936)· and the Jewish Agency to a conference to be held in September 1946.[23] The Arab Higher Committee and the Jewish Agency both rejected the invitation, the former because the British would not allow the mufti to attend and the latter because Britain did not accept its condition to discuss the partition plan. The Arab governments submitted their own plan for the creation of a unitary state that would put an end to Jewish immigration, protect both Jewish minority rights and holy sites, and conclude a treaty with Britain.[24] The conference simply lacked delegates who could make credible decisions. No real progress could be made.

In the United States, the congressional and state election campaign was in full swing. In a tight race in New York State, Governor Thomas E. Dewey found it "expedient" to come out in strong support of the Zionist demands for statehood and for large-scale immigration to Palestine. The Arabs, once again, protested that President Truman was acting contrary to earlier promises. America's staunchly pro-Zionist position encouraged Zionists not to make significant concessions. The British decided to temporarily adjourn the conference in October 1946.

Thereafter, the conference reconvened in January 1947 but continued to be dogged by difficulties. The Zionist position hardened after the Twenty-Second Jewish Congress, which demanded "nothing less than a Jewish state." And, despite meeting British officials informally, Jewish representatives continued their boycott. The Palestinian side returned when the mufti of Jerusalem was allowed to attend, but the Palestinian position had hardened considerably. Ultimately, the British government made its own proposals, providing for a trusteeship for up to five years and Jewish immigration of 100,000 over two years. But as the Arabs and the Zionists had rejected the proposal, Britain's choices were limited. In April 1947 the government asked the UN secretary general to convene a special session of the General Assembly. The objective would be to constitute a special committee to prepare for the consideration of the question of Palestine by the General Assembly.

After a breakdown in relations with Britain, which blamed the Zionists for the failure in reaching a compromise on Palestine, an increasing number of nationalist Jews became convinced that the only way to realize their dream of an independent Jewish state in Palestine was to intensify the campaign of violence against the Palestinian administration and secure more support from the American administration. For the United States too, backing the partition plan was crucial. President Roosevelt wanted good relations with Saudi Arabia and had promised Kind Saud that the United States would make no policy decisions about Palestine without consulting the Arabs and take no action which might prove hostile to the Arab people.[25] A week later Roosevelt died, and Vice President Harry Truman took over as president.

Truman had been a more ardent supporter of the Zionist cause before the war. In 1939 then senator Truman had inserted in the Congressional Record a comment condemning MacDonald's white paper as a "dishonorable repudiation by Britain of her obligations."[26] Revelations about the Holocaust had radically changed the political climate the world over, no less in the United States, which, as a newly emerged superpower, mattered. At a 1944 rally in Chicago, Truman had said, "Today, not tomorrow, we must do all that is humanly possible to provide a haven and place of safety for all those who can be grasped from the hands of Nazi butchers. Free lands must be opened to them."[27]

In his political memoir, Harry Truman wrote, "The question of Palestine as a Jewish homeland goes back to the solemn promise that had been made to them [the Jews] by the British in the Balfour Declaration of 1917—a promise which had stirred the hopes and the dreams of these oppressed people. This promise, I felt, should be kept, just as all promises made by responsible, civilized governments should be kept."[28]

For all his support for Jewish immigration, Truman had his misgivings about a Jewish state, lest it require enormous U.S. resources to defend.[29] At one stage, shortly after MacDonald issued his white paper limiting the immigration of Jews to Palestine, he wanted to bring large numbers of Jewish people to the United States. However, he encountered opposition at home. In October 1945 he wrote to Prime Minister Atlee of Britain to allow a "reasonable number of displaced people" to immigrate to Palestine; Atlee refused. In the same month, though, Senator Robert Wagner of New York and Senator Robert Taft of Ohio introduced a resolution in the chamber in open support of a Jewish state.[30] It was one of the decisive events for the eventual creation of the Israeli state. President Truman's immediate reaction was to oppose the Wagner-Taft resolution for fear of precipitating a crisis.

Truman suggested that he wanted to wait for the report of the Anglo-American Committee.[31] But the language of the Wagner-Taft resolution was both powerful and provocative; it called on the Truman administration to "use its good offices" to open Palestine to "the free entry of Jews" and to assist in establishing "the Jewish national home" there.[32] Senator Wagner then informed the White House that unless the president "vigorously backed the resolution," Republicans would be able to "turn their support for the measure into political capital."

Truman's hesitation did not stop the U.S. Congress. First, the Senate Foreign Relations Committee approved the resolution by a vote of seventeen to one. Four days later, on December 17, the full Senate endorsed the establishment of a Jewish "home" in Palestine; the House of Representatives did the same two days later. It had been Zionist strategy to cultivate congressional support for a Jewish state. That strategy had succeeded, and "the rebuke of the president was complete." When the report came, the Zionists welcomed the recommendation for the immigration of 100,000 homeless Jews but criticized the committee's opposition to a Jewish state.

Britain's opposition to immigration on such scale triggered the illegal Jewish armed groups in Palestine to step up acts of terrorism against the mandatory power.[33] Britain retaliated in mid-1946, arresting the leaders of the Jewish Agency for Palestine, which was an internationally recognized organization. The British government tried to justify its action by alleging that the agency was conspiring with the underground military force, Haganah. For many prominent Jews in Palestine, the British act was "nothing less than an act of war against the Jewish people."

The end of World War II in mid-1945 had brought profound changes in the balance of global power, which had shifted from Britain to the United States. The Soviet Union's emergence as the second superpower had all but ensured a new race between the two ex-allies. Competition for access to energy deposits in the Middle East would be at the center of geopolitics in the second half of the twentieth century, just as it had been earlier. But the actors this time were different—the Americans and the Soviets, instead of the British and the Ottoman.

The age of empires in the old sense was coming to an end with the British Empire's dissolution. However, there was a pressing need for an imperial project to ensure free access to raw materials and energy resources, routes, and markets, as the world entered the era of postwar industrialization. Control of the project moved to the United States, the leader of the capitalist world, and to the Soviet Union, its adversary. In February 1947 the British government announced that it would terminate its mandate for Palestine. Within days the issue of the future of Palestine was sent to the UN.[34]

The year 1947 will be remembered for Britain's withdrawal from two major undertakings, India and Palestine, amid bloodshed and large-scale refugee migration, which would leave tragic legacies for future generations.[35] Despite Truman's misgivings about what the establishment of a Jewish homeland in Palestine would mean for America in terms of commitment, the power of Jewish votes in U.S. domestic politics, their influence in Congress, and the sympathy generated for a group that had suffered Nazi persecution during the war combined to build an unstoppable momentum. On May 14, 1948, the state of Israel was established despite Arab rejection of the UN partition plan.[36] The British mandate of Palestine expired the next day. Palestinians commemorate the event as al Nakba (cataclysm). That year saw the forced deportation of up to a million refugees from their cities and villages, massacres of civilians, and the razing to the ground of hundreds of Palestinian villages.[37]

Subsequent Arab-Israeli wars—the Sinai campaign of 1956, the 1967 and 1973 wars—and other conflicts over the last six decades have perpetuated the humiliation and the tragedy that began a century before. It is one of the most profound lessons history has repeated but humans fail to heed—that the humiliation of a people anywhere leads to nothing but injustice, which is the seed of all violence, more injustice, and wars.

EPILOGUE

In our wildest aberrations we dream of an equilibrium we have left behind and which we naively expect to find at the end of our errors.

—*Albert Camus*

History is used to turmoil, occasionally interrupted by a dawn of hope. When World War I ended with the deaths of many millions and the defeat of the German, Austro-Hungarian, and Ottoman Empires, few would have foreseen a second war in which some sixty million would perish and the horror of the atomic bomb would be visited on humankind. We must ask whether a war of even greater ferocity a little more than twenty years after World War I meant that matters were not settled in 1918. Under the Treaty of Versailles of June 1919, Germany had to admit war guilt, pay reparations, return overseas colonies, and disarm. The victors wanted to make sure that Germany could never again threaten the peace in Europe.[1]

Imperial Germany's defeat in November 1918 seemed comprehensive. The German Revolution (1918–19) swept away Emperor Wilhelm II and forced all ruling princes to abdicate. The Weimar Republic was created, but that experiment in parliamentary democracy was short-lived. The republic collapsed with the Wall Street crash of October 1929, at a time when the humiliation of imperial Germany was still alive in the German people's minds. Germany was in crisis again, with crippling war costs, hyperinflation, and the rise of extremists—paramilitaries on the left and the right. All this prompted the rise of the Nazi Party and Adolf Hitler. The Weimar era was over by 1933; the Nazi era had begun, and Germany was a threat to peace once more.

World War II, which ended in the defeat of Germany and Japan, also did not settle matters. The victors, the United States and the Soviet Union, were soon nuclear adversaries, determined to build their own empires in their very different visions. The Cold War was in fact a series of conflicts between the two superpowers fought in regions of the world, including Vietnam, Korea, the South Asian subcontinent and

Afghanistan, the Middle East, and Central and South America, that had emerged from World Wars I and II with numerous territorial, ethnic, and religious disputes.[2] After an enormously expensive decade of war in Afghanistan, the Soviet Union was defeated and became extinct as a superpower, but matters were far from settled. New challenges in the form of extreme nationalism, ethnic conflict, and religious fundamentalism came to the fore in many parts of the world, including the West.[3]

The outcome of the Soviet Union's dissolution for West Asia was different from that in Europe. Soviet satellite states in Eastern Europe emerged from the iron curtain and walked toward the West. The transformation was by and large peaceful, but there were a few exceptions. The end of Nicolae Ceauşescu's Communist regime in Romania was particularly chaotic and violent. Yugoslavia, which was also Communist but not a Soviet satellite, endured a violent ethnic conflict between Serbs, Muslims, and Croats that ultimately broke up the federation.

In West Asia, the focus of this book, the turmoil that began with the Ottoman Empire's collapse at the end of World War I determined the history of the next century. The imperial powers' arbitrary partition of Arabia into smaller, vulnerable entities left a legacy of unresolvable disputes. The Palestinians' loss of land and livelihood and the colonization of their territory by settlers from continents far away triggered a crisis unimaginable in its early years. The discovery of oil, in Iran in 1908 and subsequently in the Arab world, gave the Western powers a long-term motive to anchor themselves in the region. Domination of the Middle East was essential for industrialization, access to transit routes, and overseas markets.

A long chapter of imperial competition—first between Britain and Russia and then between the United States and the Soviet Union—seemed to end with the Cold War. In reality, the Cold War battles in West Asia had their origins in the early twentieth century, when the Ottoman Empire was defeated and oil was discovered in the region. The defeat of Soviet Communism was greeted with hubristic euphoria in the West. Neoconservative thinker Francis Fukuyama celebrated the triumph of "liberal capitalism" in his 1989 essay and subsequent book *The End of History and the Last Man*, in which he asserted, "What we may be witnessing is not just the end of the Cold War, or the passing of a particular period of post-war history, but the end of history as such: that is, the end point of mankind's ideological evolution and the universalization of Western liberal democracy as the final form of human government."[4]

Around the same time, Samuel Huntington came out with his "clash of civilizations" theory.[5] Whereas Fukuyama proclaimed that "Western liberal democracy" had secured the final victory, that nothing would follow in terms of competing ideologies grounded in local needs and endeavors to address them, Huntington predicted continuing conflict in the world. This conflict would not be "primarily ideological or primarily economic" but would have a "cultural" source. The clash of civilizations would dominate global politics, and the future would be "the West versus the rest":

> Western military power is unrivaled. Apart from Japan, the West faces no economic challenge. It dominates international political and security institutions and with Japan international economic institutions. Global political and security issues are effectively settled by a directorate of the United States, Britain and France, world economic issues by a directorate of the United States, Germany and Japan, all of which maintain extraordinarily close relations with each other to the exclusion of lesser and largely non-Western countries. . . . The very phrase "the world community" has become the euphemistic collective noun (replacing "the Free World") to give global legitimacy to actions reflecting the desires of the world community.[6]

On the surface, Fukuyama and Huntington seemed to be saying different things. One asserted that the long ideological war was over; human evolution had arrived at its end point, and the West's victory was final. The other predicted global conflict between civilizations. However, there appeared to be a common underlying message—that the United States must maintain its global domination. Outside North America and Western Europe, the world was still crowded with autocratic regimes, repression, regional wars over disputed frontiers, and desperate poverty and hunger. Refugee crises and acquired immunodeficiency syndrome (AIDS) threatened tens of millions of people. There were no effective answers to these challenges.

In the late 1980s the Japanese economy was still enjoying one of its longest expansionary phases after World War II, but it fell into a long recession after the 1990 stock market crash and the collapse of property prices.[7] So severe was Japan's economic decline that the 1990s came to be known as the lost decade. In contrast, China was rapidly becoming an economic powerhouse. When it emerged, the term "international community" broadly referred to the Western bloc. To equate the international community with the erstwhile Free World in the wake of the Cold War was a misrepresentation of history in making. By December 1999 Russia's extreme vulnerability was ending. President Boris Yeltsin suddenly resigned, handing over power to the much younger Vladimir Putin. Signs that Russia's resurgence was about to commence a decade after the Soviet Union's fall were unmistakable.

In the absence of a real challenger, right-wing policy advocates such as Fukuyama and Huntington were among thinkers eager to influence America's future course of action in the post-Soviet world. Their intervention in the ongoing political debate in Washington was to become a self-fulfilling prophecy. Ideologically driven thinkers have a tendency to say what their sponsors would like to hear. What is said, in turn, influences policy. In February 1992 Paul Wolfowitz, undersecretary of defense in George H. W. Bush's administration, proposed that the U.S. objective in the post-Soviet world was to prevent the recmergence of a new rival in the defunct USSR or elsewhere in the future.[8]

Wolfowitz's doctrine called for America's predominance in the Middle East to "preserve U.S. access to the region's oil." But George H. W. Bush was defeated by Bill Clinton in November 1992, and the Republican plan for the post-Soviet international order had to wait. Still, many of the 1992 document's tenets emerged again in the late 1990s. The neoconservative Project for the New American Century, which played a crucial role in shaping George W. Bush's election campaign and his presidency, had a manifesto remarkably similar to the 1992 "Strategy Planning Guidance" drafted by Wolfowitz.[9]

The American response to the attacks of September 11, 2001, named the global war on terror, went way beyond the removal of Afghanistan's Taliban regime, which had provided sanctuary to militant groups. The invasion of Iraq; continuing pressure on Iran, Syria, and Lebanon; and America's support of Israel during the war on Gaza (December 27, 2008–January 18, 2009) in the final days of George W. Bush's presidency signified the execution of a plan conceived in the final decade of the twentieth century. In the Iraq War, beginning in 2003, thousands of American and allied soldiers died, many more were injured, and the breakdown of order made conflict truly multilayered as neighbor turned against neighbor, one ethnic group against another. Civilians suffered most, although the exact numbers of civilian casualties are impossible to count. Millions were internally displaced or fled as refugees to Syria, Jordan, and other countries.

In *Overcoming the Bush Legacy in Iraq and Afghanistan*, I compared Barack Obama's victory over his Republican rival John McCain in November 2008 to revolutionary events of America's past.[10] American voters lined up in huge numbers to cast their ballots in the hope of bringing a nightmarish period of history to a close. The American people had had enough of George W. Bush, who was one of the most unpopular presidents in history when he left office. Bush was despised abroad, wreaking great damage to America's moral and political international leadership. The election in which the people constitutionally and peacefully voted to overturn the neoconservative Republican order was nothing short of a "popular revolution."

Obama had promised to disengage from the war in Iraq, which he described as the "wrong war" (the Afghan war was the "right war" for him), and to promote economic recovery and reconciliation. He pledged to begin a dialogue with the Muslim world based on "mutual interests and mutual respect." He devoted his speech of June 4, 2009, in Cairo to mending the broken fences with the Muslim world (see appendix B). In sum, President Obama promised to transform the way in which the executive branch was functioning, and he hoped that eventually a transformation of the United States of America would take place.

As the end of Obama's first term approached in 2012, the United States was in the midst of a counterrevolution at home and abroad. Once a preacher of change and hope, Obama had embraced the imperialist Project for the New American Century of the Bush era. He had extended the global war on terror with a vastly escalated program of drone attacks in a growing number of countries;[11] he had taken it upon himself to go through the profiles, or "intelligence notes," about people's backgrounds, actual or alleged activities and their psychological conditions, and decide who would be killed and who would be defined as "militant."

Obama had reneged on his promise to close the Guantánamo Bay detention camp, which he had pledged to do within a year of taking office. With an executive order, he brought back indefinite detention at Guantánamo and military commission trials.[12] The number of inmates at Guantánamo went down, but at facilities abroad, such as the American military base at Bagram in Afghanistan, the prisoner populations increased many times over.[13] And despite the administration's attempts to manage the news media, revelations of atrocities involving U.S. troops continued.[14] These revelations caused more outrage abroad than in the United States, where the main concern was the deteriorating economy and unemployment.

Popular uprisings across the Middle East and North Africa, starting in Tunisia in December 2010, threatened the status quo in the region. The self-immolation of Mohammed Bouazizi, an unemployed Tunisian graduate selling vegetables, after being harassed and humiliated by municipal officials, was a momentous event.[15] It caused a strong emotional reaction in the Arab world. The uprisings threatened pro-U.S. regimes and, consequently, the West's geopolitical interests in the region. Opposition movements against friendly rulers caused anxiety in Washington. In contrast, in Iran, Syria, and Libya—which were ruled by adversarial and unpredictable leaders—antiregime sentiments provided opportunities. Regime change in these countries would greatly enhance American influence in the region. In each uprising, the immediate targets of public fury were autocratic and corrupt rulers; not far beneath the surface was resentment against the foreign powers that maintained those rulers.

The pressure from below succeeded in overthrowing Zine El Abidine Ben Ali in Tunisia in January 2011, and elections for a constituent assembly and for president were subsequently held.[16] However, events were different elsewhere. After initial protests against Algeria's elderly strongman, Abdelaziz Bouteflika, his party, the National Liberation Front (FLN), showed no sign of giving up power; FLN members won nearly half the seats in parliament in the May 2012 elections. There was widespread disbelief of the election results, which the opposition called "neither acceptable, logical or reasonable."[17]

In Egypt, the thirty-year rule of Hosni Mubarak was made possible by billions of dollars in American aid, mostly to the Egyptian armed forces. After weeks of massive demonstrations against his rule, the military withdrew support from the eighty-three-year-old ruler, forcing Mubarak to resign.[18] The Muslim Brotherhood and its Islamist allies won parliamentary elections in January 2012, but the Mubarak-era judges of the Supreme Constitutional Court annulled those elections six months later, just before the final round of the presidential election. The Muslim Brotherhood, whose candidate, Mohamed Morsi, looked likely to win against Mubarak's last prime minister, Ahmed Shafiq, warned the generals of a "life or death" struggle over the country's political future.[19] The Supreme Military Council meanwhile assumed sweeping powers to legislate and to veto any constitution. Analysts described these moves as a coup.[20] After delays and uncertainty, Morsi was declared the winner in the presidential election. But Egypt was without a constitution; the newly elected president's powers were not defined; the country was without a parliament; and the military had a firm grip over foreign and defense policies. How long would the military and the Muslim Brotherhood cohabit? And what impact would the new civilian political order have on relations with Israel and on Egyptian and regional politics? Such critical questions remained. As 2012 came to an end, President Morsi's move to grant himself sweeping powers opened up sharp divisions in Egyptian society again. And Israel launched another bombing campaign against the Hamas-ruled Gaza Strip and maintained its siege of the territory.

The contrast in American attitudes toward people's revolts in different countries in the region was stark. Washington's criticisms of friendly regimes were infrequent, mild, and ambiguous, even when they were made. On Egypt, the Obama administration would refer to its desire to "stand with the people in their aspirations to choose their own leaders." But the United States wanted the relationship based on billions of dollars of aid to the Egyptian armed forces to continue.[21] On the suppression of protests in Bahrain, a close military ally and the base of America's Fifth Fleet, Secretary of State Hillary Clinton said, "We cannot dictate the outcome." And in the same interview, she said, "We had no control over what happened in Egypt."[22] With Saudi Arabia, the closest U.S. ally other than Israel in the region, Washington's relations are reverential.[23]

"Put your sword in its place, for all who take the sword will perish by the sword." These words from the Bible speak to Muammar Gaddafi's regime in Libya and his brutal killing in October 2011. Gaddafi's assassination was also a lesson for those who fought the dictator, for the end of him left a disturbing trail of savagery from which the victors did not emerge unscathed. Whereas Western governments were complicit and the mainstream newspapers and broadcast media restrained and unchallenging, nongovernmental organizations drew on their conscience to speak out about reprisals by both sides.[24]

Gaddafi was the second Arab ruler after Iraq's Saddam Hussein to meet his end as a result of Western intervention in this, so far brief, new century. Unlike the situation in Iraq, Western powers were not in Libya as occupiers in a formal sense. That there were no "boots on the ground" was President Barack Obama's escape route. Airpower—drones in particular—had changed the nature of warfare, making it possible to control territory from the sky. Having troops on the ground was irrelevant.

The United States, Britain, and France, flying NATO's flag, embarked on a "humanitarian" bombing mission in Libya. In March 2011 the UN Security Council called for dialogue, reform, and measures to protect civilians in Benghazi via Resolution 1973, but a mere seven months later, the situation looked much different.[25] Just before Gaddafi's gruesome killing under NATO's watchful eyes, Secretary Clinton, visiting Libya, said, "We hope he can be captured or killed soon."[26] How many times had the foreign minister of one country been heard proclaiming that the leader of another be eliminated? It was an act of incitement and encouraged anti-Gaddafi fighters to hunt him down.

After Gaddafi's assassination, Secretary Clinton said, "We came, we saw, he died."[27] In London, Defence Secretary Philip Hammond told executives of British companies to "pack their suitcases" and head for Libya to secure contracts.[28] Others more in touch had words of warning. Abdel Bari Atwan, editor of the London-based pan-Arab newspaper *Al-Quds Al-Arabi*, wrote in the *Guardian*, "Pictures of his final struggle will bolster those who remain Gaddafi loyalists—and make no mistake, there are many who will lament his demise, either out of self-interest or tribal loyalty."[29]

With NATO's war in Libya over, attention turned more firmly on Iran and Syria. But China and Russia were no longer willing to support Western moves in the Security Council that would authorize military intervention.[30] Inconsistencies in Western policy had compromised the alliance's credibility, and that regime change in Syria and Iran would complete America's project in the Middle East was obvious.

But history never fails to surprise, and the future is unlikely to be any different, for those who seek greatness bring about their own downfall, and those who are humiliated wait for their day.

APPENDIX A

Declaration of Independence,
July 4, 1776

When in the course of human events, it becomes necessary for one people to dissolve the political bands which have connected them with another, and to assume among the powers of the earth, the separate and equal station to which the laws of nature and of nature's God entitle them, a decent respect to the opinions of mankind requires that they should declare the causes which impel them to the separation.

We hold these truths to be self-evident:

That all men are created equal; that they are endowed by their Creator with certain unalienable rights; that among these are life, liberty, and the pursuit of happiness; that, to secure these rights, governments are instituted among men, deriving their just powers from the consent of the governed; that whenever any form of government becomes destructive of these ends, it is the right of the people to alter or to abolish it, and to institute new government, laying its foundation on such principles, and organizing its powers in such form, as to them shall seem most likely to effect their safety and happiness. Prudence, indeed, will dictate that governments long established should not be changed for light and transient causes; and accordingly all experience hath shown that mankind are more disposed to suffer, while evils are sufferable than to right themselves by abolishing the forms to which they are accustomed. But when a long train of abuses and usurpations, pursuing invariably the same object, evinces a design to reduce them under absolute despotism, it is their right, it is their duty, to throw off such government, and to provide new guards for their future security. Such has been the patient sufferance of these colonies; and such is now the necessity which constrains them to alter their former systems of government. The history of the present King of Great Britain is a history of repeated injuries and usurpations, all having in direct object the establishment of an absolute tyranny over these states. To prove this, let facts be submitted to a candid world.

He has refused his assent to laws, the most wholesome and necessary for the public good.

He has forbidden his governors to pass laws of immediate and pressing importance, unless suspended in their operation till his assent should be obtained; and, when so suspended, he has utterly neglected to attend to them.

He has refused to pass other laws for the accommodation of large districts of people, unless those people would relinquish the right of representation in the legislature, a right inestimable to them, and formidable to tyrants only.

He has called together legislative bodies at places unusual, uncomfortable, and distant from the depository of their public records, for the sole purpose of fatiguing them into compliance with his measures.

He has dissolved representative houses repeatedly, for opposing, with manly firmness, his invasions on the rights of the people.

He has refused for a long time, after such dissolutions, to cause others to be elected; whereby the legislative powers, incapable of annihilation, have returned to the people at large for their exercise; the state remaining, in the mean time, exposed to all the dangers of invasions from without and convulsions within.

He has endeavored to prevent the population of these states; for that purpose obstructing the laws for naturalization of foreigners; refusing to pass others to encourage their migration hither, and raising the conditions of new appropriations of lands.

He has obstructed the administration of justice, by refusing his assent to laws for establishing judiciary powers.

He has made judges dependent on his will alone, for the tenure of their offices, and the amount and payment of their salaries.

He has erected a multitude of new offices, and sent hither swarms of officers to harass our people and eat out their substance.

He has kept among us, in times of peace, standing armies, without the consent of our legislatures.

He has affected to render the military independent of, and superior to, the civil power.

He has combined with others to subject us to a jurisdiction foreign to our Constitution and unacknowledged by our laws, giving his assent to their acts of pretended legislation:

> For quartering large bodies of armed troops among us;

> For protecting them, by a mock trial, from punishment for any murders which they should commit on the inhabitants of these states;

> For cutting off our trade with all parts of the world;

> For imposing taxes on us without our consent;

> For depriving us, in many cases, of the benefits of trial by jury;

> For transporting us beyond seas, to be tried for pretended offenses;

> For abolishing the free system of English laws in a neighboring province, establishing therein an arbitrary government, and enlarging its boundaries, so as to render it at once an example and fit instrument for introducing the same absolute rule into these colonies;

> For taking away our charters, abolishing our most valuable laws, and altering fundamentally the forms of our governments;

> For suspending our own legislatures, and declaring themselves invested with power to legislate for us in all cases whatsoever.

He has abdicated government here, by declaring us out of his protection and waging war against us.

He has plundered our seas, ravaged our coasts, burned our towns, and destroyed the lives of our people.

He is at this time transporting large armies of foreign mercenaries to complete the works of death, desolation, and tyranny already begun with circumstances of cruelty and perfidy scarcely paralleled in the most barbarous ages, and totally unworthy the head of a civilized nation.

He has constrained our fellow-citizens, taken captive on the high seas, to bear arms against their country, to become the executioners of their friends and brethren, or to fall themselves by their hands.

He has excited domestic insurrection among us, and has endeavored to bring on the inhabitants of our frontiers the merciless Indian savages, whose known rule of warfare is an undistinguished destruction of all ages, sexes, and conditions.

In every stage of these oppressions we have petitioned for redress in the most humble terms; our repeated petitions have been answered only by repeated injury. A prince, whose character is thus marked by every act which may define a tyrant, is unfit to be the ruler of a free people.

Nor have we been wanting in our attentions to our British brethren. We have warned them, from time to time, of attempts by their legislature to extend an unwarrantable jurisdiction over us. We have reminded them of the circumstances of our emigration and settlement here. We have appealed to their native justice and magnanimity; and we have conjured them, by the ties of our common kindred, to disavow these usurpations which would inevitably interrupt our connections and correspondence. They too, have been deaf to the voice of justice and of consanguinity. We must, therefore, acquiesce in the necessity which denounces our separation, and hold them as we hold the rest of mankind, enemies in war, in peace friends.

We, therefore, the representatives of the United States of America, in General Congress assembled, appealing to the Supreme Judge of the world for the rectitude of our intentions, do, in the name and by the authority of the good people of these colonies solemnly publish and declare, That these United Colonies are, and of right ought to be, free and independent states; that they are absolved from all allegiance to the British crown and that all political connection between them and the state of Great Britain is, and ought to be, totally dissolved; and that, as free and independent states, they have full power to levy war, conclude peace, contract alliances, establish commerce, and do all other acts and things which independent states may of right do. And for the support of this declaration, with a firm reliance on the protection of Divine Providence, we mutually pledge to each other our lives, our fortunes, and our sacred honor.

[Signed by] JOHN HANCOCK [President]

New Hampshire
JOSIAH BARTLETT,
WM. WHIPPLE,
MATTHEW THORNTON.

Massachusetts Bay
SAML. ADAMS,
JOHN ADAMS,
ROBT. TREAT PAINE,
ELBRIDGE GERRY.

Rhode Island
STEP. HOPKINS,
WILLIAM ELLERY.

Connecticut
ROGER SHERMAN,
SAM'EL HUNTINGTON,
WM. WILLIAMS,
OLIVER WOLCOTT.

New York
WM. FLOYD,
PHIL. LIVINGSTON,
FRANS. LEWIS,
LEWIS MORRIS.

New Jersey
RICHD. STOCKTON,
JNO. WITHERSPOON,
FRAS. HOPKINSON,
JOHN HART,
ABRA. CLARK.

Pennsylvania
ROBT. MORRIS
BENJAMIN RUSH,
BENJA. FRANKLIN,
JOHN MORTON,
GEO. CLYMER,

JAS. SMITH,
GEO. TAYLOR,
JAMES WILSON,
GEO. ROSS.

Delaware
CAESAR RODNEY,
GEO. READ,
THO. M'KEAN.

Maryland
SAMUEL CHASE,
WM. PACA,
THOS. STONE,
CHARLES CARROLL of Carrollton.

Virginia
GEORGE WYTHE,
RICHARD HENRY LEE,
TH. JEFFERSON,
BENJA. HARRISON,
THS. NELSON, JR.,
FRANCIS LIGHTFOOT LEE,
CARTER BRAXTON.

North Carolina
WM. HOOPER,
JOSEPH HEWES,
JOHN PENN.

South Carolina
EDWARD RUTLEDGE,
THOS. HAYWARD, JUNR.,
THOMAS LYNCH, JUNR.,
ARTHUR MIDDLETON.

Georgia
BUTTON GWINNETT,
LYMAN HALL,
GEO. WALTON.

NOTE.-Mr. Ferdinand Jefferson, Keeper of the Rolls in the Department of State, at Washington, says: " The names of the signers are spelt above as in the facsimile of the original, but the punctuation of them is not always the same; neither do the names of the States appear in the facsimile of the original. The names of the signers of each State are grouped together in the facsimile of the original, except the name of Matthew Thornton, which follows that of Oliver Wolcott."-Revised Statutes of the United States, 2d edition, 1878, p. 6.

Source: "Declaration of Independence," July 4, 1776, Avalon Project, Yale Law School, http://avalon.law.yale.edu/18th_century/declare.asp.

APPENDIX B

President Barack Obama's Cairo Speech:
Remarks on a New Beginning,
June 4, 2009

I am honored to be in the timeless city of Cairo, and to be hosted by two remarkable institutions. For over a thousand years, Al-Azhar has stood as a beacon of Islamic learning and, for over a century, Cairo University has been a source of Egypt's advancement. Together, you represent the harmony between tradition and progress. I am grateful for your hospitality, and the hospitality of the people of Egypt. I am also proud to carry with me the goodwill of the American people, and a greeting of peace from Muslim communities in my country: Assalaamu alaykum.

We meet at a time of tension between the United States and Muslims around the world—tension rooted in historical forces that go beyond any current policy debate. The relationship between Islam and the West includes centuries of coexistence and cooperation, but also conflict and religious wars. More recently, tension has been fed by colonialism that denied rights and opportunities to many Muslims and a Cold War in which Muslim-majority countries were too often treated as proxies without regard to their own aspirations. Moreover, the sweeping change brought by modernity and globalization led many Muslims to view the West as hostile to the traditions of Islam.

Violent extremists have exploited these tensions in a small but potent minority of Muslims. The attacks of September 11, 2001 and the continued efforts of these extremists to engage in violence against civilians has led some in my country to view Islam as inevitably hostile not only to America and Western countries, but also to human rights. This has bred more fear and mistrust.

So long as our relationship is defined by our differences, we will empower those who sow hatred rather than peace, and who promote conflict rather than the cooperation that can help all of our people achieve justice and prosperity. This cycle of suspicion and discord must end.

I have come here to seek a new beginning between the United States and Muslims around the world; one based upon mutual interest and mutual respect; and one based upon the truth that America and Islam are not exclusive, and need not be in competition. Instead, they overlap, and share common principles—principles of justice and progress; tolerance and the dignity of all human beings.

I do so recognizing that change cannot happen overnight. No single speech can eradicate years of mistrust, nor can I answer in the time that I have all the complex questions that brought us to this point. But I am convinced that in order to move forward, we must say openly the things we hold in our hearts, and that too often are said only behind closed doors. There must be a sustained effort to listen to each other; to learn from each other; to respect one another; and to seek common ground. As the Holy Quran tells us: "Be conscious of God and speak always the truth." That is what I will try to do—to speak the truth as best I can, humbled by the task before us, and firm in my belief that the interests we share as human beings are far more powerful than the forces that drive us apart.

Part of this conviction is rooted in my own experience. I am a Christian, but my father came from a Kenyan family that includes generations of Muslims. As a boy, I spent several years in Indonesia and heard the call of the azaan [the Muslim call to prayer] at the break of dawn and the fall of dusk. As a young man, I worked in Chicago communities where many found dignity and peace in their Muslim faith.

As a student of history, I also know civilization's debt to Islam. It was Islam—at places like Al-Azhar University—that carried the light of learning through so many centuries, paving the way for Europe's Renaissance and Enlightenment. It was innovation in Muslim communities that developed the order of algebra; our magnetic compass and tools of navigation; our mastery of pens and printing; our understanding of how disease spreads and how it can be healed. Islamic culture has given us majestic arches and soaring spires; timeless poetry and cherished music; elegant calligraphy and places of peaceful contemplation. And throughout history, Islam has demonstrated through words and deeds the possibilities of religious tolerance and racial equality.

I know, too, that Islam has always been a part of America's story. The first nation to recognize my country was Morocco. In signing the Treaty of Tripoli in 1796, our second President John Adams wrote: "The United States has in itself no character of enmity against the laws, religion or tranquility of Muslims." And since our founding, American Muslims have enriched the United States. They have fought in our wars, served in government, stood for civil rights, started businesses, taught at our universities, excelled in our sports arenas, won Nobel prizes, built our tallest building, and lit the Olympic torch. And when the first Muslim-American was recently elected to Congress, he took the oath to defend our constitution using the same Holy Quran that one of our founding fathers—Thomas Jefferson—kept in his personal library.

So I have known Islam on three continents before coming to the region where it was first revealed. That experience guides my conviction that partnership between America and Islam must be based on what Islam is, not what it isn't. And I consider it part of my responsibility as president of the United States to fight against negative stereotypes of Islam wherever they appear.

But that same principle must apply to Muslim perceptions of America. Just as Muslims do not fit a crude stereotype, America is not the crude stereotype of a self-interested empire. The United States has been one of the greatest sources of progress that the world has ever known. We were born out of revolution against an empire. We were founded upon the ideal that all are created equal, and we have shed blood and struggled for centuries to give meaning to those words—within our borders, and around the world. We are shaped by every culture, drawn from every end of the Earth, and dedicated to a simple concept: *E pluribus unum*—"Out of many, one."

Much has been made of the fact that an African-American with the name Barack Hussein Obama could be elected president. But my personal story is not so unique. The dream of opportunity for all people has not come true for everyone in America, but its promise exists for all who come to our shores—that includes nearly 7 million American Muslims in our country today who enjoy incomes and education that are higher than average.

Moreover, freedom in America is indivisible from the freedom to practice one's religion. That is why there is a mosque in every state of our union, and over 1,200 mosques within our borders. That is why the US government has gone to court to protect the right of women and girls to wear the hijab, and to punish those who would deny it.

So let there be no doubt: Islam is a part of America. And I believe that America holds within her the truth that regardless of race, religion, or station in life, all of us share common aspirations—to live in peace and security; to get an education and to work with dignity; to love our families, our communities, and our God. These things we share. This is the hope of all humanity.

Of course, recognizing our common humanity is only the beginning of our task. Words alone cannot meet the needs of our people. These needs will be met only if we act boldly in the years ahead; and if we understand that the challenges we face are shared, and our failure to meet them will hurt us all.

For we have learned from recent experience that when a financial system weakens in one country, prosperity is hurt everywhere. When a new flu infects one human being, all are at risk. When one nation pursues a nuclear weapon, the risk of nuclear attack rises for all nations. When violent extremists operate in one stretch of mountains, people are endangered across an ocean. And when innocents in Bosnia and Darfur are slaughtered, that is a stain on our collective conscience. That is what it means to share this world in the 21st century. That is the responsibility we have to one another as human beings.

This is a difficult responsibility to embrace. For human history has often been a record of nations and tribes subjugating one another to serve their own interests. Yet in this new age, such attitudes are self-defeating. Given our interdependence, any world order that elevates one nation or group of people over another will inevitably fail. So whatever we think of the past, we must not be prisoners of it. Our problems must be dealt with through partnership; progress must be shared.

That does not mean we should ignore sources of tension. Indeed, it suggests the opposite: we must face these tensions squarely. And so in that spirit, let me speak as clearly and plainly as I can about some specific issues that I believe we must finally confront together.

The first issue that we have to confront is violent extremism in all of its forms.

In Ankara, I made clear that America is not—and never will be—at war with Islam. We will, however, relentlessly confront violent extremists who pose a grave threat to our security. Because we reject the same thing that people of all faiths reject: the killing of innocent men, women, and children. And it is my first duty as president to protect the American people.

The situation in Afghanistan demonstrates America's goals, and our need to work together. Over seven years ago, the United States pursued al Qaeda and the Taliban with broad international support. We did not go by choice, we went because of necessity. I am aware that some question or justify the events of 9/11. But let us be clear: Al Qaeda killed nearly 3,000 people on that day. The victims were innocent men, women and children from America and many other nations who had done nothing to harm anybody. And yet al Qaeda chose to ruthlessly murder these people, claimed credit for the attack, and even now states their determination to kill on a massive scale. They have affiliates in many countries and are trying to expand their reach. These are not opinions to be debated; these are facts to be dealt with.

Make no mistake: we do not want to keep our troops in Afghanistan. We seek no military bases there. It is agonizing for America to lose our young men and women. It is costly and politically difficult to continue this conflict. We would gladly bring every single one of our troops home if we could be confident that there were not violent extremists in Afghanistan and Pakistan determined to kill as many Americans as they possibly can. But that is not yet the case.

That's why we're partnering with a coalition of 46 countries. And despite the costs involved, America's commitment will not weaken. Indeed, none of us should tolerate these extremists. They have killed in many countries. They have killed people of different faiths—more than any other, they have killed Muslims. Their actions are irreconcilable with the rights of human beings, the progress of nations, and with Islam. The Holy Quran teaches that whoever kills an innocent, it is as if he has killed all mankind; and whoever saves a person, it is as if he has saved all mankind. The enduring faith of over a billion people is so much bigger than the narrow hatred of a few. Islam is not part of the problem in combating violent extremism—it is an important part of promoting peace.

We also know that military power alone is not going to solve the problems in Afghanistan and Pakistan. That is why we plan to invest $1.5 [billion] each year over the next five years to partner with Pakistanis to build schools and hospitals, roads and businesses, and hundreds of millions to help those who have been displaced. And that is why we are providing more than $2.8 [billion] to help Afghans develop their economy and deliver services that people depend upon.

Let me also address the issue of Iraq. Unlike Afghanistan, Iraq was a war of choice that provoked strong differences in my country and around the world. Although I believe that the Iraqi people are ultimately better off without the tyranny of Saddam Hussein, I also believe that events in Iraq have reminded America of the need to use diplomacy and build international consensus to resolve our problems whenever possible. Indeed, we can recall the words of Thomas Jefferson, who said: "I hope that our wisdom will grow with our power, and teach us that the less we use our power the greater it will be."

Today, America has a dual responsibility: to help Iraq forge a better future—and to leave Iraq to Iraqis. I have made it clear to the Iraqi people that we pursue no bases, and no claim on their territory or resources. Iraq's sovereignty is its own. That is why I ordered the removal of our combat brigades by next August. That is why we will honor our agreement with Iraq's democratically elected government to remove combat troops from Iraqi cities by July, and to remove all our troops from Iraq by 2012. We will help Iraq train its security forces and develop its economy. But we will support a secure and united Iraq as a partner, and never as a patron.

And finally, just as America can never tolerate violence by extremists, we must never alter our principles. 9/11 was an enormous trauma to our country. The fear and anger that it provoked was understandable, but in some cases, it led us to act contrary to our ideals. We are taking concrete actions to change course. I have unequivocally prohibited the use of torture by the United States, and I have ordered the prison at Guantánamo Bay closed by early next year.

So America will defend itself, respectful of the sovereignty of nations and the rule of law. And we will do so in partnership with Muslim communities which are also threatened. The sooner the extremists are isolated and unwelcome in Muslim communities, the sooner we will all be safer.

The second major source of tension that we need to discuss is the situation between Israelis, Palestinians and the Arab world.

America's strong bonds with Israel are well known. This bond is unbreakable. It is based upon cultural and historical ties, and the recognition that the aspiration for a Jewish homeland is rooted in a tragic history that cannot be denied.

Around the world, the Jewish people were persecuted for centuries, and anti-Semitism in Europe culminated in an unprecedented Holocaust. Tomorrow, I will visit Buchenwald, which was part of a network of camps where Jews were enslaved, tortured, shot and gassed to death by the Third Reich. Six million Jews were killed—more than the entire Jewish population of Israel today. Denying that fact is baseless, ignorant, and hateful. Threatening Israel with destruction—or repeating vile stereotypes about Jews—is deeply wrong, and only serves to evoke in the minds of Israelis this most painful of memories while preventing the peace that the people of this region deserve.

On the other hand, it is also undeniable that the Palestinian people—Muslims and Christians—have suffered in pursuit of a homeland. For more than 60 years they have endured the pain of dislocation. Many wait in refugee camps in the West Bank, Gaza, and neighboring lands for a life of peace and security that they have never been able to lead. They endure the daily humiliations—large and small—that come with occupation. So let there be no doubt: the situation for the Palestinian people is intolerable. America will not turn our backs on the legitimate Palestinian aspiration for dignity, opportunity, and a state of their own.

For decades, there has been a stalemate: two peoples with legitimate aspirations, each with a painful history that makes compromise elusive. It is easy to point fingers—for Palestinians to point to the displacement brought by Israel's founding and for Israelis to point to the constant hostility and attacks throughout its history from within its borders as well as beyond. But if we see this conflict only from one side or the other, then we will be blind to the truth: the only resolution is for the aspirations of both sides to be met through two states, where Israelis and Palestinians each live in peace and security.

That is in Israel's interest, Palestine's interest, America's interest, and the world's interest. That is why I intend to personally pursue this outcome with all the patience that the task requires. The obligations that the parties have agreed to under the road map are clear. For peace to come, it is time for them—and all of us—to live up to our responsibilities.

Palestinians must abandon violence. Resistance through violence and killing is wrong and does not succeed. For centuries, black people in America suffered the lash of the whip as slaves and the humiliation of segregation. But it was not violence that won full and equal rights. It was a peaceful and determined insistence upon the ideals at the center of America's founding. This same story can be told by people from South Africa to South Asia; from eastern Europe to Indonesia. It's a story with a simple truth: that violence is a dead end. It is a sign of neither courage nor power to shoot rockets at sleeping children, or to blow up old women on a bus. That is not how moral authority is claimed; that is how it is surrendered.

Now is the time for Palestinians to focus on what they can build. The Palestinian Authority must develop its capacity to govern, with institutions that serve the needs of its people. Hamas does have support among some Palestinians, but they also have responsibilities. To play a role in fulfilling Palestinian aspirations, and to unify the Palestinian people, Hamas must put an end to violence, recognize past agreements, and recognize Israel's right to exist.

At the same time, Israelis must acknowledge that just as Israel's right to exist cannot be denied, neither can Palestine's. The United States does not accept the legitimacy of continued Israeli settlements. This construction violates previous agreements and undermines efforts to achieve peace. It is time for these settlements to stop.

Israel must also live up to its obligations to ensure that Palestinians can live, and work, and develop their society. And just as it devastates Palestinian families, the continuing humanitarian crisis in Gaza does not serve Israel's security; neither does the continuing lack of opportunity in the West Bank. Progress in the daily lives of the Palestinian people must be part of a road to peace, and Israel must take concrete steps to enable such progress.

Finally, the Arab states must recognize that the Arab Peace Initiative was an important beginning, but not the end of their responsibilities. The Arab-Israeli conflict should no longer be used to distract the people of Arab nations from other problems. Instead, it must be a cause for action to help the Palestinian people develop the institutions that will sustain their state; to recognize Israel's legitimacy; and to choose progress over a self-defeating focus on the past.

America will align our policies with those who pursue peace, and say in public what we say in private to Israelis and Palestinians and Arabs. We cannot impose peace. But privately, many Muslims recognize that Israel will not go away. Likewise, many Israelis recognize the need for a Palestinian state. It is time for us to act on what everyone knows to be true.

Too many tears have flowed. Too much blood has been shed. All of us have a responsibility to work for the day when the mothers of Israelis and Palestinians can see their children grow up without fear; when the Holy Land of three great faiths is the place of peace that God intended it to be; when Jerusalem is a secure and lasting home for Jews and Christians and Muslims, and a place for all of the children of Abraham to mingle peacefully together as in the story of Isra, when Moses, Jesus, and Mohammed (peace be upon them) joined in prayer.

The third source of tension is our shared interest in the rights and responsibilities of nations on nuclear weapons.

This issue has been a source of tension between the United States and the Islamic Republic of Iran. For many years, Iran has defined itself in part by its opposition to my country, and there is indeed a tumultuous history between us. In the middle of the Cold War, the United States played a role in the overthrow of a democratically elected Iranian government. Since the Islamic revolution, Iran has played a role in acts of hostage-taking and violence against US troops and civilians. This history is well known. Rather than remain trapped in the past, I have made it clear to Iran's leaders and people that my country is prepared to move forward. The question, now, is not what Iran is against, but rather what future it wants to build.

It will be hard to overcome decades of mistrust, but we will proceed with courage, rectitude and resolve. There will be many issues to discuss between our two countries, and we are willing to move forward without preconditions on the basis of mutual respect. But it is clear to all concerned that when it comes to nuclear weapons, we have reached a decisive point. This is not simply about America's interests. It is about preventing a nuclear arms race in the Middle East that could lead this region and the world down a hugely dangerous path.

I understand those who protest that some countries have weapons that others do not. No single nation should pick and choose which nations hold nuclear weapons. That is why I strongly reaffirmed America's commitment to seek a world in which no nations hold nuclear weapons. And any nation—including Iran—should have the right to access peaceful nuclear power if it complies with its responsibilities under the nuclear non-proliferation treaty. That commitment is at the core of the treaty, and it must be kept for all who fully abide by it. And I am hopeful that all countries in the region can share in this goal.

The fourth issue that I will address is democracy.

I know there has been controversy about the promotion of democracy in recent years, and much of this controversy is connected to the war in Iraq. So let me be clear: no system of government can or should be imposed upon one nation by any other.

That does not lessen my commitment, however, to governments that reflect the will of the people. Each nation gives life to this principle in its own way, grounded in the traditions of its own people. America does not presume to know what is best for everyone, just as we would not presume to pick the outcome of a peaceful election. But I do have an unyielding belief that all people yearn for certain things: the ability to speak your mind and have a say in how you are governed; confidence in the rule of law and the equal administration of justice; government that is transparent and doesn't steal from the people; the freedom to live as you choose. Those are not just American ideas, they are human rights, and that is why we will support them everywhere.

There is no straight line to realize this promise. But this much is clear: governments that protect these rights are ultimately more stable, successful and secure. Suppressing ideas never succeeds in making them go away. America respects the right of all peaceful and law-abiding voices to be heard around the world, even if we disagree with them. And we will welcome all elected, peaceful governments—provided they govern with respect for all their people.

This last point is important because there are some who advocate for democracy only when they are out of power; once in power, they are ruthless in suppressing the rights of others. No matter where it takes hold, government of the people and by the people sets a single standard for all who hold power: you must maintain your power through consent, not coercion; you must respect the rights of minorities, and participate with a spirit of tolerance and compromise; you must place the interests of your people and the legitimate workings of the political process above your party. Without these ingredients, elections alone do not make true democracy.

The fifth issue that we must address together is religious freedom.

Islam has a proud tradition of tolerance. We see it in the history of Andalusia and Cordoba during the Inquisition. I saw it firsthand as a child in Indonesia, where devout Christians worshipped freely in an overwhelmingly Muslim country. That is the spirit we need today. People in every country should be free to choose and live their faith based upon the persuasion of the mind, heart, and soul. This tolerance is essential for religion to thrive, but it is being challenged in many different ways.

Among some Muslims, there is a disturbing tendency to measure one's own faith by the rejection of another's. The richness of religious diversity must be upheld—whether it is for Maronites in Lebanon or the Copts in Egypt. And fault lines must be closed among Muslims as well, as the divisions between Sunni and Shi'a have led to tragic violence, particularly in Iraq.

Freedom of religion is central to the ability of peoples to live together. We must always examine the ways in which we protect it. For instance, in the United States, rules on charitable giving have made it harder for Muslims to fulfill their religious obligation. That is why I am committed to working with American Muslims to ensure that they can fulfill zakat.

Likewise, it is important for Western countries to avoid impeding Muslim citizens from practicing religion as they see fit—for instance, by dictating what clothes a Muslim woman should wear. We cannot disguise hostility towards any religion behind the pretense of liberalism.

Indeed, faith should bring us together. That is why we are forging service projects in America that bring together Christians, Muslims, and Jews. That is why we welcome efforts like Saudi Arabian King Abdullah's Interfaith dialogue and Turkey's leadership in the Alliance of Civilizations. Around the world, we can turn dialogue into interfaith service, so bridges between peoples lead to action—whether it is combating malaria in Africa, or providing relief after a natural disaster.

The sixth issue that I want to address is women's rights. I know that there is a healthy debate about this issue. I reject the view of some in the West that a woman who chooses to cover her hair is somehow less equal, but I do believe that a woman who is denied an education is denied equality. And it is no coincidence that countries where women are well-educated are far more likely to be prosperous.

Now let me be clear: issues of women's equality are by no means simply an issue for Islam. In Turkey, Pakistan, Bangladesh and Indonesia, we have seen Muslim-majority countries elect a woman to lead. Meanwhile, the struggle for women's equality continues in many aspects of American life, and in countries around the world.

Our daughters can contribute just as much to society as our sons, and our common prosperity will be advanced by allowing all humanity—men and women—to reach their full potential. I do not believe that women must make the same choices as men in order to be equal, and I respect those women who choose to live their lives in traditional roles. But it should be their choice. That is why the United States will partner with any Muslim-majority country to support expanded literacy for girls, and to help young women pursue employment through microfinancing that helps people live their dreams.

Finally, I want to discuss economic development and opportunity.

I know that for many, the face of globalization is contradictory. The internet and television can bring knowledge and information, but also offensive sexuality and mindless violence. Trade can bring new wealth and opportunities, but also huge disruptions and changing communities. In all nations—including my own—this change can bring fear. Fear that because of modernity we will lose control over our economic choices, our politics, and most importantly our identities—those things we most cherish about our communities, our families, our traditions, and our faith.

But I also know that human progress cannot be denied. There need not be contradiction between development and tradition. Countries like Japan and South Korea grew their economies while maintaining distinct cultures. The same is true for the astonishing progress within Muslim-majority countries from Kuala Lumpur to Dubai. In ancient times and in our times, Muslim communities have been at the forefront of innovation and education.

This is important because no development strategy can be based only upon what comes out of the ground, nor can it be sustained while young people are out of work. Many Gulf States have enjoyed great wealth as a consequence of oil, and some are beginning to focus it on broader development. But all of us must recognize that education and innovation will be the currency of the 21st century, and in too many Muslim communities there remains underinvestment in these areas. I am emphasizing such investments within my country. And while America in the past has focused on oil and gas in this part of the world, we now seek a broader engagement.

On education, we will expand exchange programs, and increase scholarships, like the one that brought my father to America, while encouraging more Americans to study in Muslim communities. And we will match promising Muslim students with internships in America; invest in online learning for teachers and children around the world; and create a new online network, so a teenager in Kansas can communicate instantly with a teenager in Cairo.

On economic development, we will create a new corps of business volunteers to partner with counterparts in Muslim-majority countries. And I will host a summit on entrepreneurship this year to identify how we can deepen ties between business leaders, foundations and social entrepreneurs in the United States and Muslim communities around the world.

On science and technology, we will launch a new fund to support technological development in Muslim-majority countries, and to help transfer ideas to the marketplace so they can create jobs. We will open centers of scientific excellence in Africa, the Middle East and south-east Asia, and appoint new science envoys to collaborate on programs that develop new sources of energy, create green jobs, digitize records, clean water and grow new crops. And today I am announcing a new global effort with the Organization of the Islamic Conference to eradicate polio. And we will also expand partnerships with Muslim communities to promote child and maternal health.

All these things must be done in partnership. Americans are ready to join with citizens and governments; community organizations, religious leaders, and businesses in Muslim communities around the world to help our people pursue a better life.

The issues that I have described will not be easy to address. But we have a responsibility to join together on behalf of the world we seek—a world where extremists no longer threaten our people, and American troops have come home; a world where Israelis and Palestinians are each secure in a state of their own, and nuclear energy is used for peaceful purposes; a world where governments serve their citizens, and the rights of all God's children are respected. Those are mutual interests. That is the world we seek. But we can only achieve it together.

I know there are many—Muslim and non-Muslim—who question whether we can forge this new beginning. Some are eager to stoke the flames of division, and to stand in the way of progress. Some suggest that it isn't worth the effort—that we are fated to disagree, and civilizations are doomed to clash. Many more are simply skeptical that real change can occur. There is so much fear, so much mistrust. But if we choose to be bound by the past, we will never move forward. And I want to particularly say this to young people of every faith, in every country—you, more than anyone, have the ability to remake this world.

All of us share this world for but a brief moment in time. The question is whether we spend that time focused on what pushes us apart, or whether we commit ourselves to an effort—a sustained effort—to find common ground, to focus on the future we seek for our children, and to respect the dignity of all human beings.

It is easier to start wars than to end them. It is easier to blame others than to look inward; to see what is different about someone than to find the things we share. But we should choose the right path, not just the easy path. There is also one rule that lies at the heart of every religion—that we do unto others as we would have them do unto us. This truth transcends nations and peoples—a belief that isn't new; that isn't black or white or brown; that isn't Christian, or Muslim or Jew. It's a belief that pulsed in the cradle of civilization, and that still beats in the heart of billions. It's a faith in other people, and it's what brought me here today.

We have the power to make the world we seek, but only if we have the courage to make a new beginning, keeping in mind what has been written.

The Holy Quran tells us: "O mankind! We have created you male and a female; and we have made you into nations and tribes so that you may know one another."

The Talmud tells us: "The whole of the Torah is for the purpose of promoting peace."

The Holy Bible tells us: "Blessed are the peacemakers, for they shall be called sons of God."

The people of the world can live together in peace. We know that is God's vision. Now, that must be our work here on Earth. Thank you. And may God's peace be upon you.

Source: Barack Obama, "Remarks by the President on a New Beginning," Office of the Press Secretary, White House, June 4, 2009, http://www.whitehouse.gov/the -press-office/remarks-president-cairo-university-6-04-09.

APPENDIX C

President Obama's Acceptance Speech at the
Nobel Peace Prize Ceremony,
December 10, 2009

Oslo City Hall, Oslo, Norway

THE PRESIDENT: Your Majesties, Your Royal Highnesses, distinguished members of the Norwegian Nobel Committee, citizens of America, and citizens of the world:

I receive this honor with deep gratitude and great humility. It is an award that speaks to our highest aspirations—that for all the cruelty and hardship of our world, we are not mere prisoners of fate. Our actions matter, and can bend history in the direction of justice.

And yet I would be remiss if I did not acknowledge the considerable controversy that your generous decision has generated. (Laughter.) In part, this is because I am at the beginning, and not the end, of my labors on the world stage. Compared to some of the giants of history who've received this prize—Schweitzer and King; Marshall and Mandela—my accomplishments are slight. And then there are the men and women around the world who have been jailed and beaten in the pursuit of justice; those who toil in humanitarian organizations to relieve suffering; the unrecognized millions whose quiet acts of courage and compassion inspire even the most hardened cynics. I cannot argue with those who find these men and women—some known, some obscure to all but those they help—to be far more deserving of this honor than I.

But perhaps the most profound issue surrounding my receipt of this prize is the fact that I am the Commander-in-Chief of the military of a nation in the midst of two wars. One of these wars is winding down. The other is a conflict that

America did not seek; one in which we are joined by 42 other countries—including Norway—in an effort to defend ourselves and all nations from further attacks.

Still, we are at war, and I'm responsible for the deployment of thousands of young Americans to battle in a distant land. Some will kill, and some will be killed. And so I come here with an acute sense of the costs of armed conflict—filled with difficult questions about the relationship between war and peace, and our effort to replace one with the other.

Now these questions are not new. War, in one form or another, appeared with the first man. At the dawn of history, its morality was not questioned; it was simply a fact, like drought or disease—the manner in which tribes and then civilizations sought power and settled their differences.

And over time, as codes of law sought to control violence within groups, so did philosophers and clerics and statesmen seek to regulate the destructive power of war. The concept of a "just war" emerged, suggesting that war is justified only when certain conditions were met: if it is waged as a last resort or in self-defense; if the force used is proportional; and if, whenever possible, civilians are spared from violence.

Of course, we know that for most of history, this concept of "just war" was rarely observed. The capacity of human beings to think up new ways to kill one another proved inexhaustible, as did our capacity to exempt from mercy those who look different or pray to a different God. Wars between armies gave way to wars between nations—total wars in which the distinction between combatant and civilian became blurred. In the span of 30 years, such carnage would twice engulf this continent. And while it's hard to conceive of a cause more just than the defeat of the Third Reich and the Axis powers, World War II was a conflict in which the total number of civilians who died exceeded the number of soldiers who perished.

In the wake of such destruction, and with the advent of the nuclear age, it became clear to victor and vanquished alike that the world needed institutions to prevent another world war. And so, a quarter century after the United States Senate rejected the League of Nations—an idea for which Woodrow Wilson received this prize—America led the world in constructing an architecture to keep the peace: a Marshall Plan and a United Nations, mechanisms to govern the waging of war, treaties to protect human rights, prevent genocide, restrict the most dangerous weapons.

In many ways, these efforts succeeded. Yes, terrible wars have been fought, and atrocities committed. But there has been no Third World War. The Cold War ended with jubilant crowds dismantling a wall. Commerce has stitched much of the world together. Billions have been lifted from poverty. The ideals of liberty and self-determination, equality and the rule of law have haltingly advanced. We are the heirs of the fortitude and foresight of generations past, and it is a legacy for which my own country is rightfully proud.

And yet, a decade into a new century, this old architecture is buckling under the weight of new threats. The world may no longer shudder at the prospect of war between two nuclear superpowers, but proliferation may increase the risk of catastrophe. Terrorism has long been a tactic, but modern technology allows a few small men with outsized rage to murder innocents on a horrific scale.

Moreover, wars between nations have increasingly given way to wars within nations. The resurgence of ethnic or sectarian conflicts; the growth of secessionist movements, insurgencies, and failed states—all these things have increasingly trapped civilians in unending chaos. In today's wars, many more civilians are killed than soldiers; the seeds of future conflict are sown, economies are wrecked, civil societies torn asunder, refugees amassed, children scarred.

I do not bring with me today a definitive solution to the problems of war. What I do know is that meeting these challenges will require the same vision, hard work, and persistence of those men and women who acted so boldly decades ago. And it will require us to think in new ways about the notions of just war and the imperatives of a just peace.

We must begin by acknowledging the hard truth: We will not eradicate violent conflict in our lifetimes. There will be times when nations—acting individually or in concert—will find the use of force not only necessary but morally justified.

I make this statement mindful of what Martin Luther King Jr. said in this same ceremony years ago: "Violence never brings permanent peace. It solves no social problem: it merely creates new and more complicated ones." As someone who stands here as a direct consequence of Dr. King's life work, I am living testimony to the moral force of non-violence. I know there's nothing weak—nothing passive—nothing naïve—in the creed and lives of Gandhi and King.

But as a head of state sworn to protect and defend my nation, I cannot be guided by their examples alone. I face the world as it is, and cannot stand idle in the face of threats to the American people. For make no mistake: Evil does exist in the world. A non-violent movement could not have halted Hitler's armies. Negotiations cannot convince al Qaeda's leaders to lay down their arms. To say that force may sometimes be necessary is not a call to cynicism—it is a recognition of history; the imperfections of man and the limits of reason.

I raise this point, I begin with this point because in many countries there is a deep ambivalence about military action today, no matter what the cause. And at times, this is joined by a reflexive suspicion of America, the world's sole military superpower.

But the world must remember that it was not simply international institutions—not just treaties and declarations—that brought stability to a post–World War II world. Whatever mistakes we have made, the plain fact is this: The United States of America has helped underwrite global security for more than six decades with the blood of our citizens and the strength of our arms. The service and sacrifice of our men and women in uniform has promoted peace and prosperity from Germany to Korea, and enabled democracy to take hold in places like the Balkans. We have borne this burden not because we seek to impose our will. We have done so out of enlightened self-interest—because we seek a better future for our children and grandchildren, and we believe that their lives will be better if others' children and grandchildren can live in freedom and prosperity.

So yes, the instruments of war do have a role to play in preserving the peace. And yet this truth must coexist with another—that no matter how justified, war promises human tragedy. The soldier's courage and sacrifice is full of glory, expressing devotion to country, to cause, to comrades in arms. But war itself is never glorious, and we must never trumpet it as such.

So part of our challenge is reconciling these two seemingly irreconcilable truths—that war is sometimes necessary, and war at some level is an expression of human folly. Concretely, we must direct our effort to the task that President Kennedy called for long ago. "Let us focus," he said, "on a more practical, more attainable peace, based not on a sudden revolution in human nature but on a gradual evolution in human institutions." A gradual evolution of human institutions.

What might this evolution look like? What might these practical steps be?

To begin with, I believe that all nations—strong and weak alike—must adhere to standards that govern the use of force. I—like any head of state—reserve the right to act unilaterally if necessary to defend my nation. Nevertheless, I am convinced that adhering to standards, international standards, strengthens those who do, and isolates and weakens those who don't.

The world rallied around America after the 9/11 attacks, and continues to support our efforts in Afghanistan, because of the horror of those senseless attacks and the recognized principle of self-defense. Likewise, the world recognized the need to confront Saddam Hussein when he invaded Kuwait—a consensus that sent a clear message to all about the cost of aggression.

Furthermore, America—in fact, no nation—can insist that others follow the rules of the road if we refuse to follow them ourselves. For when we don't, our actions appear arbitrary and undercut the legitimacy of future interventions, no matter how justified.

And this becomes particularly important when the purpose of military action extends beyond self-defense or the defense of one nation against an aggressor. More and more, we all confront difficult questions about how to prevent the slaughter of civilians by their own government, or to stop a civil war whose violence and suffering can engulf an entire region.

I believe that force can be justified on humanitarian grounds, as it was in the Balkans, or in other places that have been scarred by war. Inaction tears at our conscience and can lead to more costly intervention later. That's why all responsible nations must embrace the role that militaries with a clear mandate can play to keep the peace.

America's commitment to global security will never waver. But in a world in which threats are more diffuse, and missions more complex, America cannot act alone. America alone cannot secure the peace. This is true in Afghanistan. This is true in failed states like Somalia, where terrorism and piracy is joined by famine and human suffering. And sadly, it will continue to be true in unstable regions for years to come.

The leaders and soldiers of NATO countries, and other friends and allies, demonstrate this truth through the capacity and courage they've shown in Afghanistan. But in many countries, there is a disconnect between the efforts of those who serve and the ambivalence of the broader public. I understand why war is not popular, but I also know this: The belief that peace is desirable is rarely enough to achieve it. Peace requires responsibility. Peace entails sacrifice. That's why NATO continues to be indispensable. That's why we must strengthen U.N. and regional peacekeeping, and not leave the task to a few countries. That's why we honor those who return home from peacekeeping and training abroad to Oslo and Rome; to Ottawa and Sydney; to Dhaka and Kigali—we honor them not as makers of war, but of wagers—but as wagers of peace.

Let me make one final point about the use of force. Even as we make difficult decisions about going to war, we must also think clearly about how we fight it. The Nobel Committee recognized this truth in awarding its first prize for peace to Henry Dunant—the founder of the Red Cross, and a driving force behind the Geneva Conventions.

Where force is necessary, we have a moral and strategic interest in binding ourselves to certain rules of conduct. And even as we confront a vicious adversary that abides by no rules, I believe the United States of America must remain a standard bearer in the conduct of war. That is what makes us different from those whom we fight. That is a source of our strength. That is why I prohibited torture. That is why I ordered the prison at Guantanamo Bay closed. And that is why I have reaffirmed America's commitment to abide by the Geneva Conventions. We lose ourselves when we compromise the very ideals that we fight to defend. (Applause.) And we honor—we honor those ideals by upholding them not when it's easy, but when it is hard.

I have spoken at some length to the question that must weigh on our minds and our hearts as we choose to wage war. But let me now turn to our effort to avoid such tragic choices, and speak of three ways that we can build a just and lasting peace.

First, in dealing with those nations that break rules and laws, I believe that we must develop alternatives to violence that are tough enough to actually change behavior—for if we want a lasting peace, then the words of the international community must mean something. Those regimes that break the rules must be held accountable. Sanctions must exact a real price. Intransigence must be met with increased pressure—and such pressure exists only when the world stands together as one.

One urgent example is the effort to prevent the spread of nuclear weapons, and to seek a world without them. In the middle of the last century, nations agreed to be bound by a treaty whose bargain is clear: All will have access to peaceful nuclear power; those without nuclear weapons will forsake them; and those with nuclear weapons will work towards disarmament. I am committed to upholding this treaty. It is a centerpiece of my foreign policy. And I'm working with President Medvedev to reduce America and Russia's nuclear stockpiles.

But it is also incumbent upon all of us to insist that nations like Iran and North Korea do not game the system. Those who claim to respect international law cannot avert their eyes when those laws are flouted. Those who care for their own security cannot ignore the danger of an arms race in the Middle East or East Asia. Those who seek peace cannot stand idly by as nations arm themselves for nuclear war.

The same principle applies to those who violate international laws by brutalizing their own people. When there is genocide in Darfur, systematic rape in Congo, repression in Burma—there must be consequences. Yes, there will be engagement; yes, there will be diplomacy—but there must be consequences when those things fail. And the closer we stand together, the less likely we will be faced with the choice between armed intervention and complicity in oppression.

This brings me to a second point—the nature of the peace that we seek. For peace is not merely the absence of visible conflict. Only a just peace based on the inherent rights and dignity of every individual can truly be lasting.

It was this insight that drove drafters of the Universal Declaration of Human Rights after the Second World War. In the wake of devastation, they recognized that if human rights are not protected, peace is a hollow promise.

And yet too often, these words are ignored. For some countries, the failure to uphold human rights is excused by the false suggestion that these are somehow Western principles, foreign to local cultures or stages of a nation's development. And within America, there has long been a tension between those who describe themselves as realists or idealists—a tension that suggests a stark choice between the narrow pursuit of interests or an endless campaign to impose our values around the world.

I reject these choices. I believe that peace is unstable where citizens are denied the right to speak freely or worship as they please; choose their own leaders or assemble without fear. Pent-up grievances fester, and the suppression of tribal and religious identity can lead to violence. We also know that the opposite is true. Only when Europe became free did it finally find peace. America has never fought a war against a democracy, and our closest friends are governments that protect the rights of their citizens. No matter how callously defined, neither America's interests—nor the world's—are served by the denial of human aspirations.

So even as we respect the unique culture and traditions of different countries, America will always be a voice for those aspirations that are universal. We will bear witness to the quiet dignity of reformers like Aung Sang Suu Kyi; to the bravery of Zimbabweans who cast their ballots in the face of beatings; to the hundreds of thousands who have marched silently through the streets of Iran. It is telling that the leaders of these governments fear the aspirations of their own people more than the power of any other nation. And it is the responsibility of all free people and free nations to make clear that these movements—these movements of hope and history—they have us on their side.

Let me also say this: The promotion of human rights cannot be about exhortation alone. At times, it must be coupled with painstaking diplomacy. I know that engagement with repressive regimes lacks the satisfying purity of indignation. But I also know that sanctions without outreach—condemnation without discussion—can carry forward only a crippling status quo. No repressive regime can move down a new path unless it has the choice of an open door.

In light of the Cultural Revolution's horrors, Nixon's meeting with Mao appeared inexcusable—and yet it surely helped set China on a path where millions of its citizens have been lifted from poverty and connected to open societies. Pope John Paul's engagement with Poland created space not just for the Catholic Church, but for labor leaders like Lech Walesa. Ronald Reagan's efforts on arms control and embrace of perestroika not only improved relations with the Soviet Union, but empowered dissidents throughout Eastern Europe. There's no simple formula here. But we must try as best we can to balance isolation and engagement, pressure and incentives, so that human rights and dignity are advanced over time.

Third, a just peace includes not only civil and political rights—it must encompass economic security and opportunity. For true peace is not just freedom from fear, but freedom from want.

It is undoubtedly true that development rarely takes root without security; it is also true that security does not exist where human beings do not have access to enough food, or clean water, or the medicine and shelter they need to survive. It does not exist where children can't aspire to a decent education or a job that supports a family. The absence of hope can rot a society from within.

And that's why helping farmers feed their own people—or nations educate their children and care for the sick—is not mere charity. It's also why the world must come together to confront climate change. There is little scientific dispute that if we do nothing, we will face more drought, more famine, more mass displacement—all of which will fuel more conflict for decades. For this reason, it is not merely scientists and environmental activists who call for swift and forceful action—it's military leaders in my own country and others who understand our common security hangs in the balance.

Agreements among nations. Strong institutions. Support for human rights. Investments in development. All these are vital ingredients in bringing about the evolution that President Kennedy spoke about. And yet, I do not believe that we will have the will, the determination, the staying power, to complete this work without something more—and that's the continued expansion of our moral imagination; an insistence that there's something irreducible that we all share.

As the world grows smaller, you might think it would be easier for human beings to recognize how similar we are; to understand that we're all basically seeking the same things; that we all hope for the chance to live out our lives with some measure of happiness and fulfillment for ourselves and our families.

And yet somehow, given the dizzying pace of globalization, the cultural leveling of modernity, it perhaps comes as no surprise that people fear the loss of what they cherish in their particular identities—their race, their tribe, and perhaps most powerfully their religion. In some places, this fear has led to conflict. At times, it even feels like we're moving backwards. We see it in the Middle East, as the conflict between Arabs and Jews seems to harden. We see it in nations that are torn asunder by tribal lines.

And most dangerously, we see it in the way that religion is used to justify the murder of innocents by those who have distorted and defiled the great religion of Islam, and who attacked my country from Afghanistan. These extremists are not the first to kill in the name of God; the cruelties of the Crusades are amply recorded. But they remind us that no Holy War can ever be a just war. For if you truly believe that you are carrying out divine will, then there is no need for restraint—no need to spare the pregnant mother, or the medic, or the Red Cross worker, or even a person of one's own faith. Such a warped view of religion is not just incompatible with the concept of peace, but I believe it's incompatible with the very purpose of faith—for the one rule that lies at the heart of every major religion is that we do unto others as we would have them do unto us.

Adhering to this law of love has always been the core struggle of human nature. For we are fallible. We make mistakes, and fall victim to the temptations of pride, and power, and sometimes evil. Even those of us with the best of intentions will at times fail to right the wrongs before us.

But we do not have to think that human nature is perfect for us to still believe that the human condition can be perfected. We do not have to live in an idealized world to still reach for those ideals that will make it a better place. The non-violence practiced by men like Gandhi and King may not have been practical or possible in every circumstance, but the love that they preached—their fundamental faith in human progress—that must always be the North Star that guides us on our journey.

For if we lose that faith—if we dismiss it as silly or naïve; if we divorce it from the decisions that we make on issues of war and peace—then we lose what's best about humanity. We lose our sense of possibility. We lose our moral compass.

Like generations have before us, we must reject that future. As Dr. King said at this occasion so many years ago, "I refuse to accept despair as the final response to the ambiguities of history. I refuse to accept the idea that the 'isness' of man's present condition makes him morally incapable of reaching up for the eternal 'oughtness' that forever confronts him."

Let us reach for the world that ought to be—that spark of the divine that still stirs within each of our souls. (Applause.)

Somewhere today, in the here and now, in the world as it is, a soldier sees he's outgunned, but stands firm to keep the peace. Somewhere today, in this world, a young protestor awaits the brutality of her government, but has the courage to march on. Somewhere today, a mother facing punishing poverty still takes the time to teach her child, scrapes together what few coins she has to send that child to school—because she believes that a cruel world still has a place for that child's dreams.

Let us live by their example. We can acknowledge that oppression will always be with us, and still strive for justice. We can admit the intractability of depravation, and still strive for dignity. Clear-eyed, we can understand that there will be war, and still strive for peace. We can do that—for that is the story of human progress; that's the hope of all the world; and at this moment of challenge, that must be our work here on Earth.

Thank you very much. (Applause.)

Source: Barack Obama, "Remarks by the President at the Acceptance of the Nobel Peace Prize," Office of the Press Secretary, White House, December 10, 2009, http://www .whitehouse.gov/the-press-office/remarks-president-acceptance-nobel-peace-prize.

APPENDIX D

The Sykes-Picot Agreement, 1916

It is accordingly understood between the French and British governments:
That France and Great Britain are prepared to recognize and protect an independent Arab state or a confederation of Arab states (a) and (b) marked on the annexed map, under the suzerainty of an Arab chief. That in area (a) France, and in area (b) Great Britain, shall have priority of right of enterprise and local loans. That in area (a) France, and in area (b) Great Britain, shall alone supply advisers or foreign functionaries at the request of the Arab state or confederation of Arab states.

That in the blue area France, and in the red area Great Britain, shall be allowed to establish such direct or indirect administration or control as they desire and as they may think fit to arrange with the Arab state or confederation of Arab states.

That in the brown area there shall be established an international administration, the form of which is to be decided upon after consultation with Russia, and subsequently in consultation with the other allies, and the representatives of the Shereef of Mecca.

That Great Britain be accorded (1) the ports of Haifa and Acre, (2) guarantee of a given supply of water from the Tigres and Euphrates in area (a) for area (b). His Majesty's government, on their part, undertake that they will at no time enter into negotiations for the cession of Cyprus to any third power without the previous consent of the French government.

That Alexandretta shall be a free port as regards the trade of the British empire, and that there shall be no discrimination in port charges or facilities as regards British shipping and British goods; that there shall be freedom of transit for British goods through Alexandretta and by railway through the blue area, or area (b), or area (a); and there shall be no discrimination, direct or indirect, against British goods on any railway or against British goods or ships at any port serving the areas mentioned.

That Haifa shall be a free port as regards the trade of France, her dominions and protectorates, and there shall be no discrimination in port charges or facilities as regards French shipping and French goods. There shall be freedom of transit for French goods through Haifa and by the British railway through the brown area, whether those goods are intended for or originate in the blue area, area (a), or area (b), and there shall be no discrimination, direct or indirect, against French goods on any railway, or against French goods or ships at any port serving the areas mentioned.

That in area (a) the Baghdad railway shall not be extended southwards beyond Mosul, and in area (b) northwards beyond Samarra, until a railway connecting Baghdad and Aleppo via the Euphrates valley has been completed, and then only with the concurrence of the two governments.

That Great Britain has the right to build, administer, and be sole owner of a railway connecting Haifa with area (b), and shall have a perpetual right to transport troops along such a line at all times. It is to be understood by both governments that this railway is to facilitate the connection of Baghdad with Haifa by rail, and it is further understood that, if the engineering difficulties and expense entailed by keeping this connecting line in the brown area only make the project unfeasible, that the French government shall be prepared to consider that the line in question may also traverse the Polgon Banias Keis Marib Salkhad tell Otsda Mesmie before reaching area (b).

For a period of twenty years the existing Turkish customs tariff shall remain in force throughout the whole of the blue and red areas, as well as in areas (a) and (b), and no increase in the rates of duty or conversions from ad valorem to specific rates shall be made except by agreement between the two powers.

There shall be no interior customs barriers between any of the above mentioned areas. The customs duties leviable on goods destined for the interior shall be collected at the port of entry and handed over to the administration of the area of destination.

It shall be agreed that the French government will at no time enter into any negotiations for the cession of their rights and will not cede such rights in the blue area to any third power, except the Arab state or confederation of Arab states, without the previous agreement of his majesty's government, who, on their part, will give a similar undertaking to the French government regarding the red area.

The British and French government, as the protectors of the Arab state, shall agree that they will not themselves acquire and will not consent to a third power acquiring territorial possessions in the Arabian peninsula, nor consent to a third power installing a naval base either on the east coast, or on the islands, of the red sea. This, however, shall not prevent such adjustment of the Aden frontier as may be necessary in consequence of recent Turkish aggression.

The negotiations with the Arabs as to the boundaries of the Arab states shall be continued through the same channel as heretofore on behalf of the two powers.

It is agreed that measures to control the importation of arms into the Arab territories will be considered by the two governments.

I have further the honor to state that, in order to make the agreement complete, his majesty's government are proposing to the Russian government to exchange notes analogous to those exchanged by the latter and your excellency's government on the 26th April last. Copies of these notes will be communicated to your excellency as soon as exchanged. I would also venture to remind your excellency that the conclusion of the present agreement raises, for practical consideration, the question of claims of Italy to a share in any partition or rearrangement of Turkey in Asia, as formulated in article 9 of the agreement of the 26th April, 1915, between Italy and the allies.

His Majesty's government further consider that the Japanese government should be informed of the arrangements now concluded.

Source: Mark Sykes and Georges Picot, "The Sykes-Picot Agreement: 1916," Avalon Project, Yale Law School, http://avalon.law.yale.edu/20th_century/sykes.asp.

APPENDIX E

Balfour Declaration, 1917

November 2nd, 1917
Dear Lord Rothschild,

I have much pleasure in conveying to you, on behalf of His Majesty's Government, the following declaration of sympathy with Jewish Zionist aspirations which has been submitted to, and approved by, the Cabinet.

"His Majesty's Government view with favour the establishment in Palestine of a national home for the Jewish people, and will use their best endeavours to facilitate the achievement of this object, it being clearly understood that nothing shall be done which may prejudice the civil and religious rights of existing non-Jewish communities in Palestine, or the rights and political status enjoyed by Jews in any other country."

I should be grateful if you would bring this declaration to the knowledge of the Zionist Federation.

Yours sincerely,
Arthur James Balfour

Source: Arthur Balfour, "Balfour Declaration," letter to Walter Rothschild, November 2, 1917, Avalon Project, Yale Law School, http://avalon.law.yale.edu/20th_century /balfour.asp.

APPENDIX F

U.S. Recognition of Israel, Proclamation Signed by Harry Truman, May 14, 1948

This Government has been informed that a Jewish state has been proclaimed in Palestine, and recognition has been requested by the *provisional* Government thereof.

The United States recognizes the provisional government as the de facto authority of the new ~~Jewish~~ *State of* ~~state.~~ *Israel.*

Harry Truman

Approved.
May 14, 1948.

Source: "Document for May 14th: Press Release Announcing U.S. Recognition of Israel," May 14, 1948, Alphabetical Correspondence File: "Handwriting of the President," Charles Ross Papers, 1904–1967, Harry S. Truman Library, http://www.archives.gov/historical-docs/todays-doc/index.html?dod-date=514. Courtesy of Mike Hanini Odetalla.

APPENDIX G

Excerpts from Pentagon's Plan:
"Prevent the Re-Emergence
of a New Rival"

Following are excerpts from the Pentagon's Feb. 18 draft of the Defense Planning Guidance for the Fiscal Years 1994–1999:

This Defense Planning guidance addresses the fundamentally new situation which has been created by the collapse of the Soviet Union, the disintegration of the internal as well as the external empire, and the discrediting of Communism as an ideology with global pretensions and influence. The new international environment has also been shaped by the victory of the United States and its coalition allies over Iraqi aggression—the first post-cold-war conflict and a defining event in U.S. global leadership. In addition to these two victories, there has been a less visible one, the integration of Germany and Japan into a U.S.-led system of collective security and the creation of a democratic "zone of peace." . . .

Defense Strategy Objectives

Our first objective is to prevent the re-emergence of a new rival, either on the territory of the former Soviet Union or elsewhere, that poses a threat on the order of that posed formerly by the Soviet Union. This is a dominant consideration underlying the new regional defense strategy and requires that we endeavor to prevent any hostile power from dominating a region whose resources would, under consolidated control, be sufficient to generate global power. These regions include Western Europe, East Asia, the territory of the former Soviet Union, and Southwest Asia.

There are three additional aspects to this objective: First, the U.S. must show the leadership necessary to establish and protect a new order that holds the promise of convincing potential competitors that they need not aspire to a greater role or pursue a more aggressive posture to protect their legitimate interests. Second, in the non-defense areas, we must account sufficiently for the interests of the advanced industrial nations to discourage them from challenging our leadership or seeking to overturn the established political and economic order. Finally, we must maintain the mechanisms for deterring potential competitors from even aspiring to a larger regional or global role. An effective reconstitution capability is important here, since it implies that a potential rival could not hope to quickly or easily gain a predominant military position in the world.

The second objective is to address sources of regional conflict and instability in such a way as to promote increasing respect for international law, limit international violence, and encourage the spread of democratic forms of government and open economic systems. These objectives are especially important in deterring conflicts or threats in regions of security importance to the United States because of their proximity (such as Latin America), or where we have treaty obligations or security commitments to other nations. While the U.S. cannot become the world's "policeman," by assuming responsibility for righting every wrong, we will retain the pre-eminent responsibility for addressing selectively those wrongs which threaten not only our interests, but those of our allies or friends, or which could seriously unsettle international relations. Various types of U.S. interests may be involved in such instances: access to vital raw materials, primarily Persian Gulf oil; proliferation of weapons of mass destruction and ballistic missiles, threats to U.S. citizens from terrorism or regional or local conflict, and threats to U.S. society from narcotics trafficking. . . .

It is improbable that a global conventional challenge to U.S. and Western security will re-emerge from the Eurasian heartland for many years to come. Even in the highly unlikely event that some future leadership in the former Soviet Union adopted strategic aims of recovering the lost empire or otherwise threatened global interests, the loss of Warsaw Pact allies and the subsequent and continuing dissolution of military capability would make any hope of success require several years or more of strategic and doctrinal re-orientation and force regeneration and redeployment, which in turn could only happen after a lengthy political realignment and re-orientation to authoritarian and aggressive political and economic control. Furthermore, any such political upheaval in or among the states of the former U.S.S.R. would be much more likely to issue in internal or localized hostilities, rather than a concerted strategic effort to marshal capabilities for external expansionism—the ability to project power beyond their borders.

There are other potential nations or coalitions that could, in the further future, develop strategic aims and a defense posture of region-wide or global domination.

Our strategy must now refocus on precluding the emergence of any potential future global competitor. But because we no longer face either a global threat or a hostile, non-democratic power dominating a region critical to our interests, we have the opportunity to meet threats at lower levels and lower costs—as long as we are prepared to reconstitute additional forces should the need to counter a global threat re-emerge. . . .

Regional Threats and Risk

With the demise of a global military threat to U.S. interests, regional military threats, including possible conflicts arising in and from the territory of the former Soviet Union, will be of primary concern to the U.S. in the future. These threats are likely to arise in regions critical to the security of the U.S. and its allies, including Europe, East Asia, the Middle East and Southwest Asia, and the territory of the former Soviet Union. We also have important interests at stake in Latin America, Oceania, and Sub-Saharan Africa. In both cases, the U.S. will be concerned with preventing the domination of key regions by a hostile power. . . .

Former Soviet Union

The former Soviet state achieved global reach and power by consolidating control over the resources in the territory of the former U.S.S.R. The best means of assuring that no hostile power is able to consolidate control over the resources within the former Soviet Union is to support its successor states (especially Russia and Ukraine) in their efforts to become peaceful democracies with market-based economies. A democratic partnership with Russia and the other republics would be the best possible outcome for the United States. At the same time, we must also hedge against the possibility that democracy will fail, with the potential that an authoritarian regime bent on regenerating aggressive military power could emerge in Russia, or that similar regimes in other successor republics could lead to spreading conflict within the former U.S.S.R. or Eastern Europe. . . .

For the immediate future, key U.S. concerns will be the ability of Russia and the other republics to demilitarize their societies, convert their military industries to civilian production, eliminate or, in the case of Russia, radically reduce their nuclear weapons inventory, maintain firm command and control over nuclear weapons, and prevent leakage of advanced military technology and expertise to other countries. . . .

Western Europe

NATO continues to provide the indispensable foundation for a stable security environment in Europe. Therefore, it is of fundamental importance to preserve NATO as the primary instrument of Western defense and security, as well as the channel for U.S. influence and participation in European security affairs. While the United States supports the goal of European integration, we must seek to prevent the emergence of European-only security arrangements which would undermine NATO, particularly the alliance's integrated command structure. . . .

East-Central Europe

The end of the Warsaw Pact and the dissolution of the Soviet Union have gone a long way toward increasing stability and reducing the military threat to Europe. The ascendancy of democratic reformers in the Russian republic, should this process continue, is likely to create a more benign policy toward Eastern Europe. However, the U.S. must keep in mind the long history of conflict between the states of Eastern Europe, as well as the potential for conflict between the states of Eastern Europe and those of the former Soviet Union. . . .

The most promising avenues for anchoring the east-central Europeans into the West and for stabilizing their democratic institutions is their participation in Western political and economic organizations. East-central European membership in the (European Community) at the earliest opportunity, and expanded NATO liaison. . . .

The U.S. could also consider extending to the east-central European states security commitments analogous to those we have extended to Persian Gulf states. . . .

Should there be a re-emergence of a threat from the Soviet Union's successor state, we should plan to defend against such a threat in Eastern Europe, should there be an alliance decision to do so.

East Asia and Pacific

. . . Defense of Korea will likely remain one of the most demanding major regional contingencies. . . . Asia is home to the world's greatest concentration of traditional Communist states, with fundamental values, governance, and policies decidedly at variance with our own and those of our friends and allies.

To buttress the vital political and economic relationships we have along the Pacific rim, we must maintain our status as a military power of the first magnitude in the area. This will enable the U.S. to continue to contribute to regional security and stability by acting as a balancing force and prevent emergence of a vacuum or a regional hegemon. . . .

Middle East and Southwest Asia

In the Middle East and Southwest Asia, our overall objective is to remain the predominant outside power in the region and preserve U.S. and Western access to the region's oil. We also seek to deter further aggression in the region, foster regional stability, protect U.S. nationals and property, and safeguard our access to international air and seaways. As demonstrated by Iraq's invasion of Kuwait, it remains fundamentally important to prevent a hegemon or alignment of powers from dominating the region. This pertains especially to the Arabian peninsula. Therefore, we must continue to play a strong role through enhanced deterrence and improved cooperative security. . . .

We will seek to prevent the further development of a nuclear arms race on the Indian subcontinent. In this regard, we should work to have both countries, India and Pakistan, adhere to the Nuclear Non-Proliferation Treaty and to place their nuclear energy facilities under International Atomic Energy Agency safeguards. We should discourage Indian hegemonic aspirations over the other states in South Asia and on the Indian Ocean. With regard to Pakistan, a constructive U.S.-Pakistani military relationship will be an important element in our strategy to promote stable security conditions in Southwest Asia and Central Asia. We should therefore endeavor to re-build our military relationship given acceptable resolution of our nuclear concerns....

Latin America

Cuba's growing domestic crisis holds out the prospect for positive change, but over the near term, Cuba's tenuous internal situation is likely to generate new challenges to U.S. policy. Consequently, our programs must provide capabilities to meet a variety of Cuban contingencies which could include an attempted repetition of the Mariel boatlift, a military provocation against the U.S. or an American ally, or political instability and internal conflict in Cuba.

Source: "Excerpts from Pentagon's Plan: 'Prevent the Re-Emergence of a New Rival,'" *New York Times,* March 8, 1992.

NOTES

Prologue

1. Agnes Savill, *Alexander the Great and His Time* (New York: Barnes & Noble, 1993), 133.
2. Niccolò Machiavelli, *The Prince*, trans. George Bull (London: Penguin, 2003), 18.
3. David Owen, "Hubris: The New Iraq War Syndrome," *Observer*, October 29, 2006.
4. The first was when George W. Bush was inaugurated in January 2001.
5. See "Obama's World: How Will a 21st-Century President Fare in a 19th-Century World?" *Economist*, November 6, 2008, http://www.economist.com/displaystory .cfm?story_id=12551938.
6. Project for the New American Century, "Statement of Principles," June 3, 1997, http://www.newamericancentury.org/statementofprinciples.htm.
7. Ramzy Baroud, "Europe's Identity Crisis: A Growing Anti-Muslim Sentiment throughout Europe," *Global Research*, December 24, 2009, http://www.global research.ca/index.php?context=va&aid=16655.
8. See, for example, "Obama spells out plans for change," ElectionCenter2008, CNN Politics.com, http://edition.cnn.com/2008/POLITICS/08/29/obama.promises/ index.html.
9. Obama for America, "President Obama's Stance on Israel: Myths vs. Facts," 2012, http://assets.bostatic.com/pdfs/jewish-american/Israel_myths_facts.pdf, accessed December 9, 2012.
10. See Abraham Lincoln, "First Inaugural Address of Abraham Lincoln," March 4, 1861, Avalon Project, Yale Law School, http://avalon.law.yale.edu/19th_century/ lincoln1.asp, accessed December 9, 2012.

11. John F. Kennedy, "Inaugural Address of John F. Kennedy," January 20, 1961, Avalon Project, Yale Law School, http://avalon.law.yale.edu/20th_century /kennedy.asp, accessed December 9, 2012.

12. Barack Obama, "Inaugural Address of Barack Obama," January 20, 2009, Avalon Project, Yale Law School, 2009, http://avalon.law.yale.edu/21st_century/obama.asp.

13. "Declaration of Independence, July 4, 1776," Avalon Project, Yale Law School, http://avalon.law.yale.edu/18th_century/declare.asp, accessed December 4, 2012.

14. For the text of the Bill of Rights, see The Charters of Freedom, National Archives and Records Administration, http://www.archives.gov/exhibits/charters/ bill_of_rights.html, accessed December 4, 2012.

15. Peter Finn and Anne E. Kornblut, "Guantanamo Bay: Why Obama Hasn't Fulfilled His Promise to Close the Facility," *Washington Post*, April 24, 2011.

16. Barack Obama, "Remarks by President Obama to the Turkish Parliament," Office of the Press Secretary, White House, April 6, 2009, http://www.whitehouse.gov/ the-press-office/remarks-president-obama-turkish-parliament.

17. "Barack Obama Backs Turkey over EU Membership," *Daily Telegraph*, April 6, 2009.

18. "Obama Pledges New US Engagement," BBC News, April 7, 2009.

19. Nobel Foundation, "The Nobel Peace Prize 2009" Announcement, October 9, 2009, http://www.nobelprize.org/nobel_prizes/peace/laureates/2009 /announcement.html.

20. "Obama Promotes Nuclear-Free World," BBC News, April 5, 2009.

21. Barack Obama, "Remarks by President Obama in Prague, Czech Republic," Office of the Press Secretary, White House, April 5, 2009, http://www.whitehouse .gov/the_press_office/Remarks-By-President-Barack-Obama-In-Prague -As-Delivered.

22. "Obama Promotes Nuclear-Free World."

23. For an overview, see Chris Woods, "A Drone Strike Every Four Days under Obama," *Express Tribune* (Pakistan), August 11, 2011, http://tribune.com.pk /story/228690/exclusive-a-drone-strike-every-four-days-under-obama/.

24. Lolita C. Balder, "Terror Attacks Spike in Pakistan, Afghanistan: Thousands of Mostly Muslim Civilians Are Slaughtered in Extremist Strikes," MSNBC, April 28, 2009.

25. Barack Obama, "A New Strategy for Afghanistan and Pakistan," Office of the Press Secretary, White House, March 27, 2009, http://www.whitehouse.gov/the_press _office/Remarks-by-the-President-on-a-New-Strategy-for-Afghanistan-and -Pakistan/.

26. George Santayana, *The Life of Reason*, Volume 1–3 (Charleston, SC: BiblioLife, 2009), 217.

27. "UN Official Criticizes US over Drone Attacks," BBC News, June 2, 2010.

28. Office of the UN High Commissioner for Human Rights, "Gaza Aid Convoy Killings: 'Those Responsible Must Be Held Criminally Responsible'—UN Expert," May 31, 2010, http://unispal.un.org/UNISPAL.NSF/0/FC8B241DD08E 470885257735004FEB7F.

29. Natasha Mozgovaya, "Biden: Israel Right to Stop Gaza Flotilla from Breaking Blockade," *Ha'aretz*, June 3, 2010.

1. DYNAMIC OF IMPERIALISM

1. "Stoic" as defined in the *Merriam-Webster's Collegiate Dictionary*.

2. Marsilio Ficino, quoted in James Hankins, *Plato in the Italian Renaissance* (Leiden, Netherlands: E. J. Brill, 1990), 304.

3. George Washington, "Inaugural Address," April 30, 1789, National Archives and Records Administration, http://www.archives.gov/exhibits/american_originals/ inaugtxt.html, December 5, 2012.

4. John Tirman, *100 Ways America Is Screwing Up the World* (New York: HarperCollins, 2006), 1–14.

5. Kennedy, "Inaugural Address of John F. Kennedy."

6. For communication between the CIA officer in Saigon, Lucien Conein, and South Vietnamese generals plotting the 1963 coup, see "DCI Briefing," July 9, 1963; for Washington's view, see State Department, Cable 243 to the U.S. embassy in Saigon, August 24, 1963; and State Department, "Check-List of Possible U.S. Actions in Case of Coup," memorandum, October 25, 1963, in John Prados, *JFK and Diem Coup* (Washington, DC: National Security Archive, November 5, 2003), http://www.gwu.edu/~nsarchiv/NSAEBB/NSAEBB101/index.htm.

7. "1975: Saigon Surrenders," BBC News, April 30, 1975.

8. See, for example, "Superpowers' Mistakes in Afghanistan," BBC News, December 24, 2004.

9. Liz Thurgood and Jonathan Steele, "Last Soviet Troops Leave Afghanistan," *Guardian*, February 16, 1989.

10. A company employee on the eightieth floor of 1 World Trade Center. See "United in Courage," People Magazine, September 12, 2001, http://whatreallyhappened .com/WRHARTICLES/people.html.

11. Michael O'Hanlon, "A Flawed Masterpiece," *Foreign Affairs* 81, no. 3 (March/April 2002): 47.

12. Andrew Bacevich, "Prophets and Poseurs: Niebuhr and Our Times," *World Affairs*, Winter 2008, http://www.worldaffairsjournal.org/articles/2008-Winter/full -prophets.html.

13. U.S. Department of Defense, "Contracts," Office of the Assistant Secretary of Defense (Public Affairs), September 28, 2007, http://www.defenselink.mil/contracts/contract.aspx?contractid=3615; and Suzanne Goldenberg, "E-mail Shows Cheney 'Link' to Oil," *Guardian*, June 1, 2004.

14. See, for example, "Army to End Expansive, Exclusive Halliburton Deal," *Washington Post*, July 12, 2006.

15. Patrick Cockburn, "A 'Fraud' Bigger than Madoff," *Independent*, February 16, 2009.

16. "Gulf War Illness Is Real, New Federal Report Says," *Veterans Today*, November 17, 2008.

17. *NewsHour*, hosted by Jim Lehrer, PBS, November 10, 2008.

18. Plato, *The Republic*, trans. Desmond Lee (London: Penguin, 2007), 60–63.

19. See ibid., 61.

20. Michael Hardt and Antonio Negri, *Empire* (Cambridge, MA: Harvard University Press, 2001).

21. Ibid., xi–xvii.

22. George W. Bush, "President's State of the Union Address," January 29, 2002, White House Archives, Washington, DC.

23. Johan Galtung, "On the Coming Decline and Fall of the US Empire," Transnational Foundation for Peace and Future Research, January 28, 2004, http://www.oldsite.transnational.org/SAJT/forum/meet/2004/Galtung_USempireFall.html.

24. Ralph Peters, *Fighting for the Future: Will America Triumph?* (Mechanicsburg, PA: Stackpole Books, 1999), 141; also see Susan George, "The WTO and the Global War System," Transnational Institute, November 28, 1999, http://www.tni.org/archives/archives_george_utopian.

25. See Kathleen R. Gibson, "Customs and Cultures in Animals and Humans: Neurobiological and Evolutionary Considerations," in *Anthropology in Theory: Issues in Epistemology*, ed. Henrietta Moore and Todd Sanders (Malden, MA: Wiley Blackwell, 2006), 193.

26. Robert Murphy, *Cultural and Social Anthropology: An Overture*, 2nd ed. (Englewood Cliffs, NJ: Prentice-Hall, 1986), 14.

2. A QUESTION OF SANITY

1. Ferenc Szasz, "Quotes about History," History News Network, George Mason University, December 26, 2005, http://www.hnn.us/articles/1328.html.

2. "McCain Lambasts Bush Years," *Washington Times*, October 23, 2008.

3. See National Intelligence Estimate, *Prospects for Iraq's Stability: A Challenging Road Ahead* (Washington, DC, 2007).

4. UN High Commissioner for Refugees, "UNHCR Worried about Effect of Dire Security Situation on Iraq's Displaced," October 13, 2006, http://www.unhcr .org/452fa9954.html.

5. "Bush Will Add More than 20,000 Troops to Iraq," CNN, January 11, 2007.

6. See Enoch Powell, *Joseph Chamberlain* (London: Thames and Hudson, 1977), 151.

7. James Carafano, *The Long War against Terrorism* (Washington, DC: Heritage Foundation, September 8, 2003).

8. "Rumsfeld Offers Strategies for Current War," *Washington Post*, February 3, 2006.

9. Sun Tzu, "Calculations," in *The Art of War*, http://www.sonshi.com/sun1.html, accessed December 5, 2012.

10. Gabriel Kolko, "The Age of Perpetual Conflict," *Defense and the National Interest*, February 3, 2006, extract from *The Age of War: The United States Confronts the World* (Boulder, CO: Lynne Rienner, 2006).

11. See "McCain Calls War 'Necessary and Just,'" *Washington Post*, April 12, 2007.

12. "Hillary Clinton: No Regret over Iraq Vote," CNN, April 21, 2004.

13. Barack Obama, "2002 Speech Against the Iraq War," October 2, 2002, http:// obamaspeeches.com/001-2002-Speech-Against-the-Iraq-War-Obama-Speech .htm.

14. Ibid.

15. See appendix B.

16. Barack Obama, "Remarks by the President in the State of the Union Address," Office of the Press Secretary, White House, January 27, 2010, http://www .whitehouse.gov/the-press-office/remarks-president-state-union-address.

17. Hillary Rodham Clinton, "Remarks at the U.S.–Islamic World Forum," U.S. Department of State, February 14, 2010, http://www.state.gov/secretary /rm/2010/02/136678.htm.

18. International Crisis Group, *Failed Responsibility: Iraqi Refugees in Syria, Jordan and Lebanon*, Middle East Report No. 77 (Brussels, July 10, 2008), 3–42.

19. Ibid., 36.

20. Barack Obama's remarks in Democratic Presidential Candidates Debate in Manchester, New Hampshire, January 5, 2008, http://www.presidency.ucsb.edu/ws /index.php?pid=76224.

21. Juan Cole, "Obama Is Saying the Wrong Things about Afghanistan," Salon.com, July 23, 2008.

22. Barack Obama, "Statement by the President on Afghanistan," February 17, 2009, http://www.whitehouse.gov/the-press-office/statement-president-afghanistan.

23. See "Profile: Gen. Stanley McChrystal," BBC News, May 11, 2009.

24. Gallup Poll in Pakistan for *Al Jazeera*, August 9, 2009, http://www.aljazeera.com /news/asia/2009/08/20098910857878664.html.

25. Ben Farmer and David Blair, "Afghanistan Election: Low Turnout as Voters Fear Taliban Attacks," *Daily Telegraph*, August 20, 2009; Carlotta Gall, "Intimidation and Fraud Observed in Afghan Election," *New York Times*, August 22, 2009; and Paul Rogers, "Afghanistan: The Point of Decision," *openDemocracy*, July 27, 2009.

26. John Burns, "An Old Afghanistan Hand Offers Lessons of the Past," *New York Times*, October 19, 2008.

27. For annual figures since 2001, see "Operation Enduring Freedom," iCasualties.org, 2009, http://icasualties.org/oef/.

28. Burns, "Old Afghanistan Hand Offers Lessons."

3. The Axis of Evil and the Great Satan

1. See Farzaneh Roudi, "Youth, Women's Rights, and Political Change in Iran," Population Reference Bureau, July 2009, http://www.prb.org/Articles/2009/iranyouth.aspx?p=1; and John Simpson, "Iran's Revolution Turns 30," BBC News, February 10, 2009.

2. Djavad Salehi-Isfahani, *Tough Times Ahead for the Iranian Economy* (Washington, DC: Brookings Institution, April 6, 2009); also Mahtab Alam Rizvi, *An Assessment of Iran's Presidential Elections 2009* (New Delhi: Institute for Defense Studies, June 19, 2009).

3. Robert Tait, "It's the Economy, Mr Ahmadinejad," *Guardian*, September 19, 2007.

4. "Top Iran Clerics Criticise President over Economy," *Jordan Times*, April 20, 2008, quoting *Aftab-e Yazd*.

5. The other candidates were Mohsen Rezaee (the conservative ex-commander of the Iranian Revolutionary Guard and secretary of the Expediency Discernment Council, which advises the Supreme Leader) and Mehdi Karroubi (ex-speaker of the Majlis, another reformist).

6. Rafsanjani later criticized mass arrests and called for freedom of expression after his daughter was detained by plainclothes officers while taking part in a protest alleging fraud in the June 2009 election. See, for example, Ali Akbar Dareini, "Top Iranian Cleric Criticises Hard-Liners in Sermon," *Independent*, July 17, 2009.

7. "Ahmadinejad Accuses Obama of Meddling in Iran," *Hurriyet*, June 16, 2010.

8. "Iran Accuses UK of Vote Sabotage, Kicks Out BBC," *Al Arabiya*, June 21, 2009.

9. "Bush's 'Axis of Evil' Comes to Haunt United States," *Washington Post*, October 10, 2006.

10. Amy S. Clark, "IAEA: Iran Nuclear Report Outrageous," CBS News, September 14, 2006.

11. Dick Cheney, interview with Don Imus, MSNBC, January 20, 2005.

12. Agence France-Presse, "Clinton Warns Iran That Patience Has Limits," Canada.com, October 31, 2009.

13. See "Director General's Report to Board," IAEA, September 7, 2009.

14. See "New Iran Sanctions Likely after Nuclear Talks Stalemate," *Guardian*, September 7, 2009.

15. "Iran Accuses US of Forging Nuclear Documents," VOA News, September 5, 2009.

16. "Iran accuses US of giving IAEA forged documents," *Al Arabiya News* quoting the Iranian news agency report from Vienna, September 5, 2009.

17. Mohamed ElBaradei, "Statement of the Director General," IAEA, September 7, 2009, http://www.iaea.org/newscenter/statements/2009/ebsp2009n009.html #syria.

18. Neil MacFarquhar, "U.N. Approves New Sanctions to Deter Iran," *New York Times*, June 9, 2010.

19. Ian Traynor, "EU to Introduce New Iran Sanctions," *Guardian*, June 15, 2010.

20. Ali Sheikholeslami, Anthony DiPaola, and Alaric Nightingale, "Iran Sanctions Leave China, Russia as Winners in Trade," *Bloomberg*, August 9, 2010.

21. "Muammar Gaddafi Killed as Sirte Falls," *Al Jazeera*, October 21, 2011.

22. Stewart Patrick, "Libya and the Future of Humanitarian Intervention," *Foreign Affairs*, August 26, 2011.

23. Louis Charbonneau, "Russia, China Veto U.N. Resolution Condemning Syria," Reuters, October 4, 2011; and "Russia, China Veto U.N. Security Council Resolution on Syria," *Russia Today*, February 4, 2012.

24. For an overview of Iran's progress, see Ervand Abrahamian, *A History of Modern Iran* (Cambridge: Cambridge University Press, 2008), 1–7.

25. Ibid., 32–33.

26. See "The Constitutional Revolution" in *Iran: A Country Study*, ed. Helem Chapin Metz (Washington, DC: GPO, 1987), http://countrystudies.us/iran/13.htm; and Abrahamian, *History of Modern Iran*, 34.

27. "Constitutional Revolution."

28. Abrahamian, *History of Modern Iran*, 49–50; and "Qajars and the Constitutional Revolution of 1906," Qajar Dynasty Pages, http://www.qajarpages.org/qajrevol .html.

29. For an overview of British attempts to achieve oil independence and Anglo-American diplomacy, see B. S. McBeth, *British Oil Policy 1919–1939* (London: Frank Cass, 1985), 15–85. The Anglo-Iranian agreement was never approved by the Majlis.

30. Abrahamian, *History of Modern Iran*, 63–64.

31. Cyrus Ghani, *Iran and the Rise of Reza Shah: From Qajar Collapse to Pahlavi Power* (London: I. B. Tauris, 2000), 372.

32. Abrahamian, *History of Modern Iran*, 64.

33. Ibid., 67–72. For Millspaugh's term and how it ended see "PERSIA: Millspaugh Out," *Time*, August 8, 1927.

34. For a survey of the Reza Shah period, see Stephanie Cronin, ed., *The Making of Modern Iran: State and Society under Reza Shah 1921–1941* (London: Routledge, 2003), 59–61.

35. See Farhad Khosrakhavar, "Postrevolutionary Iran and the New Social Movements," in *Twenty Years of Islamic Revolution: Political and Social Transition in Iran since 1979*, ed. Eric Hooglund (Syracuse, NY: Syracuse University Press, 2002), 4.

4. IRAN'S DIALECTIC OF ANTI-AMERICANISM

1. Barack Obama, Nicholas Sarkozy, and Gordon Brown, "Statements by President Obama, French President Sarkozy, and British Prime Minister Brown on Iranian Nuclear Facility," Office of the Press Secretary, White House, September 25, 2009, http://www.whitehouse.gov/the_press_office/Statements-By-President-Obama -French-President-Sarkozy-And-British-Prime-Minister-Brown-On-Iranian -Nuclear-Facility/.

2. Julian Borger, "Why Iran Confessed to Secret Nuclear Site Built Inside Mountain," *Guardian*, September 26, 2009.

3. Scott Ritter, "Keeping Iran Honest," *Guardian*, September 25, 2009.

4. Article 42: Pursuant to Article 8, design information in respect of existing facilities shall be provided to the Agency during the discussion of the Subsidiary Arrangements. The time limits for the provision of design information in respect of the new facilities shall be specified in the Subsidiary Arrangements and such information shall be provided as early as possible before nuclear material is introduced into a new facility. For full text of the agreement between IAEA and Iran, see IAEA, "Agreement between Iran and the International Atomic Energy Agency for the Application of Safeguards in Connection with the Treaty on the Non-Proliferation of Nuclear Weapons," *IAEA Information Circular* 214, December 13, 1974.

5. Reza Ladjevardian, *From Ancient Persia to Contemporary Iran* (Washington, DC: Mage Publishers, 2005).

6. Abbas Milani, *Eminent Persians: The Men and Women Who Made Modern Iran, 1941–1979* (Syracuse, NY: Syracuse University Press, 2008), 1:11.

7. See Ryszard Kapuscinski, *Shah of Shahs* (London: Penguin, 2006), 25.

8. Shahbaz Shahnavaz, *Britain and the Opening Up of South-West Persia 1880–1914: A Study in Imperialism and Economic Dependence* (Abingdon, UK: Routledge, 2005), 135.

9. Keith McLachlan, *The Neglected Garden: The Politics and Ecology of Agriculture in Iran* (London: I. B. Tauris, 1988), 41–42.

10. Mehran Kamrava, *The Modern Middle East: The Political History since the First World War* (Berkeley: University of California Press, 2005), 141.

11. Abrahamian, *History of Modern Iran*, 93–94.

12. Kamrava, *Modern Middle East*, 141.

13. Eric V. Thompson, comp., "A Brief History of Major Oil Companies in the Gulf Region," Petroleum Archives Project, University of Virginia, http://www.virginia.edu/igpr/APAG/apagoilhistory.html, accessed December 6, 2012.

14. Leonardo Maugeri, *The Age of Oil: The Mythology, History, and the Future of the World's Most Controversial Resource* (Westport, CT: Praeger, 2006), 63–64.

15. Ibid., 64.

16. Michael Clark, "Premier Quits as Iran Speeds Nationalization of Oil Fields," *New York Times*, April 28, 1951.

17. Maugeri, *Age of Oil*, 64.

18. "The Present Situation in Iran," NSC 136/1, November 20, 1952, in *Mohammad Mosaddeq and the 1953 Coup in Iran*, ed. Mark J. Gasiorowski and Malcolm Byrne (Washington, DC: National Security Archive, June 22, 2004), http://www.gwu.edu/~nsarchiv/NSAEBB/NSAEBB126/iran521120.pdf.

19. Ibid.

20. See Donald Wilber, "Overthrow of Premier Mossadeq of Iran, November 1952–August 1953," CIA Clandestine Service History, March 1954, in *The Secret CIA History of the Iran Coup, 1953*, ed. Malcolm Byrne (Washington, DC: National Security Archive, November 29, 2000), http://www.gwu.edu/~nsarchiv/NSAEBB/NSAEBB28/, I:1. Present at the meeting on the American side were Kermit Roosevelt, chief of the Near East and Africa Division; John Levitt, chief of Iran Branch; and James Darling, chief of Near East Africa Paramilitary Staff.

21. "First Progress Report on Paragraph 5–a of NSC 136/1, 'U.S. Policy Regarding the Present Situation in Iran,'" March 20, 1953, National Security Archive, Washington, DC.

22. Wilber, "Overthrow of Premier Mossadeq," V, VI.

23. Ibid., V:22.

24. Ibid., VI:39–43.

25. Ibid., VIII:65–77.

26. See Iran Chamber Society, "A Short Account of 1953 Coup," http://www.iranchamber.com/history/coup53/coup53p2.php, 2, accessed December 6, 2012.

27. Wilber, "Overthrow of Premier Mossadeq," VIII:68–69.

28. Ibid., VIII:67.

29. Ibid., 71.

30. Ibid., 76.

31. Douglas Hurd, quoted in Arash Norouzi, "Glory and Humiliation: Iran, Britain and That Coup," The Mossadegh Project, February 12, 2006, http://www.mohammadmossadegh.com/news/house-of-lords/.

5. AMERICAN EMPIRE IN CHAOS

1. Jalal Matini, "Quotes from Ayatollah Khomeini," trans. Farhad Mafie, *Iran Heritage*, July 25, 2003, http://www.iran-heritage.org/interestgroups/government-article2.htm.

2. Council of the League of Nations, "The Palestine Mandate," July 24, 1922, Avalon Project, Yale Law School, http://avalon.law.yale.edu/20th_century/palmanda.asp, accessed December 9, 2012.

3. Ali M. Ansari, *Confronting Iran* (London: Hurst, 2006), 41.

4. See Thomas L. McNaugher, *Arms and Oil: US Military Strategy and the Persian Gulf* (Washington, DC: Brookings Institution, 1985), 47.

5. Ibid.

6. U.S. Department of State, "Second Arab Oil Embargo, 1973–1974," http://2001-2009.state.gov/r/pa/ho/time/dr/96057.htm, accessed December 7, 2012.

7. "Business: Oil Squeeze," *Time*, February 5, 1979.

8. "Iran: Another Crisis for the Shah," *Time*, November 13, 1978.

9. "The Khomeini Era Begins," *Time*, February 12, 1979.

10. Jimmy Carter Library and Museum, "The Hostage Crisis in Iran," November 6, 2012, http://www.jimmycarterlibrary.gov/documents/hostages.phtml.

11. John Dumbrell, *American Foreign Policy: From Carter to Clinton* (Basingstoke, UK: Palgrave Macmillan, 1997), 35.

12. "Khomeini Calls for Stricter Islamic Policy," *Guardian*, March 2, 1979.

13. For an overview, see Vasiliy Mitrokhin, *The KGB in Afghanistan* (Washington, DC: Cold War International History Project, Woodrow Wilson International Center for Scholars, July 2009), http://www.wilsoncenter.org/publication/the-kgb-afghanistan, 17–80.

14. See Bill Blum, trans., "The CIA Intervention in Afghanistan," *Le Nouvel Observateur*, January 15–21, 1998, http://www.globalresearch.ca/articles/BRZ110A.html.

15. Robert Gates, a career CIA officer, served as the agency's director between 1991 and 1993. See his book *From the Shadows: The Ultimate Insider's Story of Five Presidents and How They Won the Cold War* (New York: Simon & Schuster, 1997), 143–49.

16. This and the following quotes in this paragraph are taken from "CIA Intervention in Afghanistan."

17. See Hussain Haqqani, *Pakistan: Between Mosque and Military* (Washington, DC: Carnegie Endowment for International Peace, 2005), 131.

18. Ibid., 132.

19. Federation of American Scientists, "Pakistan's Nuclear Weapons," December 11, 2002, http://www.fas.org/nuke/guide/pakistan/nuke/.

20. See Shafqat Ali Khan, chapter 8 in *Nuclear Weapons after the Comprehensive Test Ban: Implications for Modernization and Proliferation*, ed. Eric H. Arnett (Oxford: Oxford University Press, 1996), 75.

21. Gates, *From the Shadows*, 146.

22. Peter Dale Scott, *Drug, Oil and War: The United States in Afghanistan, Columbia and China* (Lanham, MD: Rowman & Littlefield, 2003), 49.

23. Based on his contacts in the CIA, John Cooley provides an account of how the American-led operation to help the Afghan insurgents was forged. See John Cooley, *Unholy Wars: Afghanistan, America and International Terrorism* (London: Pluto Press, 2002), 41–43.

24. See Mohammad Yousaf and Mark Adkin, *Afghanistan: The Bear Trap* (Barnsley, UK: Leo Cooper, 2001), 97.

25. Pakistan carried out a series of nuclear tests in May 1998—two weeks after India tested its own devices. India had carried out its first test in May 1974.

26. "U.S. Non-Proliferation Policy and Renewed Assistance to Pakistan," State Department cable 25686, January 30, 1980, in *The United States and Pakistan's Quest for the Bomb*, ed. William Burr (Washington, DC: National Security Archive, December 21, 2010), http://www.gwu.edu/~nsarchiv/nukevault/ebb333/index.htm.

27. Except for America's brief interventions in some regional conflicts: for example, humanitarian mission in Somalia, 1992–94; Haiti to restore President Jean-Bertrand Aristide, 1994; NATO bombing of Serbia, 1999. See Zoltan Grossman, "From Wounded Knee to Libya: A Century of U.S. Military Interventions," http://academic.evergreen.edu/g/grossmaz/interventions.html, accessed December 7, 2012.

28. Pervez Musharraf, "Statement by the President of Pakistan, September 12, 2001," Avalon Project, Yale Law School, http://avalon.law.yale.edu/sept11/pakistan_001.asp, accessed December 7, 2012.

29. Pervez Musharraf, "Address to the Nation, 19 Sept 2001," *Our Leader—Musharraf* (blog), July 13, 2006, http://presidentmusharraf.wordpress.com/2006/07/13/address-19-september-2001/.

30. Ashley J. Tellis, *Pakistan and the War on Terror: Conflicted Goals, Compromised Performance* (Washington, DC: Carnegie Endowment for International Peace, January 2008), 3.

31. For example, see "Bush Admits to CIA Secret Prisons," BBC News, September 7, 2006. Among those captured in Pakistan was Khalid Sheikh Mohammed, described by the Americans as the mastermind of the 9/11 attacks, and sent to Guantánamo, where he was subjected to simulated drowning to extract confession.

32. Tellis, *Pakistan and the War on Terror*, 1.

33. Michael Howard, *War and the Liberal Conscience* (New York: Columbia University Press, 2008), 113.

34. For an authoritative overview of what was known as Iran's White Revolution, see Abrahamian, *Modern History of Iran*, 123–54.

6. ARABIA AND THE WEST

1. Edward Said, *Orientalism* (New York: Penguin, 2003), 204.

2. Bernard Lewis, "The Roots of Muslim Rage," *Atlantic*, September 1990, http://www.theatlantic.com/magazine/archive/1990/09/the-roots-of-muslim-rage/4643/2/.

3. For an overview of the rise and fall of the East India Company, see Joe Bindloss and others, *India*, 12th rev. ed. (London: Lonely Planet Publications, 2007), 48–49.

4. Said, *Orientalism*, 206.

5. Some examples are depictions of exotic or naked women in Turkish baths and the Oriental societies, which were extremely conservative, in general; Rudyard Kipling's poem *Gunga Din* depicting the relationship between a British soldier and a water bearer (*Bhishti*); colonial masters and their subjects; and corrupt, despotic rulers.

6. Lydia Saad, "Anti-Muslim Sentiments Fairly Commonplace," Gallup News Service, August 10, 2006, http://www.gallup.com/poll/24073/antimuslim-sentiments-fairly-commonplace.aspx#1.

7. David Sapsted, "UK Poll Finds Profound Anti-Muslim Sentiment," *The National*, January 14, 2010.

8. Evelin Lindner, *Making Enemies: Humiliation and International Conflict* (Westport, CT: Praeger, 2006), 89.

9. Ibid., 94–95.

10. Christopher Blanchard, *Saudi Arabia: Background and U.S. Relations* (Washington, DC: Congressional Research Service, July 9, 2009), 2.

11. "Second Saudi State," *Encyclopaedia Britannica*, http://www.britannica.com/EBchecked/topic/525348/Saudi-Arabia/45226/Second-Saudi-state, accessed December 7, 2012.

12. Ami Isseroff, "Saudi Arabia: A Brief History," MidEastWeb, 2003, http://www.mideastweb.org/arabiahistory.htm.

13. Blanchard, *Saudi Arabia*, 2; and Isseroff, "Saudi Arabia: A Brief History."

14. See Rachel Bronson, *Thicker Than Oil* (Oxford: Oxford University Press, 2006), 9.

15. Ibid., 149.

16. See Anne-Marie Slaughter, "U.S.-Saudi Relations in a World without Equilib-

rium," Session 3 conference transcript, Saudi–US Relations Information Center, May 18, 2009, http://www.saudi-us-relations.org/articles/2009/ioi/090518-ussa -slaughter.html.

17. Oil exploration rights were granted to California Arabian Standard Oil Company, an affiliate of Standard Oil of California, later to be known as Arabian American Oil Company. See Bronson, *Thicker Than Oil*, 14–21.

18. "US Saudi Relation," citing U.S.–Saudi Arabia Business Council, http://ddi08 .wikispaces.com/SS+Saudi+Relations+Oil+DA, accessed December 7, 2012.

19. See "Saudi Arabia: Country Analysis Brief," U.S. Energy Information Administration, last modified October 16, 2012, http://www.eia.doe.gov/emeu/cabs/Saudi _Arabia/Background.html.

20. See Applied Information Systems, "U.S. Oil Imports," http://www.appinsys.com /oil/, accessed December 7, 2012.

21. Lionel Beehner and Toni Johnson, "Global Oil Trends," *Backgrounder*, October 18, 2007, http://www.cfr.org/publication/9484/global_oil_trends.html.

22. See Paul Roberts, *The End of Oil* (New York: Mariner, 2005), 96.

23. James L. Williams, "Oil Price History and Analysis," WTRG Economics, http:// www.wtrg.com/prices.htm, accessed December 7, 2012.

24. Jay Hakes, "35 Years after the Arab Oil Embargo," *Journal of Energy Security*, October 6, 2008, http://www.ensec.org/index.php?option=com_content&view=article& id=155:35yearsafterthearaboilembargo&catid=83:middle-east&Itemid=324.

25. History.com, "OPEC Enacts Oil Embargo," http://www.history.com/this-day-in -history/opec-enacts-oil-embargo, December 7, 2012.

26. See Bassam Fattouh, "Spare Capacity and Oil Price Dynamics," *Petroleum World*, http://www.petroleumworld.com/SunOPF021206.htm, accessed December 9, 2012.

27. Williams, "Oil Price History and Analysis."

28. Ashraf Laidi, *Currency Trading and the Intermarket Analysis: How to Profit from the Shifting Currents in Global Markets* (Hoboken, NJ: Wiley, 2009), 32.

29. Colin Wells, *The Complete Idiot's Guide to Understanding Saudi Arabia* (New York: Penguin, 2003), 159.

30. Nino P. Tollitz, *Saudi Arabia: Terrorism, US Relations and Oil* (New York: Nova Science Publishers, 2006), 18.

31. Lawrence E. Walsh, "Part I. Iran/contra: The Underlying Facts," in *Final Report of the Independent Counsel for Iran/Contra Matters*, vol. 1 (Washington, DC: GPO, 1993), http://www.fas.org/irp/offdocs/walsh/part_i.htm.

32. See John Pike, "National Union for the Total Independence of Angola," Intelligence Resource Program, Federation of American Scientists, May 7, 2003, http:// www.fas.org/irp/world/para/unita.htm.

33. Tetteh Hormeku, "US Intervention in Africa: Through Angolan Eyes," Third World Network, http://www.twnside.org.sg/title/tett-cn.htm, accessed December 9, 2012.

34. Bronson, *Thicker Than Oil*, 33.

35. Ibid., 34.

36. There are too many groups to name here. Some examples are Armenians, Azeris, Chechens, Kazakhs, Tatars, Uighurs, and Uzbeks.

37. Modern-day Syria and Lebanon were ruled under a French mandate granted by the League of Nations after World War I and the collapse of the Ottoman Empire. Even before the League of Nations was formed, the Sykes-Picot Agreement, a secret deal reached in 1916 between Britain and France with the assent of Imperial Russia, carved up large parts of West Asia between Britain and France.

38. William Quandt, *Saudi Arabia in the 1980s: Foreign Policy, Security and Oil* (Washington, DC: Brookings Institution, 1981), 9–35.

39. Uriya Shavit, "Al-Qaeda's Saudi Origins," *Middle East Quarterly* 13, no. 4 (2006): 3–13.

7. IRAQ UNDER OCCUPATION AND DICTATORSHIP

1. Bruce Preston, *A Brief Modern Political History of Iraq*, http://www.e-book.com.au/iraqhistory.htm (Strawberry Hills, NSW, Australia: e-books Australia), accessed December 7, 2012.

2. Ibid.

3. Efraim Karsh, *Islamic Imperialism: A History* (New Haven, CT: Yale University Press, 2007), 90.

4. Charles Tripp, *A History of Iraq*, 3rd ed. (Cambridge: Cambridge University Press, 2007), 8.

5. Ibid., 30.

6. Ibid., 13.

7. Christian Coates Ulrichsen, "The British Occupation of Mesopotamia, 1914–1922," *Journal of Strategic Studies* 30, no. 2 (April 2007): 349–77.

8. Ibid., 349.

9. Ibid.

10. Deepak Tripathi, chapter 5 in *Overcoming the Bush Legacy in Iraq and Afghanistan* (Washington, DC: Potomac Books, 2010).

11. "Conference of San Remo," *Encyclopaedia Britannica*, http://www.britannica.com/EBchecked/topic/521598/Conference-of-San-Remo, accessed December 7, 2012. The prime ministers of Britain, France, and Italy, as well as representatives of Japan, Greece, and Belgium, attended the conference (April 19–26, 1920).

The purpose of the conference was to decide the future of the territories of the former Ottoman Empire, one of the defeated Central Powers in World War I (the other Central Powers were the German Empire, the Austro-Hungarian Empire, and the Kingdom of Bulgaria). The mandates to administer Mesopotamia and Palestine were granted to Britain, and France received the mandates for Syria and Lebanon.

12. "British Mandate of Mesopotamia," Student Reader, September 3, 2011, http://studentreader.com/timeline-of-mesopotamia-british-mandate/.

13. "The Great Iraqi Revolution 1929," Armed Conflict Events Data, December 16, 2000, http://www.onwar.com/aced/data/india/iraq1920.htm.

14. Graham E. Fuller and Rend Rahim Franche, *The Arab Shi'a: The Forgotten Muslims* (New York: St. Martin's, 1999), 46. For the significance of the 1920 revolt, see Marion Farouk-Sluglett and Peter Sluglett, *Iraq since 1958: From Revolution to Dictatorship* (London: Routledge and Kegan Paul, 1987), 10.

15. Fuller and Franche, *The Arab Shi'a*, 46.

16. Tareq Y. Ismael and Jacqueline S. Ismael, "Iraq and the New World Order," in *The Gulf War and the New World Order: International Relations of the Middle East*, ed. Tareq Y. Ismael and Jacqueline S. Ismael (Gainesville: University Press of Florida, 1994), 269.

17. Tripp, *History of Iraq*, 44–45.

18. Michael Graham Fry, Eric Goldstein, and Richard Langhorne, *Guide to International Relations and Diplomacy* (London: Continuum, 2002), 200.

19. Ibid.

20. Tripp, *History of Iraq*, 47.

21. Helen Chapin Metz, ed., *Iraq: A Country Study* (Whitefish, MT: Kessinger Publishing, 2004), 50.

22. Gareth Stansfield, *Iraq* (Cambridge, UK: Polity Press, 2007), 47.

23. Michael Joseph Cohen, *Churchill and the Jews*, 2nd ed. (Abingdon, UK: Frank Cass, 2003), 82–83.

24. See, for example, Don Peretz, *The Middle East Today*, 6th ed. (Westport, CT: Praeger, 1994), 107; also, Tareq Y. Ismael, *International Relations of the Contemporary Middle East* (Syracuse, NY: Syracuse University Press, 1986), 84.

25. For the ratification of the 1922 treaty and the subsequent oil discovery, see Tripp, *History of Iraq*, 51–59.

26. Royal Dutch Shell was jointly British and Dutch owned.

27. Stansfield, *Iraq*, 49.

28. Ibid., 50.

29. See Tripp, "The Hashemite Monarchy 1932–41," chapter 3 in *History of Iraq*, 75–104.

30. Abbas Alnasrawi, *The Economy of Iraq: Oil, Wars, Destruction of Development and Prospects* (Westport, CT: Greenwood Press, 1994).

31. Sequence of events from "The Iraq Crisis—Timeline: Chronology of Modern Iraqi History," MidEastWeb, 2002–3, http://www.mideastweb.org/iraqtimeline .htm; also, Preston, *Brief Modern History of Iraq.*

32. From his infancy until he reached the age of eighteen in 1953, King Faisal II remained on the throne under his uncle acting as regent, in effect king. Abd al-Ilah was a pro-British member of the royal family.

33. Liam D. Anderson and Matthew Elliot, *The Future of Iraq: Dictatorship, Democracy, or Division* (New York: Palgrave Macmillan, 2004), 18.

34. Matthew Elliot, *"Independent Iraq": The Monarchy and British Influence, 1941–58* (London: I. B. Tauris, 1996), 12.

35. Tripp, *History of Iraq*, 96–99.

36. Helen Chapin Metz, "Iraq: A Country Study," in *Iraq: Issues, Historical Background, Bibliography*, ed. Leon M. Jeffries (New York: Nova Science Publishers, 2003), 152.

37. Ibid.

38. The formal leader of the coup was Gen. Mohammad Naquib, but the real power behind the takeover was Nasser, who assumed the presidency in January 1955 following a bitter power struggle with Naquib, who was jailed.

39. Editorial, "Coup D'État," *Times* (London), July 15, 1958, 9.

40. "Significance of the Coup in Syria," *Times* (London), November 16, 1970.

41. "King Idris Deposed by Military Junta in Libya Coup," *Times* (London), September 2, 1969.

42. Tripp, *History of Iraq*, xiii–xv, 158.

8. THE BETRAYAL OF PALESTINIANS

1. Ian Richard Netton, comp. and ed., *Middle East Sources: A MELCOM Guide to Middle Eastern and Islamic Books and Materials in the United Kingdom and Irish Libraries* (Richmond, UK: Curzon Press, 1998), 35.

2. Peter Tertzakian, *A Thousand Barrels a Second: The Coming Oil Break Point and the Challenges Facing an Energy Dependent World* (New York: McGraw-Hill, 2007), 35–42; also, Gerald D. Nash, *United States Oil Policy, 1890–1964: Business and Government in Twentieth Century America* (Pittsburgh, PA: University of Pittsburgh Press, 1968), 5–6.

3. Mark Sykes and Georges Picot, "The Sykes-Picot Agreement: 1916," Avalon Project, Yale Law School, http://avalon.law.yale.edu/20th_century/sykes.asp; also, BBC, "The Sykes–Picot Agreement," *Israel and the Palestinians: Key Documents*, November 29, 2001.

4. Keith Wheeler, "In an Angry Arab World," *Life*, April 1, 1957, 118.

5. Arthur Balfour, "The Balfour Declaration," letter to Walter Rothschild, November 2, 1917, Israel Ministry of Foreign Affairs, Jerusalem.

6. Jean Allain, *International Law in the Middle East: Closer to Power than Justice* (Aldershot, UK: Ashgate Publishing, 2004), 76, quoting Benny Morris, *Righteous Victims: A History of the Zionist-Arab Conflict, 1881–1999* (New York: Random House, 1999), 71.

7. Allain, *International Law in the Middle East*, 77.

8. See, for example, C. L. Mowat, *The New Cambridge Modern History*, volume 12, *The Shifting Balance of World Forces, 1898–1945* (Cambridge: Cambridge University Press, 1968), 289.

9. Institute of Palestine Studies (IPS), "Palestinian History: A Chronology," http://www.palestine-studies.org/enakba/Chronology/Before%20Their%20 Diaspora%20Chronology.pdf.

10. Winston Churchill, "British White Paper of June 1922," Avalon Project, Yale Law School, http://avalon.law.yale.edu/20th_century/brwh1922.asp, accessed December 7, 2012.

11. Ibid.

12. IPS, "Palestinian History." The Revisionist Party was a predecessor of the Herut Party (1948), which later became Likud.

13. Palestine Facts. "British Mandate: McDonald White Paper," http://208.84.118 .121/pf_mandate_whitepaper_1939.php, accessed December 7, 2012.

14. Ibid.

15. Haim Hillel Ben-Sasson, ed., *A History of the Jewish People* (London: Weidenfeld & Nicolson, 1976), 1044.

16. Robert Kumamoto, *International Terrorism and American Foreign Policy, 1945–1976* (Boston: Northeastern University Press, 1999), 17.

17. Ibid., 17–18.

18. Sol Scharfstein, *Understanding Israel* (Jersey City, NJ: Ktav Publishing House, 1994), 112.

19. Malcolm Kerr, *The Elusive Peace in the Middle East* (New York: State University of New York Press, 1975), 179.

20. Ibid., 181.

21. Fred J. Khouri, *The Arab-Israeli Dilemma*, 3rd ed. (Syracuse, NY: Syracuse University Press, 1985), 36.

22. Ibid.

23. The initiative for the Arab Higher Committee came from Hajj Amin al-Husayni. The committee consisted of the leaders of Palestinian Arab clans under the mufti's chairmanship.

24. Khouri, *Arab-Israeli Dilemma*, 36–37.

25. Franklin D. Roosevelt, letter to King Ibn Saud, April 5, 1945, Avalon Project, Yale Law School, http://avalon.law.yale.edu/20th_century/decad161.asp.

26. "The Recognition of the State of Israel: Chronology," Harry S. Truman Library, http://www.trumanlibrary.org/whistlestop/study_collections/israel/large/index .php?action=chrono, accessed December 7, 2012.

27. "Truman and the Creation of the Jewish Army," *Middle East Studies Online Journal*, August 30, 2009, http://www.middle-east-studies.net/?p=1707.

28. Harry S. Truman, *Memoirs: Years of Trial and Hope* (New York: Doubleday, 1956), 132.

29. Ami Isseroff, "President Harry S. Truman and U.S. Support for Israeli Statehood," MidEastWeb, 2003, http://www.mideastweb.org/us_supportforstate.htm.

30. Raymond H. Geselbracht, comp., "The United States and the Recognition of Israel: A Chronology," Harry S. Truman Library, http://www.trumanlibrary.org /israel/palestin.htm, December 7, 2012.

31. Michael J. Devine, Robert P. Watson, Robert J. Wolz, eds., *Israel and the Legacy of Harry S. Truman* (Kirksville, MO: Truman State University Press, 2008), 97.

32. John Snetsinger, *Truman, the Jewish Vote and the Creation of Israel* (Stanford, CA: Hoover Institution Press, 1974), 24–25.

33. Ibid., 29–30.

34. See Geselbracht, "The United States and the Recognition of Israel."

35. The UN Security Council approved the Partition Plan for Palestine in November 1947.

36. American-Israeli Cooperative Enterprise, "The American Position on Partition," Jewish Virtual Library, http://www.jewishvirtuallibrary.org/jsource/History /US_position_on_partition.html, accessed December 7, 2012. Also see Israel Ministry of Foreign Affairs, "The Declaration of the Establishment of the State of Israel, May 14, 1948," http://www.mfa.gov.il/MFA/Peace%20Process/Guide%20 to%20the%20Peace%20Process/Declaration%20of%20Establishment%20of%20 State%20of%20Israel; "Palestinian History, A Chronology," PalestineRemembered .com, September 9, 2001, http://www.palestineremembered.com/Acre/Palestine -Remembered/Story564.html#1947.

37. See the online Palestinian resource *al Nakba*, http://www.alnakba.org/.

Epilogue

1. See J. Rickard, "First World War, 1914–1918," History of War, February 18, 2001, http://www.historyofwar.org/articles/wars_wwI.html.

2. Odd Arne Westad, *The Global Cold War: Third World Interventions and the Making of Our Times* (Cambridge: Cambridge University Press, 2007); John Lewis Gaddis, *The Cold War: A New History* (New York: Penguin, 2006); Ronald E. Powaski, *The Cold War: The United States and the Soviet Union, 1917–1991* (Oxford: Oxford University Press, 1998).

3. See Deepak Tripathi, *Breeding Ground: Afghanistan and the Origins of Islamist Terrorism* (Washington, DC: Potomac Books, 2011); and Tripathi, *Overcoming the Bush Legacy*.

4. See Francis Fukuyama, "The End of History?," *National Interest* 16 (Summer 1989): 3–18; Fukuyama, *The End of History and the Last Man* (New York: Avon Books, 1992), xi.

5. Samuel Huntington, "Clash of Civilizations?," *Foreign Affairs* 73, no. 3 (1993): 22–49; *The Clash of Civilizations and the Making of the World Order* (New York: Simon & Schuster, 1998).

6. Huntington, "Clash of Civilizations?," 39.

7. See Kazuyuki Motohashi, "Japan's Long-Term Recession in the 1990s: Fall of Industrial Competitiveness?," 2004, http://www.mo.t.u-tokyo.ac.jp/seika /files/WP04-08motohashi1.pdf, 2.

8. "Excerpts from Pentagon's Plan: Prevent the Re-Emergence of a New Rival," *New York Times*, March 8, 1992.

9. Project for the New American Century, "Statement of Principles." Also see Tripathi, *Overcoming the Bush Legacy*.

10. Tripathi, *Overcoming the Bush Legacy*, 117.

11. See Jo Becker and Scott Shane, "Secret 'Kill List' Proves a Test of Obama's Principles and Will," *New York Times*, May 29, 2012.

12. Peter Finn and Anne E. Kornblut, "Obama Creates Indefinite Detention System for Prisoners at Guantanamo Bay," *Washington Post*, March 8, 2011.

13. See Seth Doane, "Bagram Air Base Larger Military Prison than Gitmo," CBS News, November 13, 2011, http://www.cbsnews.com/video/watch/?id=7388152n.

14. Matthias Gebauer and Hasnain Kazim, "The 'Kill Team' Images: US Army Apologizes for Horrific Photos from Afghanistan," *Spiegel*, March 21, 2011; also, "US Marines Identify Afghanistan 'Urination' Troops," BBC News, January 13, 2012; "Obama Apology to Afghans for Quran Burning: All Forgiven?," *Christian Science Monitor*, February 28, 2012; "US Soldier Kills Afghan Civilians in Kandahar," BBC News, March 11, 2012.

15. Frank Gardner, "Tunisia One Year On: Where the Arab Spring Started," BBC News, December 17, 2011.

16. "Moderate Islamist Party Claims Election Win in Tunisia," BBC News, October 24, 2011; "Tunisia Installs Moncef Marzouki as President," *Guardian*, December 13, 2011.

17. Adam Nossiter, "Algerian Election Results Draw Disbelief," *New York Times*, May 11, 2012.

18. "Hosni Mubarak Resigns as President," *Al Jazeera*, February 11, 2011.

19. See Jack Shenker and Abdul-Rahman Hussein, "Muslim Brotherhood Warns Egypt's Generals," *Guardian*, June 18, 2012.

20. Ekram Ibrahim, "Egypt's January 25 Revolution Haunted by 'Military Coup,' Warn Analysts," *Al Ahram,* June 18, 2012.

21. "U.S. Concerned by Egyptian Military Moves," Voice of America, June 18, 2012.

22. Hillary Clinton, interview with Christiane Amanpour, *ABC This Week,* February 20, 2011, http://www.youtube.com/watch?v=IlCEVKmIOJA.

23. Reena Ninan, "Secretary of State Hillary Clinton Pushes Gulf Security and Aid for Syria," ABC News, March 31, 2012.

24. "Libya: Investigate Deaths of Gaddafi and Son," Human Rights Watch, October 22, 2011, http://www.hrw.org/news/2011/10/22/libya-investigate-deaths -gaddafi-and-son.

25. "UN Security Council Resolution 1973 (2011) on Libya—Full Text," *Guardian,* March 17, 2011.

26. "Clinton Pledges More Aid in Surprise Libya Visit," CBS News, October 18, 2011.

27. "Clinton on Qaddafi: We Came, We Saw, He Died," CBS News, October 20, 2011.

28. Jo Adetunji, "British Firms Urged to 'Pack Suitcases' in Rush for Libya Business," *Guardian,* October 21, 2011.

29. Abdel Bari Atwan, "Libya's Bloody Victory over Gaddafi Is Just the Beginning," *Guardian,* October 20, 2011.

30. "China and Russia Veto UN Resolution Condemning Syria," BBC News, October 5, 2011; Column Lynch and Alice Fordham, "Russia, China Veto U.N. Resolution on Syria," *Washington Post,* February 4, 2012.

BIBLIOGRAPHY

Archives, Government Documents, and Primary Sources

Balfour, Arthur. "The Balfour Declaration." Letter to Walter Rothschild, November 2, 1917. Avalon Project, Yale Law School. http://avalon.law.yale.edu/20th_century/balfour.asp.

BBC. "The Sykes-Picot Agreement." *Israel and the Palestinians: Key Documents*, November 29, 2001.

"Bill of Rights." The Charters of Freedom, National Archives and Records Administration. http://www.archives.gov/exhibits/charters/bill_of_rights_transcript.html. Accessed December 4, 2012.

"British Mandate of Mesopotamia." Student Reader, September 3, 2011. http://studentreader.com/timeline-of-mesopotamia-british-mandate/.

Burr, William, ed. *The United States and Pakistan's Quest for the Bomb*. Washington, DC: National Security Archive, December 21, 2010. Doc. 46. http://www.gwu.edu/~nsarchiv/nukevault/ebb333/index.htm.

Bush, George W. "President's State of the Union Address," January 29, 2002. White House Archives, Washington, DC.

Churchill, Winston. "British White Paper of June 1922." Avalon Project, Yale Law School. http://avalon.law.yale.edu/20th_century/brwh1922.asp. Accessed December 7, 2012.

Clinton, Hillary Rodham. "Remarks at the U.S.–Islamic World Forum." U.S. Department of State, February 14, 2010. http://www.state.gov/secretary/rm/2010/02/136678.htm.

Council of the League of Nations. "The Palestine Mandate," July 24, 1922. Avalon Project, Yale Law School. http://avalon.law.yale.edu/20th_century/palmanda.asp. Accessed December 9, 2012.

"Declaration of Independence, July 4, 1776." Avalon Project, Yale Law School. http:// avalon.law.yale.edu/18th_century/declare.asp. Accessed December 4, 2012.

Gasiorowski, Mark J., and Malcolm Byrne, eds. *Mohammad Mosaddeq and the 1953 Coup in Iran*. Washington, DC: National Security Archive, June 22, 2004. Docs. 1 and 2. http://www.gwu.edu/~nsarchiv/NSAEBB/NSAEBB126/iran521120.pdf.

International Atomic Energy Agency. "Agreement between Iran and the International Atomic Energy Agency for the Application of Safeguards in Connection with the Treaty on the Non-Proliferation of Nuclear Weapons." *IAEA Information Circular* 214 (December 13, 1974).

Kennedy, John F. "Inaugural Address of John F. Kennedy," January 20, 1961. Avalon Project, Yale Law School. http://avalon.law.yale.edu/20th_century/kennedy.asp. Accessed December 9, 2012.

Lincoln, Abraham. "First Inaugural Address of Abraham Lincoln," March 4, 1861. Avalon Project, Yale Law School. http://avalon.law.yale.edu/19th_century/lincoln1 .asp. Accessed December 9, 2012.

Mitrokhin, Vasiliy. *The KGB in Afghanistan*. Washington, DC: Cold War International History Project, Woodrow Wilson International Center for Scholars, July 2009. http://www.wilsoncenter.org/publication/the-kgb-afghanistan.

Musharraf, Pervez. "Address to the Nation, 19 Sept. 2001." *Our Leader—Musharraf* (blog), July 13, 2006. http://presidentmusharraf.wordpress.com/2006/07/13 /address-19-september-2001/.

———. "Statement by the President of Pakistan, September 12, 2001." Avalon Project, Yale Law School. http://avalon.law.yale.edu/sept11/pakistan_001.asp. Accessed December 7, 2012.

National Intelligence Estimate. *Prospects for Iraq's Stability: A Challenging Road Ahead*. Washington, DC, January 2007.

Obama, Barack. "Inaugural Address of Barack Obama," January 20, 2009 Avalon Project, 2009, http://avalon.law.yale.edu/21st_century/obama.asp.

———. "A New Strategy for Afghanistan and Pakistan." Office of the Press Secretary, White House, March 27, 2009. http://www.whitehouse.gov/the_press_office /Remarks-by-the-President-on-a-New-Strategy-for-Afghanistan-and-Pakistan/.

———. "Remarks by President Obama in Prague, Czech Republic." Office of the Press Secretary, White House, April 5, 2009. http://www.whitehouse.gov/the _press_office/Remarks-By-President-Barack-Obama-In-Prague-As-Delivered.

———. "Remarks by President Obama to the Turkish Parliament." Office of the Press Secretary, White House, April 6, 2009. http://www.whitehouse.gov/the-press -office/remarks-president-obama-turkish-parliament.

———. "Remarks by the President at the Acceptance of the Nobel Peace Prize."

Office of the Press Secretary, White House, December 10, 2009. http://www
.whitehouse.gov/the-press-office/remarks-president-acceptance-nobel-peace-prize.

―――. "Remarks by the President in the State of the Union Address." Office of the
Press Secretary, White House, January 27, 2010. http://www.whitehouse.gov
/the-press-office/remarks-president-state-union-address.

―――. "Remarks by the President on a New Beginning." Office of the Press Secretary, White House, June 4, 2009. http://www.whitehouse.gov/the-press-office
/remarks-president-cairo-university-6-04-09.

―――. "Senator Obama's Remarks during the Democratic Presidential Debate,"
January 5, 2008. http://www.presidency.ucsb.edu/ws/index.php?pid=76224.

―――. "Statement by the President on Afghanistan," February 17, 2009. http://www
.whitehouse.gov/the-press-office/statement-president-afghanistan.

―――. "2002 Speech Against the Iraq War," October 2, 2002. http://obamaspeeches
.com/001-2002-Speech-Against-the-Iraq-War-Obama-Speech.htm.

Obama, Barack, Nicholas Sarkozy, and Gordon Brown. "Statements by President
Obama, French President Sarkozy, and British Prime Minister Brown on Iranian
Nuclear Facility." Office of the Press Secretary, White House, September 25,
2009. http://www.whitehouse.gov/the_press_office/Statements-By-President
-Obama-French-President-Sarkozy-And-British-Prime-Minister-Brown
-On-Iranian-Nuclear-Facility/.

Obama for America. "President Obama's Stance on Israel: Myths vs. Facts." http://
assets.bostatic.com/pdfs/jewish-american/Israel_myths_facts.pdf. Accessed December 9, 2012.

Prados, John, ed. *JFK and Diem Coup.* Washington, DC: National Security Archive, November 5, 2003. Docs. 1, 2, and 17. http://www.gwu.edu/~nsarchiv/NSAEBB
/NSAEBB101/index.htm.

Project for the New American Century. "Statement of Principles." June 3, 1997. http://
www.newamericancentury.org/statementofprinciples.htm.

Roosevelt, Franklin. Letter to King Ibn Saud, April 5, 1945. Avalon Project, Yale
Law School. http://avalon.law.yale.edu/20th_century/decad161.asp. Accessed
December 9, 2012.

Sykes, Mark, and Georges Picot. "The Sykes-Picot Agreement: 1916." Avalon Project.
Yale Law School. http://avalon.law.yale.edu/20th_century/sykes.asp. Accessed
December 9, 2012.

Truman, Harry S. *Memoirs: Years of Trial and Hope.* New York: Doubleday, 1956.

U.S. Department of Defense. "Contracts." Office of the Assistant Secretary of Defense
(Public Affairs), September 28, 2007. http://www.defense.gov/contracts/contract
.aspx?contractid=3615.

U.S. Department of State. "Second Arab Oil Embargo, 1973–1974." http://2001
-2009.state.gov/r/pa/ho/time/dr/96057.htm. Accessed December 7, 2012.

Washington, George. "Inaugural Address," April 30, 1789. National Archives and
Records Administration, Washington, DC. http://www.archives.gov/exhibits
/american_originals/inaugtxt.html. Accessed December 5, 2012.

Wilber, Donald. "Overthrow of Premier Mossadeq of Iran, November 1952–August
1953." CIA Clandestine Service History, March 1954. In *The Secret CIA History
of the Iran Coup, 1953*. Edited by Malcolm Byrne. Washington, DC: National Security Archive, November 29, 2000. http://www.gwu.edu/~nsarchiv/NSAEBB
/NSAEBB28/.

ARTICLES, BOOKS, AND REPORTS

Abrahamian, Ervand. *A History of Modern Iran.* Cambridge: Cambridge University Press,
2008.

Allain, Jean. *International Law in the Middle East: Closer to Power than Justice.* Aldershot,
UK: Ashgate Publishing, 2004.

Alnasrawi, Abbas. *The Economy of Iraq: Oil, Wars, Destruction of Development and Prospects.*
Westport, CT: Greenwood Press, 1994.

Anderson, Liam D., and Matthew Elliot. *The Future of Iraq: Dictatorship, Democracy, or
Division.* New York: Palgrave Macmillan, 2004.

Ansari, Ali M. *Confronting Iran.* London: Hurst, 2006.

Arnett, Eric H., ed. *Nuclear Weapons after the Comprehensive Test Ban: Implications for Modernization and Proliferation.* Oxford: Oxford University Press, 1996.

Bacevich, Andrew. "Prophets and Poseurs: Niebuhr and Our Times." *World Affairs,* Winter
2008. http://www.worldaffairsjournal.org/articles/2008Winter/full-prophets.html.

Ben-Sasson, Haim Hillel, ed. *A History of the Jewish People.* London: Weidenfeld &
Nicolson, 1976.

Bindloss, Joe, and others. *India.* 12th rev. ed. London: Lonely Planet Publications, 2007.

Blanchard, Christopher. *Saudi Arabia: Background and U.S. Relations.* Washington, DC:
Congressional Research Service, July 9, 2009.

Blum, Bill, trans. "The CIA Intervention in Afghanistan." *Le Nouvel Observateur,* January
15–21, 1998. http://www.globalresearch.ca/articles/BRZ110A.html.

Bronson, Rachel. *Thicker Than Oil.* Oxford: Oxford University Press, 2006.

Carafano, James. *The Long War against Terrorism.* Washington, DC: Heritage Foundation,
September 8, 2003.

Cohen, Michael Joseph. *Churchill and the Jews.* 2nd ed. Abingdon, UK: Frank Cass, 2003.

Cooley, John. *Unholy Wars: Afghanistan, America and International Terrorism.* London: Pluto
Press, 2002.

Cronin, Stephanie, ed. *The Making of Modern Iran: State and Society under Reza Shah 1921–1941.* London: Routledge, 2003.

Devine, Michael J., Robert P. Watson, Robert J. Wolz, eds. *Israel and the Legacy of Harry S. Truman.* Kirksville, MO: Truman State University Press, 2008.

Dumbrell, John. *American Foreign Policy: From Carter to Clinton.* Basingstoke, UK: Palgrave Macmillan, 1997.

Elliot, Matthew. *"Independent Iraq": The Monarchy and British Influence, 1941–58.* London: I. B. Tauris, 1996.

Farouk-Sluglett, Marion, and Peter Sluglett. *Iraq since 1958: From Revolution to Dictatorship.* London: Routledge and Kegan Paul, 1987.

Fattouh, Bassam. "Spare Capacity and Oil Price Dynamics." *Petroleum World.* http://www.petroleumworld.com/SunOPF021206.htm. Accessed December 9, 2012.

Fry, Michael Graham, Eric Goldstein, and Richard Langhorne. *Guide to International Relations and Diplomacy.* London: Continuum, 2002.

Fukuyama, Francis. "The End of History?" *National Interest* 16 (Summer 1989): 3–18.

———. *The End of History and the Last Man.* New York: Avon Books, 1992.

Fuller, Graham E., and Rend Rahim Franche. *The Arab Shi'a: The Forgotten Muslims.* New York: St. Martin's, 1999.

Gaddis, John Lewis. *The Cold War: A New History.* New York: Penguin, 2006.

Gates, Robert. *From the Shadows: The Ultimate Insider's Story of Five Presidents and How They Won the Cold War.* New York: Simon & Schuster, 1997.

Ghani, Cyrus. *Iran and the Rise of Reza Shah: From Qajar Collapse to Pahlavi Power.* London: I. B. Tauris, 2000.

Gibson, Kathleen R. "Customs and Cultures in Animals and Humans: Neurobiological and Evolutionary Considerations." In *Anthropology in Theory: Issues in Epistemology*, edited by Henrietta Moore and Todd Sanders. Malden, MA: Wiley Blackwell, 2006.

Hakes, Jay. "35 Years after the Arab Oil Embargo." *Journal of Energy Security*, October 6, 2008. http://www.ensec.org/index.php?option=com_content&view=article&id=155:35yearsafterthearaboilembargo&catid=83:middle-east&Itemid=324.

Hankins, James. *Plato in the Italian Renaissance.* Leiden, Netherlands: E. J. Brill, 1990.

Haqqani, Hussain. *Pakistan: Between Mosque and Military.* Washington, DC: Carnegie Endowment for International Peace, 2005.

Hardt, Michael, and Antonio Negri. *Empire.* Cambridge, MA: Harvard University Press, 2001.

Howard, Michael. *War and the Liberal Conscience.* New York: Columbia University Press, 2008.

Huntington, Samuel. "Clash of Civilizations?" *Foreign Affairs* 73, no. 3 (1993): 22–49.

———. *The Clash of Civilizations and the Making of the World Order.* New York: Simon & Schuster, 1998.

International Crisis Group. *Failed Responsibility: Iraqi Refugees in Syria, Jordan and Lebanon.* Middle East Report No. 77. Brussels, July 10, 2008.

Ismael, Tareq Y. *International Relations of the Contemporary Middle East.* Syracuse, NY: Syracuse University Press, 1986.

Ismael, Tareq Y., and Jacqueline S. Ismael. "Iraq and the New World Order." In *The Gulf War and the New World Order: International Relations of the Middle East,* edited by Tareq Y. Ismael and Jacqueline S. Ismael. Gainesville: University Press of Florida, 1994.

Kamrava, Mehran. *The Modern Middle East: The Political History since the First World War.* Berkeley: University of California Press, 2005.

Kapuscinski, Ryszard. *Shah of Shahs.* London: Penguin, 2006.

Karsh, Efraim. *Islamic Imperialism: A History.* New Haven, CT: Yale University Press, 2007.

Kerr, Malcolm. *The Elusive Peace in the Middle East.* New York: State University of New York Press, 1975.

Khosrakhavar, Farhad. "Postrevolutionary Iran and the New Social Movements." In *Twenty Years of Islamic Revolution: Political and Social Transition in Iran since 1979,* edited by Eric Hooglund. Syracuse, NY: Syracuse University Press, 2002.

Khouri, Fred J. *The Arab-Israeli Dilemma.* 3rd ed. Syracuse, NY: Syracuse University Press, 1985.

Kolko, Gabriel. *The Age of War: The United States Confronts the World.* Boulder, CO: Lynne Rienner, 2006.

Kumamoto, Robert. *International Terrorism and American Foreign Policy, 1945–1976.* Boston: Northeastern University Press, 1999.

Ladjevardian, Reza. *From Ancient Persia to Contemporary Iran.* Washington, DC: Mage Publishers, 2005.

Laidi, Ashraf. *Currency Trading and the Intermarket Analysis: How to Profit from the Shifting Currents in Global Markets.* Hoboken, NJ: Wiley, 2009.

Lewis, Bernard. "The Roots of Muslim Rage." *Atlantic,* September 1990. http://www.theatlantic.com/magazine/archive/1990/09/the-roots-of-muslim-rage/4643/2/.

Lindner, Evelin. *Making Enemies: Humiliation and International Conflict.* Westport, CT: Praeger, 2006.

Machiavelli, Niccolò. *The Prince.* Translated by George Bull. London: Penguin, 2003.

Maugeri, Leonardo. *The Age of Oil: The Mythology, History, and the Future of the World's Most Controversial Resource.* Westport, CT: Praeger, 2006.

McBeth, B. S. *British Oil Policy 1919–1939.* London: Frank Cass, 1985.

McLachlan, Keith. *The Neglected Garden: The Politics and Ecology of Agriculture in Iran.* London: I. B. Tauris, 1988.

McNaugher, Thomas L. *Arms and Oil: US Military Strategy and the Persian Gulf.* Washington, DC: Brookings Institution, 1985.

Metz, Helen Chapin, ed. "The Constitutional Revolution." In *Iran: A Country Study*. Washington, DC: GPO, 1987. http://countrystudies.us/iran/13.htm.

———. "Iraq: A Country Study." In *Iraq: Issues, Historical Background, Bibliography*, edited by Leon M. Jeffries. New York: Nova Science Publishers, 2003.

———. *Iraq: A Country Study*. Whitefish, MT: Kessinger Publishing, 2004.

Milani, Abbas. *Eminent Persians: The Men and Women Who Made Modern Iran, 1941–1979*. Syracuse, NY: Syracuse University Press, 2008.

Mowat, C. L. *The New Cambridge Modern History*. Vol. 12, *The Shifting Balance of World Forces, 1898–1945*. Cambridge: Cambridge University Press, 1968.

Murphy, Robert. *Cultural and Social Anthropology: An Overture*. 2nd ed. Englewood Cliffs, NJ: Prentice-Hall, 1986.

Nash, Gerald D. *United States Oil Policy, 1890–1964: Business and Government in Twentieth Century America*. Pittsburgh, PA: University of Pittsburgh Press, 1968.

Netton, Ian Richard, comp. and ed. *Middle East Sources: A MELCOM Guide to Middle Eastern and Islamic Books and Materials in the United Kingdom and Irish Libraries*. Richmond, UK: Curzon Press, 1998.

O'Hanlon, Michael. "A Flawed Masterpiece." *Foreign Affairs* 81, no. 3 (March/April 2002): 47.

Patrick, Stewart. "Libya and the Future of Humanitarian Intervention." *Foreign Affairs*, August 26, 2011.

Peretz, Don. *The Middle East Today*. 6th ed. Westport, CT: Praeger, 1994.

Peters, Ralph. *Fighting for the Future: Will America Triumph?* Mechanicsburg, PA: Stackpole Books, 1999.

Plato. *The Republic*. Translated by Desmond Lee. London: Penguin, 2007.

Powaski, Ronald E. *The Cold War: The United States and the Soviet Union, 1917–1991*. Oxford: Oxford University Press, 1998.

Powell, Enoch. *Joseph Chamberlain*. London: Thames and Hudson, 1977.

Preston, Bruce. *A Brief Modern Political History of Iraq*. Strawberry Hills, NSW, Australia. http://www.e-book.com.au/iraqhistory.htm. Accessed December 7, 2012.

Quandt, William. *Saudi Arabia in the 1980s: Foreign Policy, Security and Oil*. Washington, DC: Brookings Institution, 1981.

Rizvi, Mahtab Alam. *An Assessment of Iran's Presidential Elections 2009*. New Delhi: Institute for Defense Studies, June 19, 2009.

Roberts, Paul. *The End of Oil*. New York: Mariner, 2005.

Said, Edward. *Orientalism*. New York: Penguin, 2003.

Salehi-Isfahani, Djavad. *Tough Times Ahead for the Iranian Economy*. Washington, DC: Brookings Institution, April 6, 2009.

Santayana, George. *The Life of Reason*. Vols. 1–3. Charleston, SC: BiblioBazaar, 2009.

Savill, Agnes. *Alexander the Great and His Time*. New York: Barnes & Noble, 1993.

Scharfstein, Sol. *Understanding Israel*. Jersey City, NJ: Ktav Publishing House, 1994.

Scott, Peter Dale. *Drug, Oil and War: The United States in Afghanistan, Columbia and China*. Lanham, MD: Rowman & Littlefield, 2003.

Shahnavaz, Shahbaz. *Britain and the Opening Up of South-West Persia 1880–1914: A Study in Imperialism and Economic Dependence*. Abingdon, UK: Routledge, 2005.

Shavit, Uriya. "Al-Qaeda's Saudi Origins." *Middle East Quarterly* 13, no. 4 (2006): 3–13.

Snetsinger, John. *Truman, the Jewish Vote and the Creation of Israel*. Stanford, CA: Hoover Institution Press, 1974.

Stansfield, Gareth. *Iraq*. Cambridge, UK: Polity Press, 2007.

Tellis, Ashley J. *Pakistan and the War on Terror: Conflicted Goals, Compromised Performance*. Washington, DC: Carnegie Endowment for International Peace, January 2008.

Tertzakian, Peter. *A Thousand Barrels a Second: The Coming Oil Break Point and the Challenges Facing an Energy Dependent World*. New York: McGraw-Hill, 2007.

Tirman, John. *100 Ways America Is Screwing Up the World*. New York: HarperCollins, 2006.

Tollitz, Nino P. *Saudi Arabia: Terrorism, US Relations and Oil*. New York: Nova Science Publishers, 2006.

Tripp, Charles. *A History of Iraq*. 3rd ed. Cambridge: Cambridge University Press, 2007.

"Truman and the Creation of the Jewish Army." *Middle East Studies Online Journal*, August 30, 2009. http://www.middle-east-studies.net/?p=1707.

Tzu, Sun. *The Art of War*. http://www.sonshi.com/sun1.html. Accessed 5, 2012.

Ulrichsen, Christian Coates. "The British Occupation of Mesopotamia, 1914–1922." *Journal of Strategic Studies* 30, no. 2 (April 2007): 349–77.

Walsh, Lawrence E. "Part I. Iran/Contra: The Underlying Facts." In *Final Report of the Independent Counsel for Iran/Contra Matters*. Vol. 1. Washington, DC: GPO, 1993. http://www.fas.org/irp/offdocs/walsh/part_i.htm.

Wells, Colin. *The Complete Idiot's Guide to Understanding Saudi Arabia*. New York: Penguin, 2003.

Westad, Odd Arne. *The Global Cold War: Third World Interventions and the Making of Our Times*. Cambridge: Cambridge University Press, 2007.

Yousaf, Mohammad, and Mark Adkin. *Afghanistan: The Bear Trap*. Barnsley, UK: Leo Cooper, 2001.

Newspapers and Broadcast Media

Adetunji, Jo. "British Firms Urged to 'Pack Suitcases' in Rush for Libya Business." *Guardian*, October 21, 2011.

Agence France-Presse. "Clinton Warns Iran That Patience Has Limits." Canada.com, October 31, 2009.

Al Arabiya. "Iran Accuses UK of Vote Sabotage, Kicks Out BBC." June 21, 2009.

Al Jazeera. "Hosni Mubarak Resigns as President." February 11, 2011.

————. "Muammar Gaddafi Killed as Sirte Falls." October 21, 2011.

Atwan, Abdel Bari. "Libya's Bloody Victory over Gaddafi Is Just the Beginning." *Guardian,* October 20, 2011.

Balder, Lolita C. "Terror Attacks Spike in Pakistan, Afghanistan: Thousands of Mostly Muslim Civilians Are Slaughtered in Extremist Strikes." MSNBC, April 28, 2009.

BBC News. "Bush Admits to CIA Secret Prisons." September 7, 2006.

————. "China and Russia Veto UN Resolution Condemning Syria." October 5, 2011.

————. "Moderate Islamist Party Claims Election Win in Tunisia." October 24, 2011.

————. "1975: Saigon Surrenders." April 30, 1975.

————. "Obama Pledges New US Engagement." April 7, 2009.

————. "Obama Promotes Nuclear-Free World." April 5, 2009.

————. "Profile: Gen. Stanley McChrystal." May 11, 2009.

————. "Superpowers' Mistakes in Afghanistan." December 24, 2004.

————. "UN Official Criticizes US over Drone Attacks." June 2, 2010.

————. "US Marines Identify Afghanistan 'Urination' Troops." January 13, 2012.

————. "US Soldier Kills Afghan Civilians in Kandahar." March 11, 2012.

Becker, Jo, and Scott Shane. "Secret 'Kill List' Proves a Test of Obama's Principles and Will." *New York Times,* May 29, 2012.

Borger, Julian. "Why Iran Confessed to Secret Nuclear Site Built Inside Mountain." *Guardian,* September 26, 2009.

Burns, John. "An Old Afghanistan Hand Offers Lessons of the Past." *New York Times,* October 19, 2008.

CBS News. "Clinton on Qaddafi: We Came, We Saw, He Died." October 20, 2011.

————. "Clinton Pledges More Aid in Surprise Libya Visit." October 18, 2011.

Charbonneau, Louis. "Russia, China Veto U.N. Resolution Condemning Syria." Reuters, October 4, 2011.

Cheney, Dick. Interview with Don Imus. MSNBC, January 20, 2005.

Christian Science Monitor. "Obama Apology to Afghans for Quran Burning: All Forgiven?" February 28, 2012.

Clark, Amy S. "IAEA: Iran Nuclear Report Outrageous." CBS News, September 14, 2006.

Clark, Michael. "Premier Quits as Iran Speeds Nationalization of Oil Fields." *New York Times,* April 28, 1951.

Clinton, Hillary. Interview with Christiane Amanpour. *ABC This Week,* February 20, 2011. http://www.youtube.com/watch?v=IlCEVKmIOJA.

CNN. "Bush Will Add More than 20,000 Troops to Iraq." January 11, 2007.

————. "Hillary Clinton: No Regret over Iraq Vote." April 21, 2004.

————. "Obama Looking for 'Whose Ass to Kick.'" June 8, 2010.

Cockburn, Patrick. "A 'Fraud' Bigger than Madoff." *Independent*, February 16, 2009.

Cole, Juan. "Obama Is Saying the Wrong Things About Afghanistan." Salon.com, July 23, 2008.

Daily Telegraph. "Barack Obama Backs Turkey over EU Membership." April 6, 2009.

Dareini, Ali Akbar. "Top Iranian Cleric Criticises Hard-Liners in Sermon." *Independent*, July 17, 2009.

Doane, Seth. "Bagram Air Base Larger Military Prison than Gitmo." CBS News, November 13, 2011. http://www.cbsnews.com/video/watch/?id=7388152n.

Economist. "Obama's World: How Will a 21st-Century President Fare in a 19th-Century World?" November 6, 2008. http://www.economist.com/displaystory.cfm?story_id=12551938.

Editorial. "Coup D'État." *Times* (London), July 15, 1958.

Farmer, Ben, and David Blair. "Afghanistan Election: Low Turnout as Voters Fear Taliban Attacks." *Daily Telegraph*, August 20, 2009.

Finn, Peter, and Anne E. Kornblut. "Guantanamo Bay: Why Obama Hasn't Fulfilled His Promise to Close the Facility." *Washington Post*, April 24, 2011.

———. "Obama Creates Indefinite Detention System for Prisoners at Guantanamo Bay." *Washington Post*, March 8, 2011.

Gall, Carlotta. "Intimidation and Fraud Observed in Afghan Election." *New York Times*, August 22, 2009.

Gardner, Frank. "Tunisia One Year On: Where the Arab Spring Started." BBC News, December 17, 2011.

Gebauer, Matthias, and Hasnain Kazim. "The 'Kill Team' Images: US Army Apologizes for Horrific Photos from Afghanistan." *Spiegel*, March 21, 2011.

Goldenberg, Suzanne. "E-mail Shows Cheney 'Link' to Oil." *Guardian*, June 1, 2004.

Guardian. "Khomeini Calls for Stricter Islamic Policy." March 2, 1979.

———. "New Iran Sanctions Likely after Nuclear Talks Stalemate." September 7, 2009.

———. "Tunisia Installs Moncef Marzouki as President." December 13, 2011.

———. "UN Security Council Resolution 1973 (2011) on Libya—Full Text." March 17, 2011.

Hurriyet. "Ahmadinejad Accuses Obama of Meddling in Iran." June 16, 2010.

Ibrahim, Ekram. "Egypt's January 25 Revolution Haunted by 'Military Coup,' Warn Analysts." *Al Ahram*, June 18, 2012.

"Iran accuses US of giving IAEA forged documents," *Al Arabiya News*, September 5, 2009.

Jordan Times. "Top Iran Clerics Criticise President over Economy." April 20, 2008.

Lehrer, Jim. *NewsHour*. PBS, November 10, 2008.

Lynch, Column, and Alice Fordham. "Russia, China Veto U.N. Resolution on Syria." *Washington Post*, February 4, 2012.

MacFarquhar, Neil. "U.N. Approves New Sanctions to Deter Iran." *New York Times*, June 9, 2010.

Mozgovaya, Natasha. "Biden: Israel Right to Stop Gaza Flotilla from Breaking Blockade." *Ha'aretz*, June 3, 2010.

New York Times. "Excerpts from Pentagon's Plan: Prevent the Re-Emergence of a New Rival." March 8, 1992.

Ninan, Reena. "Secretary of State Hillary Clinton Pushes Gulf Security and Aid for Syria." ABC News, March 31, 2012.

Nossiter, Adam. "Algerian Election Results Draw Disbelief." *New York Times*, May 11, 2012.

Owen, David. "Hubris: The New Iraq War Syndrome." *Observer*, October 29, 2006.

Ritter, Scott. "Keeping Iran Honest." *Guardian*, September 25, 2009.

Rogers, Paul. "Afghanistan: The Point of Decision." *openDemocracy*, July 27, 2009.

Russia Today. "Russia, China Veto U.N. Security Council Resolution on Syria." February 4, 2012.

Saad, Lydia. "Anti-Muslim Sentiments Fairly Commonplace." Gallup News Service, August 10, 2006. http://www.gallup.com/poll/24073/antimuslim-sentiments -fairly commonplace.aspx#1.

Sapsted, David. "UK Poll Finds Profound Anti-Muslim Sentiment." *The National*, January 14, 2010.

Sheikholeslami, Ali, Anthony DiPaola, and Alaric Nightingale. "Iran Sanctions Leave China, Russia as Winners in Trade." *Bloomberg*, August 9, 2010.

Shenker, Jack, and Abdul-Rahman Hussein. "Muslim Brotherhood Warns Egypt's Generals." *Guardian*, June 18, 2012.

Simpson, John. "Iran's Revolution Turns 30." BBC News, February 10, 2009.

Tait, Robert. "It's the Economy, Mr Ahmadinejad." *Guardian*, September 19, 2007.

Thurgood, Liz, and Jonathan Steele. "Last Soviet Troops Leave Afghanistan." *Guardian*, February 16, 1989.

Time. "Business: Oil Squeeze." February 5, 1979.

———. "Iran: Another Crisis for the Shah." November 13, 1978.

———. "The Khomeini Era Begins." February 12, 1979.

———. "PERSIA: Millspaugh Out." August 8, 1927.

Times (London). "King Idris Deposed by Military Junta in Libya Coup." September 2, 1969.

———. "Significance of the Coup in Syria." November 16, 1970.

Traynor, Ian. "EU to Introduce New Iran Sanctions." *Guardian*, June 15, 2010.

Veterans Today. "Gulf War Illness Is Real, New Federal Report Says." November 17, 2008.

VOA News. "Iran Accuses US of Forging Nuclear Documents." September 5, 2009.

Voice of America. "U.S. Concerned by Egyptian Military Moves." June 18, 2012.

Washington Post. "Army to End Expansive, Exclusive Halliburton Deal." July 12, 2006.

———. "Bush's 'Axis of Evil' Comes to Haunt United States." October 10, 2006.

———. "McCain Calls War 'Necessary and Just.'" April 12, 2007.

———. "Rumsfeld Offers Strategies for Current War." February 3, 2006.

Washington Times. "McCain Lambasts Bush Years." October 23, 2008.

Wheeler, Keith. "In an Angry Arab World." *Life,* April 1, 1957.

Woods, Chris. "A Drone Strike Every Four Days under Obama." *Express Tribune* (Pakistan), August 11, 2011. http://tribune.com.pk/story/228690/exclusive-a-drone-strike-every-four-days-under-obama/.

WEB SOURCES

American-Israeli Cooperative Enterprise. "The American Position on Partition." Jewish Virtual Library. http://www.jewishvirtuallibrary.org/jsource/History/US_position_on_partition.html. Accessed December 7, 2012.

Applied Information Systems. "U.S. Oil Imports." http://www.appinsys.com/oil/. Accessed December 7, 2012.

Baroud, Ramzy. "Europe's Identity Crisis: A Growing Anti-Muslim Sentiment throughout Europe." *Global Research,* December 24, 2009. http://www.globalresearch.ca/index.php?context=va&aid=16655.

Beehner, Lionel, and Toni Johnson. "Global Oil Trends." *Backgrounder,* October 18, 2007. http://www.cfr.org/publication/9484/global_oil_trends.html.

ElBaradei, Mohamed. "Statement of the Director General." IAEA, September 7, 2009. http://www.iaea.org/newscenter/statements/2009/ebsp2009n009.html#syria.

Encyclopaedia Britannica. "Conference of San Remo." http://www.britannica.com/EBchecked/topic/521598/Conference-of-San-Remo. Accessed December 7, 2012.

———. "Second Saudi State." http://www.britannica.com/EBchecked/topic/525348/Saudi-Arabia/45226/Second-Saudi-state. Accessed December 7, 2012.

Federation of American Scientists. "Pakistan's Nuclear Weapons." December 11, 2002. http://www.fas.org/nuke/guide/pakistan/nuke/.

Galtung, Johan. "On the Coming Decline and Fall of the US Empire." Transnational Foundation for Peace and Future Research, January 28, 2004.

George, Susan. "The WTO and the Global War System." Transnational Institute, November 28, 1999. http://www.tni.org/archives/archives_george_utopian.

Geselbrach, Raymond H., comp. "The United States and the Recognition of Israel: A Chronology." Harry S. Truman Library. http://www.trumanlibrary.org/israel/palestin.htm. Accessed December 7, 2012.

"The Great Iraqi Revolution 1929." Armed Conflict Events Data, December 16, 2000. http://www.onwar.com/aced/data/india/iraq1920.htm.

Grossman, Zoltan. "From Wounded Knee to Libya: A Century of U.S. Military Interventions." http://academic.evergreen.edu/g/grossmaz/interventions.html. Accessed December 7, 2012.

Harry S. Truman Library. "The Recognition of the State of Israel: Chronology." http://www.trumanlibrary.org/whistlestop/study_collections/israel/large/index.php?action=chrono. Accessed December 7, 2012.

History.com. "OPEC Enacts Oil Embargo." http://www.history.com/this-day-in-history/opec-enacts-oil-embargo. Accessed December 7, 2012.

Hormeku, Tetteh. "US Intervention in Africa: Through Angolan Eyes." Third World Network. http://www.twnside.org.sg/title/tett-cn.htm. Accessed December 9, 2012.

Human Rights Watch. "Libya: Investigate Deaths of Gaddafi and Son." October 22, 2011. http://www.hrw.org/news/2011/10/22/libya-investigate-deaths-gaddafi-and-son.

Institute of Palestine Studies. "Palestinian History: A Chronology." http://www.palestine-studies.org/enakba/Chronology/Before%20Their%20Diaspora%20Chronology.pdf.

Iran Chamber Society. "A Short Account of 1953 Coup." http://www.iranchamber.com/history/coup53/coup53p2.php. Accessed December 6, 2012.

Iraq Coalition Casualty Count. iCasualties.org. Accessed December 9, 2012.

Isseroff, Ami. "President Harry S. Truman and U.S. Support for Israeli Statehood." MidEastWeb, 2003. http://www.mideastweb.org/us_supportforstate.htm.

————. "Saudi Arabia: A Brief History." MidEastWeb, 2003. http://www.mideastweb.org/arabiahistory.htm.

Jimmy Carter Library and Museum. "The Hostage Crisis in Iran." November 6, 2012. http://www.jimmycarterlibrary.gov/documents/hostages.phtml.

Matini, Jalal. "Quotes from Ayatollah Khomeini." Translated by Farhad Mafie. *Iran Heritage*, July 25, 2003. http://www.iran-heritage.org/interestgroups/government-article2.htm.

Motohashi, Kazuyuki. "Japan's Long-Term Recession in the 1990s: Fall of Industrial Competitiveness?" 2004. http://www.mo.t.u-tokyo.ac.jp/seika/files/WP04–08 moto-hashi1.pdf.

al Nakba. http://www.alnakba.org/. Accessed December 9, 2012.

Nobel Foundation. "The Nobel Peace Prize 2009." Announcement, October 9, 2009. http://www.nobelprize.org/nobel_prizes/peace/laureates/2009/announcement.html.

Norouzi, Arash. "Glory and Humiliation: Iran, Britain, and That Coup." The Mossadegh Project, February 12, 2006. http://www.mohammadmossadegh.com/news/house-of-lords/.

Office of the UN High Commissioner for Human Rights. "Gaza Aid Convoy Killings: 'Those Responsible Must Be Held Criminally Responsible'—UN Expert." May 31, 2010. http://unispal.un.org/UNISPAL.NSF/0/FC8B241DD08E470885257735004FEB7F.

Palestine Facts. "British Mandate: McDonald White Paper." http://208.84.118.121/pf_mandate_whitepaper_1939.php. Accessed December 7, 2012.

Pike, John. "National Union for the Total Independence of Angola." Intelligence Resource Program, Federation of American Scientists, May 7, 2003. http://www.fas.org/irp/world/para/unita.htm.

Rickard, J. "First World War, 1914–1918." History of War, February 18, 2001. http://www.historyofwar.org/articles/wars_wwI.html.

Roudi, Farzaneh. "Youth, Women's Rights and Political Change in Iran." Population Reference Bureau, July 2009. http://www.prb.org/Articles/2009/iranyouth.aspx?p=1.

Slaughter, Anne-Marie. "U.S.-Saudi Relations in a World without Equilibrium." Session 3 conference transcript. Saudi-US Relations Information Center, May 18, 2009. http://www.saudi-us-relations.org/articles/2009/ioi/090518-ussa-slaughter.html.

Szasz, Ferenc. "Quotes about History." History News Network, George Mason University, December 26, 2005. http://www.hnn.us/articles/1328.html.

Thompson, Eric V., comp. "A Brief History of Major Oil Companies in the Gulf Region." Petroleum Archives Project, University of Virginia. http://www.virginia.edu/igpr/APAG/apagoilhistory.html. Accessed December 6, 2012.

UN High Commissioner for Refugees. "UNHCR Worried about Effect of Dire Security Situation on Iraq's Displaced." October 13, 2006. http://www.unhcr.org/452fa9954.html.

U.S. Energy Information Administration. "Saudi Arabia: Background." http://www.eia.gov/countries/cab.cfm?fips=SA. Last updated October 16, 2012.

"US Saudi Relations." http://ddi08.wikispaces.com/SS+Saudi+Relations+Oil+DA. Accessed December 7, 2012.

Williams, James L. "Oil Price History and Analysis." WTRG Economics. http://www.wtrg.com/prices.htm. Accessed December 7, 2012.

INDEX

ABOUT THE AUTHOR

Dr. Deepak Tripathi, fellow of the Royal Historical Society, is a British historian and former journalist whose long career (1974–2000) was spent primarily with the BBC, where he was a correspondent, editor, and commentator. In the early 1990s Tripathi set up the BBC bureau in Kabul and was the resident correspondent in Afghanistan. He has also reported from Syria, Pakistan, Sri Lanka, and India. This is the third book in a trilogy that includes *Overcoming the Bush Legacy in Iraq and Afghanistan* (2010) and *Breeding Ground: Afghanistan and the Origins of Islamist Terrorism* (2011), both published by Potomac Books. Tripathi received his PhD from the University of Roehampton, where he is an honorary research fellow in social sciences. He lives near London.